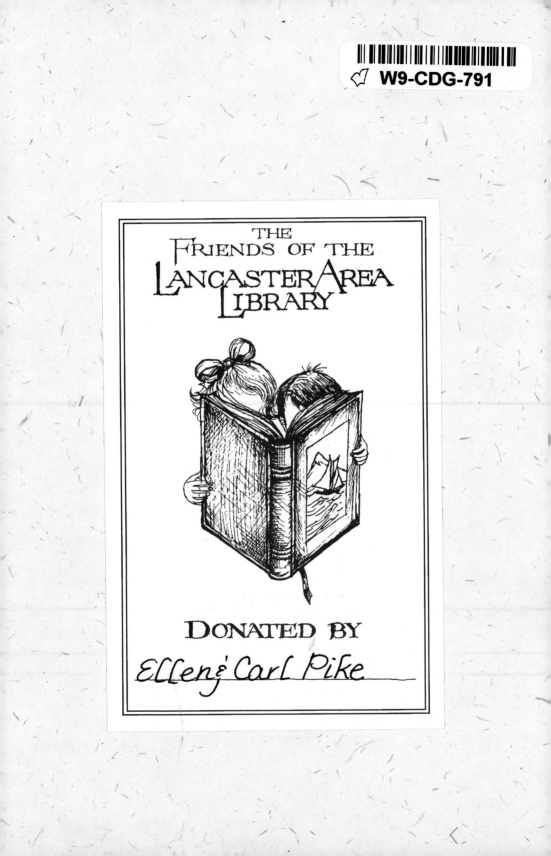

Florida A&M University, Tallahassee
Florida Atlantic University, Boca Raton
Florida Gulf Coast University, Ft. Myers
Florida International University, Miami
Florida State University, Tallahassee
University of Central Florida, Orlando
University of Florida, Gainesville
University of North Florida, Jacksonville
University of South Florida, Tampa
University of West Florida, Pensacola

El Niño IN HISTORY

Storming Through the Ages

César N. Caviedes

University Press of Florida

Gainesville · Tallahassee · Tampa · Boca Raton
Pensacola · Orlando · Miami · Jacksonville · Ft. Myers

06 05 04 03 02 01 6 5 4 3 2 1

Library of Congress Cataloging-in-Publication Data
Caviedes, César, 1936-
El Niño in history: storming through the ages / César N. Caviedes.
p. cm.
Includes bibliographical references and index.
ISBN 0-8130-2099-9 (alk. paper)
1. El Niño Current—Environmental aspects. 2. La Niña Current—
Environmental aspects. 3. Weather. I. Title.
GC296.8.E4 C39 2001
551.6—dc21 2001027591

The University Press of Florida is the scholarly publishing agency
for the State University System of Florida, comprising Florida A&M
University, Florida Atlantic University, Florida Gulf Coast University,
Florida International University, Florida State University, University of
Central Florida, University of Florida, University of North Florida,
University of South Florida, and University of West Florida.

University Press of Florida
15 Northwest 15th Street
Gainesville, FL 32611–2079
http://www.upf.com

Contents

Illustrations

Color Plates (following page 114)

Tables

Preface

As the main controlling factor of contemporary climate, El Niño no longer requires introduction. This recurrent warming of the Pacific Ocean is now widely known through its catastrophic effects: torrential rains, river flooding, and landslides that destroy property and take lives in some regions of the world, while triggering severe droughts and wildfires in other areas. Warm ocean temperatures destroy large populations of fish, kill corals in tropical waters, and prompt large-scale migrations of marine life. Furious storms, bred over the heated waters, erode beaches and destroy coastal property and in the past caused numerous shipwrecks.

On the heels of El Niño usually comes La Niña. Now the waters of the Pacific Ocean cool down, while the tropical Atlantic heats up, producing conditions favorable for the development of frequent and strong tropical cyclones and hurricanes.

Only in recent decades was it understood that most of these natural catastrophes stem from El Niño and La Niña. As early as the 1960s I became interested in the variations of precipitation along the west coast of South America that were tied to these phenomena. In those days only a handful of climatologists conducted research on this subject, including Hermann Flohn, Jakob Bjerknes, Adalberto Serra, and Jerome Namias. Their curiosity about the ways in which the oceans and the air above them interact led them to explore El Niño as the primary determinant of contemporary climate. Most of their ideas about global climate variations have stood the test of time, and the works of numerous followers are but variations of themes first developed by these visionaries.

Through the years, a limiting factor for the validation of their theories has been the relatively short period for which climatological and oceanic data are available. Because climatic and oceanographic records were not kept consistently prior to 1850, searching for hints of past El Niño/La Niña occurrences in other sources before that date constitutes a fascinating challenge. Recently, written history, archives, indirect evidence, and surrogate observations (proxy data), such as treerings, have all been utilized to retrace El Niño and La Niña events that go back as far as historical sources, traditional accounts, and archeological findings can allow. These expanded El Niño series offer astonishing details concerning the widespread extent of past occurrences and provide a new perspective on environmental history.

This book examines numerous events in political, military, social, economic, and cultural history that were influenced by El Niño. It is based on indirect historical references that I have collected since the 1960s, ranging from specialized publications in various languages to references to unusual weather contained in literary texts. This is the first comprehensive account of the history of El Niño that shifts the research focus from the physical mechanisms of the phenomenon to its past and present impact on humans.

The first chapter introduces concepts about the oceanic and meteorological processes associated with El Niño and explains how heat and humidity from the South Pacific are exported to distant parts of the world. Chapter 2 details the methods used for tracking down past El Niño/La Niña occurrences and brings contributions from environmental history into the discourse. Chapter 3 investigates the origin of the term in colonial northern Peru and unearths references to past events that serve as building blocks for a chronology of El Niño against which climatic crises around the world are measured. Chapter 4 delves into the storms bred in the South Pacific and the Atlantic Ocean during years when El Niño struck. Accounts of shipwrecks off the coasts of Chile, New Zealand, South Africa, California, and the North Atlantic are used to cast light on the effects of past El Niños.

In the 1970s climatological research revealed that regions far distant from the Pacific coast of the Americas suffered rainfall shortages in El

Niño years. Chapter 5 offers evidence of historical droughts in the highlands of Bolivia, northeastern Brazil, Mexico, Australia, Indonesia, India, and Sahelian Africa extracted from instrumental observations and varied historical sources. In chapter 6 the brisk passages from a disturbed state of nature (El Niño) to its opposite (La Niña) are interpreted; this chapter also explores the relationship between La Niña and Atlantic hurricanes that rage over the Caribbean Islands, Central America, and the U.S. Gulf Coast.

Chapter 7 examines the indirect role played by El Niño in precipitating some dramatic turns in historical events. Droughts in Africa's Sahel immediately preceded the fall of Emperor Haile Selassie in 1974 and contributed to the ousting of General Haile-Mariam Mengistu in Ethiopia in 1991. Hitler's change of fortune in Stalingrad during the winter of 1942 and the annihilation of Napoleon's Grande Armée after the siege of Moscow in 1812 are also attributed to severe Russian winters associated with aftermaths of El Niño.

Also linked to past climatic crises are droughts and famines in India, China, and Japan recorded in traditional archives, as well as fierce Atlantic storms during the cold and stormy period known as Little Ice Age. Chapter 8 examines research in the fields of anthropology, stratigraphy, geology, and glaciology that point to major El Niños with deep-reaching cultural implications in the distant past. For example, it is likely that past El Niños were the elicitors of audacious voyages of discovery by Polynesian seafarers, which resulted in the extraordinary discovery of Easter Island.

The final chapter places the evidence in a coherent framework that underlines the strength of global interrelations, and it invites the reader to look for clues of climatic crises in local and national history that may be linked to documented El Niño or La Niña occurrences.

As in previous endeavors, I express deep gratitude to my wife, Christiana Donauer-Caviedes, who patiently edited the manuscript through its several stages. Our friend Dolores Jenkins, of the Smathers Library at the University of Florida, added the needed stylistic touch. My colleagues Peter R. Waylen and Edward J. Malecki may not suspect that they have been longtime contributors to this work; through the years, they faithfully put in my office mailbox newspaper clippings and other articles relating to my pet subject. I also thank Michael Binford for volunteering chrono-logical information and Jim Sloan for his excellent illustrations. Finally, I must mention my thirty-year relationship with the Hispanic Division of the U.S. Library of Congress through *The Handbook of Latin American Studies*, a relationship that provided me access to rare publications and other research materials in this incomparable facility.

1

~

Grasping the Basic Concepts

Even though the earth is referred to as the "blue planet," we often fail to appreciate the implications of the fact that three-fourths of its surface is covered by water. The huge bodies of water are largely responsible for supplying our atmosphere with humidity: 419,000 cubic kilometers of water evaporate annually from the oceans, of which 106,000 cubic kilometers fall on continents as rain or snow. The oceans are also the main storage areas of carbon dioxide, the most important chemical compound for maintaining a balanced atmospheric temperature. Given that a quarter of the water provided by the oceans falls on continental surfaces, where it feeds the rivers, lakes, snow fields, ice masses, and vegetation that allow the existence of human settlements and the cultivation of fields, we can appreciate the oceans' importance for our survival.

Further, oceans have the physical ability to capture solar radiation and convert it into caloric energy (heat), which is distributed all over the globe. The Gulf Stream, as an example, exports to the British Isles and western Europe the caloric energy it has acquired while meandering through the Gulf of Mexico and the Caribbean Sea. Inversely, cold from subpolar latitudes is exported to lower latitudes by cold water flows, such as the California or Peru currents. Thus the oceans play a crucial role as major suppliers of humidity and regulators of our global temperature.

As you can observe in any kitchen when you heat a pot of water on the stove, the water begins to pass into the air as steam before it reaches the boiling point; water that is kept at room temperature, however, takes much longer to be converted into water vapor and in some cases may not even become a vapor at all. This basic observation—that the transformation of water from a liquid to a vapor state depends on temperature conditions—helps us understand that warm ocean surfaces transfer more humidity and heat into the atmosphere than do cold ocean surfaces.

Not only are water masses slower than continental masses to absorb energy from the sun, they are also slower to release it. This means that regions in the vicinity of the sea enjoy milder temperatures in the summer months, while regions in the heart of continents get very hot in the summer but their temperatures drop drastically with the arrival of autumn. Referring to the diverse pace of temperature transfers, climatologists speak of oceans having a "long thermal memory" and continental masses having a "short thermal memory."

Of all the oceans of the earth, the Pacific Ocean is the uncontested giant, accounting for three-fifths of all water masses. This fact alone explains the Pacific's dominant influence over the continental masses that surround it—North America, Asia, Australia, and South America—and over regions that are farther removed, such as the Caribbean basin, the islands of Indonesia, and even the Malayan Peninsula and the Indian Subcontinent. To put the huge dimensions of this body of water into perspective, let's compare it with the Atlantic Ocean: at its widest extension (from the Gulf of Panama to the Celebes Sea), the Pacific spans 11,447 miles, or 45 percent of the earth's circumference; by contrast, the widest part of the Atlantic (from the littorals of Georgia to the coast of Morocco) is roughly 4,200 miles.

Another important difference is that the widest part of the Pacific coincides roughly with the equator line, whereas the widest part of the Atlantic lies within the middle latitudes. Therefore, the Pacific Ocean possesses a much larger surface for collecting solar energy in equatorial latitudes, and passes much more humidity and heat into the atmosphere, than the other oceans. On top of this, when an ocean of the dimensions of the Pacific undergoes inter-annual variations of sea temperatures due to solar inputs or by virtue of some non-annual cycles that affect its "memory," these *variations* are also reflected in proportionally higher humidity and temperature exports to contiguous and distant lands. One of these variations, and perhaps the most important climatic oscillation of our times, is El Niño.

Oceanic and Climatological Aspects of El Niño

The coastal communities of northern Peru have traditionally been highly dependent on the sea. Farming was practiced in the few river oases of that desertic region, but the main source of animal protein was the abundant fish in the cool Peru Current. Cold water fish differ from warm water fish in that they are lean, streamlined, firm, and live in shoals. Warm water fish have a rounder shape, their meat is softer and lighter, and—with the exception of tuna—they do not commonly swim in schools.

These distinctions have been well known to north Peruvian fishing villagers since precolonial times. They observed that in December—the beginning of the southern summer—tepid waters began to move into the domain between the Gulf of Guayaquil and Pariñas Point. This annual invasion of warmer-than-usual waters caused not only changes in fish populations (a decline in the species they commonly caught and an increase in tropical fish) but also a surge in air humidity in this arid coastal region, leading to frequent summer showers. Since this set of changes happened around Christmastime, the fishermen called it *El Niño,* meaning the Child Jesus.

Erwin Schweigger, a German marine biologist who spent most of his professional life in Peru, observed that in certain years this annual occurrence—called *minor El Niño*—was supplanted by extensive invasions of equatorial warm waters that would expand much farther south than Pariñas Point and last throughout the southern summer. He also noticed that these events were accompanied by considerable variations in the weather—dense cloudiness, high air humidity, frequent thunderstorms, and heavy rains—and posited that these changes had to do with sizable alterations in the behavior of water and air masses across the entire tropical Pacific, and not with the short-lived El Niño episodes of early summer. These severe events he called *major El Niños.*

For quite a while, the regionally restricted phenomenon did not arouse the curiosity of the scientific community, although some dramatic El Niño events, such as those of 1911, 1925, and 1953, made it into the pages of reputable journals. It was only with the 1957 occurrence—coinciding with the International Geophysical Year in which particular attention was paid to global geophysical phenomena—that earth scientists turned their attention toward this oddity on the west coast of South America.

In the 1960s, Hermann Flohn, of the University of Bonn, suspected that this phenomenon had an impact on the climate of South America and directed his students Rolf Doberitz and Karin Schütte to investigate the rain patterns and wind frequencies on Pacific islands located along the equator and to correlate their findings with weather events on the Galapagos Islands and in coastal Ecuador and Peru. Also in the 1960s, Professor Jacob Bjerknes, at the University of California–Los Angeles, began to investigate the coupling of sea-surface temperatures with dry and rainy episodes on several tropical islands in the Pacific. In their studies, both men and their disciples pointedly identified El Niño as the major catalyst for climate variations in the Pacific and in western South America. Concurrently, Klaus Wyrtki, an oceanographer at the University of Hawaii, was studying the dynamics that explain the circulation of water masses in the Pacific. These three scientists laid the foundations for our present knowledge of the oceanic and climatic peculiarities of the El Niño phenomenon.

The early investigations indicated that there were two aspects to this recurring event: the *oceanic aspect,* which related to anomalies of sea temperatures across the tropical Pacific, and the *meteorological aspect,* which had to do with variations in the atmosphere above.

The Oceanic Aspect

Under normal conditions, the segment of the tropical Pacific from the coast of Ecuador/Peru to longitude 120°W is dominated by westward-flowing cold waters that are the prolongation of the Peru, or Humboldt, Current. Off the north Peruvian coast, the current turns away from the continent and forms a flow that is abnormally cold for equatorial latitudes; the cold water makes both the Galapagos penguin (*Sphoenicus mendiculus*) and seals feel at home on the Galapagos Islands. Near longitude 120°W and under the hot equatorial sun, sea temperatures start to rise, reaching near-normal equatorial values to the west of the International Date Line. It should be noted, however, that due to the stable air conditions caused by the cool sea surface, there is little evaporation, which is why the islands of Christmas, Fanning, Palmira, Jarvis, and Malden near the equator are dry and vegetation free, colonized only by seabirds and myriads of crabs.

Driven by the constantly blowing easterly winds, the superficial waters eventually reach the western Pacific in New Guinea and south of the Philippines, where the *excess* water that accumulates on the western edge of the equatorial Pacific feeds two warm currents: the East Australian Current and the Kuro Shio, or Japan Current, which moves northward along the coasts of China and Japan. Oceanographers working on El Niño pointed out very early that due to this westward transport of superficial waters caused by the *wind shear* of the easterly winds, the ocean layer directly heated by the sun is thinner on the eastern side of the equatorial Pacific and thicker on the western side, where the warm waters, driven by the easterlies, tend to pile up. The "thickness" of the superficial layer is determined by the *thermocline*, or lower boundary of the sun-heated upper layer that around 20°C marks the beginning of cooler water temperatures underneath. Under normal oceanic conditions, the thermocline between Peru and the Galapagos Islands runs at a depth of some 40 meters, while on the Asian side of the Pacific, it dips as low as 120 meters, revealing a marked asymmetry in the thickness of the sun-heated layer across the Pacific (Figure 1.1).

During abnormal warm years—synonymous with El Niño years—many of the above-mentioned conditions are drastically altered. First, the westward flow of cooler waters weakens or ceases to exist; second, there is less or no wind shear from the easterly winds; third, the thermocline in the eastern half of the equatorial Pacific may reach depths of up to 80 meters; fourth, there is horizontal transport (*advection*) of warm waters from west to east, which is caused by the development of Kelvin waves (explained later in this chapter) in the upper 100 meters of the tropical Pacific. This eastward movement, originally believed to be a massive outflow, prompted coinage of the term *El Niño current*, in use into the late 1950s. Today, the invasion of warm waters from the west Pacific is pic-

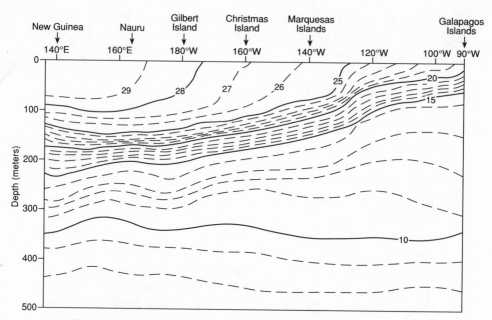

1.1. The thermocline across the equatorial Pacific Ocean. Arrows indicate the location of Pacific equatorial islands mentioned in the text.

tured as an oil slick pouring out of a damaged tanker, that is, as oil patches constantly changing shape and direction under the influence of the variable winds and the Kelvin waves.

During El Niño years, these events begin at the onset of the southern spring, that is, in September and October, and during the following months the warm waters proceed eastward, reaching the area between the Galapagos Islands and the Ecuadorian/Peruvian coast in the month of December. The eastward migration of warm water can start earlier, as it did in 1997, when advection in the western Pacific began in May, or in other instances the warm waters may stall before reaching the Galapagos Islands, which results in an "aborted" El Niño, as happened in 1976.

The Meteorological Aspect

Before proceeding any farther, we need to understand that the superficial circulations of the sea are prompted by the winds blowing above it. Surely, the water's response to episodic winds is the formation of waves and swells, but with winds of seasonal character—that is, blowing in one direction during one time of the year and in a different direction at another—the entire surface circulation reacts with prolonged seasonal flows.

The wind source over the South Pacific—the cradle of El Niño—is a cell of high air pressure centered on Easter Island (27°S, 110°W); this cell is known as the South Pacific anticyclone. Its counterpart is the North Pacific anticyclone located north of Hawaii. Emanating from these two high pressure centers, the so-called trade winds flow toward a band of low pressure cells that are situated north of the equator and known as the Inter-Tropical Convergence Zone (ITCZ). In the southern hemisphere the trade winds blow from the southeast, and in the northern hemisphere from the northeast. As they approach the equator, they take an east-west course, due to the Coriolis force (the deviating effect of the rotating earth), and are henceforth known as equatorial easterlies. Trade winds, equatorial easterlies, and the westward water transport intensify when the two high pressure cells are strong. In those years, the waters of the eastern Pacific are moderately cold, and the thermocline runs not far below the ocean surface.

However, when—for reasons still not well understood—the South Pacific anticyclone loses intensity, the whole wind system that it supports collapses. The trade winds slacken or cease altogether, the thermocline thickens in the eastern tropical Pacific, and westerly winds replace the easterlies in the tropical belt. Coupled with these changes is the onset of the eastward advection of warm waters, described in the previous section. In addition, a phenomenon occurs that may be even more important: hot and humid air masses—uncommon in the tropical Pacific—glide on top of the warm waters and begin their progression to the east, dumping along the way torrential rains on the dry equatorial islands mentioned above, as well as on the arid coasts of Ecuador and northern Peru, which are not accustomed to such downpours.

These highly visible oceanic and atmospheric changes in the eastern Pacific during El Niño years are some of the indicators of large-scale climate variations in progress. As early as 1924, Sir Gilbert Walker, working with the Indian Meteorological Service, noticed a counterbalancing tendency between air pressures at Djakarta (Indonesia) and those measured at Tahiti (French Polynesia), which suggested an interrelation between the pressure cells over the two locations notwithstanding the distance

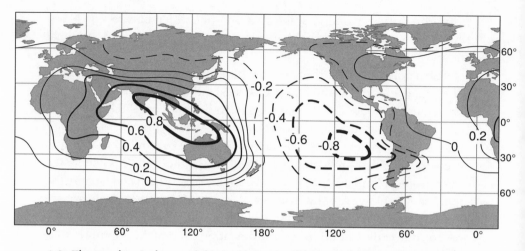

1.2. The two hemispheres of the Southern Oscillation. Solid lines show positive correlations of air pressures with Darwin/Djakarta in the "eastern hemisphere," and broken lines show negative correlations with Tahiti in the "western hemisphere," during El Niño years.

involved. Thirty years later, the Dutch climatologist H. P. Berlage proposed the concept *Southern Oscillation* to refer to the counterbalancing of pressures within the southern half of the tropics. The Southern Oscillation expresses the difference between the high pressure cell of the South Pacific and the low pressure cell over Indonesia. Meteorologists use an index to quantify this difference. A high Southern Oscillation Index (SOI) signifies dominance of easterly winds and cooler sea conditions in the Pacific, while a low (or negative) SOI means weakness or absence of easterlies, high humidity in the tropical atmosphere, and warm ocean conditions. Walker and Berlage were the first to realize that the pressure field of the South Pacific was interlocked with the pressures over Indonesia in a way that fitted the development of El Niño. That is, during El Niño events, the South Pacific anticyclone is weak while the Indonesia low is strong—triggering a series of anomalies in the Indian and Pacific Oceans.

The Southern Oscillation Index has become the established yardstick against which most climate variations in the tropics and middle latitudes are gauged. Knowing how to interpret these variations allows predictions of the degree to which El Niño conditions in the tropical Pacific will affect other world regions within a few months. During major El Niño events, when the whole tropical belt is engulfed by atmospheric and oceanic anomalies, the areas influenced by the Southern Oscillation are so vast that one can clearly identify two hemispheres (Figure 1.2): a western hemisphere that comprises the Pacific basin, western South America, Central America, and the western half of North America, where abnormally low air pressures, warm coastal waters, and unusually heavy rains occur; and an eastern hemisphere centered on Indonesia, where air pressures are high, ocean waters are cooler than normal, and severe droughts are visited upon certain regions. Included in this eastern hemisphere are Southeast Asia, Australia, India, Africa, the Atlantic basin, and northeast Brazil. Readers should now understand why, when El Niño makes it into the news for pounding California with rainstorms and wreaking havoc in the islands of the Pacific or in Peru, they also hear about wildfires in Indonesia, livestock mortality in Australia and South Africa, drought, starvation, and death in sub-Saharan Africa, and—more so in the past than lately—famine in India and northeast Brazil. The long-distance implications, or teleconnections, of El Niño and other climatic developments are covered in the next section.

Any study of El Niño and the Southern Oscillation, or ENSO—to use the acronym—should address the frequency of occurrence of such events. Table 1.1 lists El Niños since the early 1800s, and La Niñas from 1870 onward, for it was not until the nineteenth century that air and sea temperatures, pressures, and precipitation began to be systematically recorded in reliable and continuous series. Sporadic observations and unreliable measurements from earlier times do not permit comparisons with the existing series from developed parts of the world.

Early observations seemed to indicate that ENSO events occurred at intervals of about eleven years, a circumstance that led to speculation that these flare-ups of heat and humidity in the Pacific were prompted by "sunspots" that tend to peak at eleven-year intervals. However, the surge in frequency of ENSO events after 1970 and their occurrence also in years of low sunspot activity have forced researchers to look for other explanations. Today, accurate studies of the frequency of ENSO events show that they occur at intervals of about three and a half years, and that the major events tend to repeat themselves every six years. What processes are responsible for these return intervals is a question that still keeps geophysicists busy and that we will return to in the final chapter of this book.

Table 1.1
Warm (El Niño) and cold (La Niña) Pacific episodes since 1800

El Niño	La Niña	El Niño	La Niña
	1802*	1900	1903
1803			1904
1804			1908
		1911	1910
		1912	
1812			
1814			1917
		1919	
1817			
1819	1822*		1924
	1825*	1925	192?
1828		1926	
	1832*	1932	1933
			1938
1844		1940	1939
1845		1941	1945
			1950
1850		1953	1955
	1857*	1957	
		1958	1960
1864	1863*		
		1965	1964
			1968
1871	1872	1972	
	1873	1973	1974
	1875		
	1876	1976	
1877			
1878		1982	
1884		1983	1984
	1886		
	1887	1986	1988
	1890		
1891		1992	
	1893	1993	1994
1897	1898	1997	
		1998	1999

* Estimated from dry periods in western South America. All others inferred from low sea surface temperatures in the eastern tropical Pacific.

The Distant Effects: Teleconnections

We rarely stop to think about the fact that the weather we are experiencing locally may be the result of climatic developments in a distant region of the globe. If we were to tell a man in Buffalo who shovels the snow from yet another winter storm that this "white stuff" is actually coming from the Pacific, he would probably reply that he could not care less, for all he wants is this miserable winter to end. Of similar irrelevance to him would be the fact that the earth rotates from west to east and that, dragged by the momentum of this rotation, most of the weather systems that travel over North America, or across South America, and Europe follow a distinct *west-east* trajectory. However, these points are central to understanding how the effects of El Niños in the Pacific can be "exported" to distant regions.

Nevertheless, the workings of these processes were difficult to visualize before the advent of satellites that could track and transmit images of weather systems. Unlike static weather maps, contemporary satellite images actually show movements of clouds, storms, and fronts. On the screen we see how white streaks (cloud bands) or rotating swirls (traveling cyclones or depressions) make their way across the oceans and onto continental North America or Europe, and we begin to understand how dependent local daily weather is on the events occurring over oceans.

In the early decades of El Niño research, climatologists did not have the tools we work with today. My initial investigations of rainfall variations in temperate central Chile were conducted at a time when satellite imagery was affordable only in the industrialized countries of the northern hemisphere. So when I explained to my countrymen in Chile that the precipitation they received depended on the sea temperatures in the eastern Pacific Ocean, more than a few eyebrows were raised in disbelief. However, subsequent research proved that El Niño had important implications for regions beyond the restricted realm of northern Peru and Ecuador. Finally, the informed public grasped the large areal involvement of the Southern Oscillation and was ready to accept the notion that weather developing over the South Pacific not only bore upon the circum-Pacific regions but involved Indonesia, India, Africa, and Europe. The distant relations between local weather and the vagaries of ENSO (that is, El Niño and the Southern Oscillation) are known as *teleconnections*.

To understand how teleconnections operate, it is necessary to consider the different circulations that drive the movement of air masses on the globe. Circulations consist of "circuits" that are fueled by heat engines and pressure differences scattered over continents and water masses. The main circuit is the thermal-driven Hadley circulation, which involves warm air rising in equatorial latitudes due to surface heating and descending in subtropical latitudes once the air has cooled in higher elevations (Figure 1.3). Thus the warm equatorial belt constantly provides heat to other latitudes and feeds the subtropical high pressure cells from which the trade winds emanate. Another circuit, known as Walker circulation, entails the less dramatic but equally effective exchange of air from warm oceans or continents to cooler waters and land masses. While the Hadley circulation activates movement of air away from the equator, the Walker circulation propels air masses along the equator, as seen in Figure 1.4. Ascending branches are located over heated waters and superheated continental interiors—such as the Amazon and Congo basins; descending branches sit over cooler waters and dry continental margins—such as those of coastal Peru and Chile, and of Angola.

Complicating this picture are other interactions between pressure cells. We have already discussed the Southern Oscillation (SO), which interlaces the centers of the South Pacific and Indonesia. There is also the North Atlantic Oscillation (NAO), which expresses the differences between the Azores high and the low pressure over Iceland and influences air masses circulating over the tropical or midlatitudinal Atlantic Ocean and conterminous lands. NAO closely reflects the strength or weakness of the trade winds in the North Atlantic and controls, to a certain degree, the passage of hurricanes during the summer and fall seasons. While the Southern Oscillation rules air circulation in the direction of the parallels, the North Atlantic Oscillation runs along the meridians and across the parallels, thereby fostering exchanges between cold and warm air masses in the northern Atlantic basin.

The interactions between these circuits can be compared to the communications between computer nodes whose impulses cause varied responses depending on the nature of the intervening systems. Included in this cacaphony of communications are warm and cold oceans, rising or descending circuit branches, dry and humid air masses, warm continental interiors and cool coastal margins whose various circulation circuits can be greatly upset by oceanic El Niños or La Niñas. Obviously, the energy input into different latitudes and longitudes also varies from case to case.

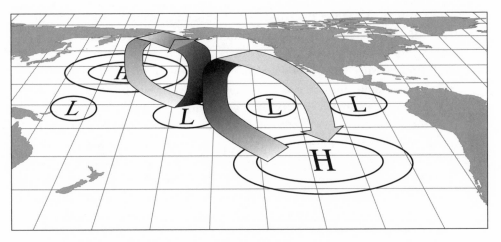

1.3. The Hadley circulation. Air from the subtropical highs converges to the equatorial lows, or doldrums.

Let us now look at the teleconnections triggered by El Niño. The warming anomalies that indicate the onset of an El Niño are first felt over the western half of the equatorial Pacific, usually at the beginning of the southern spring. It takes two to three months for the warm surface water to flow into the intervening space between the Galapagos Islands and the northern coast of Peru. The movement of this superficial water mass occurs in the form of Kelvin waves, pulsating advances of warm waters that were pooled in the western Pacific during the preceding period of dominating easterlies. Under slackening easterlies that normally keep these waters confined to the west Pacific, they begin to spread from west to east along the equator, temporarily raising sea levels by as much as two feet (seventy centimeters). Upon reaching South America, the Kelvin waves

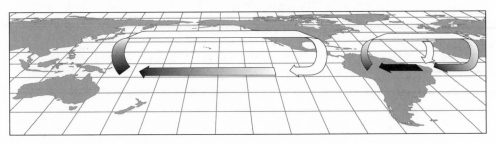

1.4. The Walker circulation. Surface air along the equator flows from east to west and returns east at high elevations.

swirl northward along the coast of Colombia and southward along the coast of Peru, expanding the warm water conditions that characterize the Pacific off western South America during El Niño years.

Riding on top of these warm waters are humid equatorial air masses that release their humidity as they move eastward along the equator. A direct connection exists between the eastward-progressing sea warming and the occurrence of torrential precipitation. At the same time, the ocean heating stimulates the atmosphere above, and these effects are transferred to regions farther east, where they are felt at certain lags *after* the initial warming of the equatorial waters. Based on this principle, the meteorological consequences of a warm Pacific in other regions are said to occur at the same time (lag 0), one month later (lag 1), two months later (lag 2), three months later (lag 3), and so on.

After decades of studying the thermal behavior of the tropical Pacific, as well as related precipitation and temperature conditions in distant regions, oceanographers discerned a distinct pattern of El Niño manifestations and divided the tropical Pacific into four major quadrants, or "regions" (Figure 1.5). El Niño 1 region comprises the coastal waters off Peru, which heat up only during major oceanic warming events. High water temperatures in this quadrant correlate with simultaneous torrential rains in the conterminous countries and with severe droughts in the Peruvian Andes and on the Altiplano of Bolivia. Across the continent, in northeastern Brazil, these El Niño episodes are associated with devastating droughts.

Warm waters in El Niño 2 region, comprising the ocean between the Galapagos Islands and the coast of Ecuador, correlate closely with increased rainfall in the Pacific lowlands and the Andes of Ecuador and decreased precipitation in the interior Amazon basin. When the waters in El Niño 3 region heat up, high precipitation occurs—after two or three months' delay—in central Chile and the Rio de la Plata basin (southern Brazil, Paraguay, Uruguay, and central Argentina). The coast of California is also affected. In most of western Mexico and on the Pacific slope of Central America, by contrast, rain deficits occur in phase with warm waters in the tropical Pacific. Oceanic warmings that remain confined to El Niño 4 region and do not intrude into the coastal waters of Peru or Ecuador tend to produce milder winters in northern California, Oregon, Washington, British Columbia, and the U.S.-Canadian prairies. Inverse relations between this El Niño region and lowered precipitation are

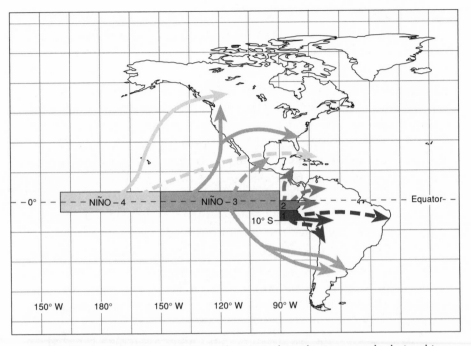

1.5. The four quadrants of El Niño in the tropical Pacific Ocean and relationships with rain in the Americas.

experienced in most of the Antilles, as well as along the Caribbean coasts of Colombia and Venezuela.

However, since sea temperature changes of the tropical Pacific are the result of atmospheric forcing, that is, pressure variations and resulting winds in the southern hemisphere, these precipitation and temperature anomalies are also related to the Southern Oscillation Index (SOI), since the latter is an accurate expression of the atmospheric variabilities affecting the circulation over tropical oceans. In fact, most of the studies on teleconnections with ENSO-related anomalies use the SOI as the main scale of reference.

Keeping the role played by the Southern Oscillation in mind, as well as its division into two distinct halves, we can easily see that while the SO's "western hemisphere" experiences high humidity, torrential rains, and above-average temperatures during El Niño events, the "eastern hemisphere" is subject to severe dryness. Heavy downpours all across the Pacific, catastrophic rains and river flooding in Ecuador and Peru, and heightened rains and winter storms on the Pacific coast of North America are coupled with droughts in Indonesia, China, Australia, and India, as well as eastern and sub-Saharan Africa, although the brunt of these catastrophic events is felt several months after the onset of an El Niño in the tropical Pacific.

What is the conveyor of these variabilities generated in a warmed Pacific Ocean? It is the tropical jet stream, a band of high-elevation winds that is established at the boundary between warm equatorial air and temperate air from subtropical latitudes. In this encounter zone, 12 to 15 kilometers above ground, winds reaching velocities up to 200 kilometers per hour weave their way from west to east over oceans and continental masses (Figure 1.6). To gain an appreciation of the steadiness and intensity of this jet stream, one might consider the following feat: in March of 1999, Brian Jones of Great Britain and Bertrand Piccard of Switzerland, impelled by these strong winds, were able to circumnavigate the globe in a balloon in only nineteen days. The jet stream rises over continental masses and mountain ranges (particularly in the summer) and dips over oceans, picking up humidity that eventually is dropped over distant continents.

Only after grasping the dynamics operating in the high troposphere (12,000 to 15,000 meters up) can one understand how stimuli generated in the distant tropical Pacific can be responsible for unusually mild winters in western Canada, rainy springs in the southeastern United States, and cold, snowy winters in western Europe during El Niño events.

Nature's Reactions to El Niño and La Niña

So far we have reviewed a series of disturbances that characterize the atmospheric and oceanic aspects of El Niño and its counterpart, La Niña. Since these changes represent brisk departures from normal conditions, they exert enormous stress on natural environments through high humidity and heavy rains in certain regions and severe droughts in others.

A sudden surplus of water in dry areas may bring dormant vegetation to bloom and cause an explosive multiplication of insects, reptiles, and small mammals, which, in normal years, stay within controlled population levels. Lack of water in other regions has the opposite effect: not only does the usual vegetation dry up or go dormant, but animal life that consumes it is drastically reduced. The fact that El Niño is basically an alteration of oceanic conditions makes its impact on the oceans even more

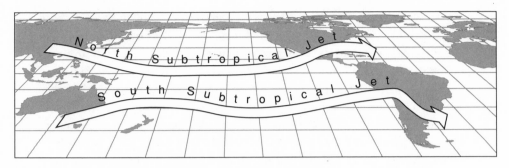

1.6. The meandering paths of the subtropical jet streams

serious. Ocean warming usually involves an increase in salinity and a reduction in oxygen and carbon, a life-threatening change for plankton—microorganisms of vegetal nature (phytoplankton) or animal nature (zooplankton)—on which many fish feed. A reaction in the marine food chain follows: not only the oceans' predators, but also seabirds and mammals (seals, sea otters, and small whales) that feed on the fish, suffer famine and a severe reduction in numbers.

Let us now turn to a selection of ecological crises caused by El Niño and La Niña in natural systems and their effect on human activities that depend on these resources.

The Collapse of the Peruvian Fisheries

Not until the occurrence of El Niño in 1972–73 did the industrialized world become aware of this phenomenon, which was affecting the distant country of Peru in South America, and have to start dealing with the consequences. Peru had moved into the limelight toward the end of the 1950s, when Peruvian gunboats began harassing or seizing fishing trawlers from San Diego for entering their "territorial waters" in pursuit of tuna. The "tuna war" between the United States and Peru was still simmering in 1968, when Juan Velasco-Alvarado, a general of nationalist leanings who had seized power in a military coup, confiscated the U.S.-owned oil wells on the northern coast of the country. The escalating friction became a cause of concern for the Americans, especially when Peru called on the Soviet Union for support. The Soviets were only too eager to oblige, thereby gaining access to the rich fishing grounds of the eastern Pacific and strengthening their geopolitical presence in Latin America.

In those years Peru was the major fishing nation of the world (with Japan and the Soviet Union close behind). Its catches consisted mostly of anchovies (*Engraulis ringens*), a cold water fish that lives in voluminous shoals in the plankton-rich waters of the Peru Current. In 1970, Peru harvested nearly 10 million metric tons of that fish, and marine biologists warned that if these high harvesting levels were to coincide with the occurrence of an El Niño, the survival of the species would be threatened. The call was not heeded, as the exports of fish meal and fish oil derived from the anchovies provided a fiscal bonanza for the Peruvian government.

Then, El Niño 1972–73 struck. Although this event was not one of the most intense ENSO episodes of the century, it hit the coastal waters of Peru with particular ferocity. In 1971, the anchovy catches had reached a whopping 12 million metric tons, and when the west coast of South America was invaded by the warm waters, the anchovy stocks, weakened by overfishing, were unable to spawn at normal rates; fishing trawlers started to return empty to their ports of origin, seabirds began to starve, and the rookeries of seabirds and mammals that abound along the arid coast dwindled. Traveling down the coast of Peru in 1973, I witnessed scenes of misery: processing plants that produced fish meal were paralyzed, fishing trawlers lay idle in bays and coves, and the beaches were littered with bird and seal carcasses.

Of the estimated 27.5 million seabirds in 1970, only 1.8 million survived the crisis. By 1982, numbers were up to 8 million, but in the course of the 1990s, they never rose above the 10-million mark. Among these birds, the *guanay* (cormorant) is particularly noteworthy. It nests in large colonies on rocky islets off the coast, and its droppings, known as *guano*, are a coveted natural fertilizer. While guano was one of Peru's main exports in the middle of the nineteenth century, its exploitation today is negligible.

For the first time since the collapse of the Pacific sardines of California in the 1940s and the depletion of the Sakhalin sardines in the 1920s, a major world fishery was crumbling before the very eyes of the alarmed world fishery authorities. The catches for the year 1973 show the magnitude of the anchovy catastrophe: Peru landed only 2.3 million tons that year, and Chile as little as 668,000 tons (Figure 1.7). From 1973 to 1983 (another El Niño year), Peru endured an unstable fishing period, with catches hovering around 2 million tons per year. Chile chose a different path. In those years of military rulers, the Chilean general Augusto Pinochet ordered all industrial fishing operations to stop immediately, and after the 1972–73 low, he changed the focus from anchovies to jack mackerel (*Trachurus murphii*)—a larger subtropical fish—and sardines (*Sardinops sagax*), which thrive in temperate waters. With this change Chile moved ahead of Peru between 1979 and 1985. While Peru had its absolute lowest landings in the El Niño year of 1983, the rising trend continued in Chile thanks to species diversification. Only after 1985 did Peru start on the road to recovery, initially also by switching to sardines and jack mackerel. Since the early 1990s, a comeback of the anchovy stock has allowed the industrial fisheries to include that species in their ventures again.

During the 1990s, world fisheries underwent some interesting changes, for which El Niño acted as catalyst. The repeated oceanic warming episodes of the 1980s had led to contractions in the volume of catches, but by 1990, the combined annual landings of Peru, Chile, and Ecuador soared to a total of 14 million tons—which broke all prior records. In

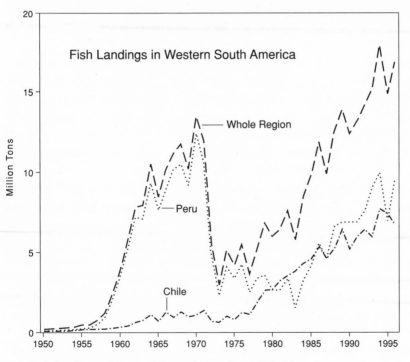

1.7. Fish landings of Peru, Chile, and Ecuador, 1950–96

1994, landings from the cold waters of the Peru Current totaled 18 million tons, a volume that would have been unthinkable twenty years earlier and that demonstrates the resilience of the Peru Current ecosystem. In the 1990s, Peru regained the top position it had enjoyed in the 1960s, and Chile secured third place among the major fishing nations of the world. Recently, however, China has taken second place from Japan, which has slipped to fourth position. It should be pointed out in this context, though, that while Peru and Chile keep their activities in the adjacent coastal waters, Chinese and Japanese fishing vessels operate far from their territorial waters, harvesting resources that are not theirs but the patrimony of all humankind.

The changing fortunes of fisheries along the west coast of South America illustrate the impact a natural disaster, such as El Niño, can have on resources believed to be inexhaustible when it is coupled with overexploitation.

The collapse of the anchovy-based fisheries on the west coast of South America prompted an unexpected global revolution in the domain of agricultural specialization. Fish meal from Peru and Chile was used mainly as animal feed in the industrialized countries of the world. When the sudden shortfall in this protein-rich product elicited a frantic search for a substitute, soybean meal seemed the most suitable. In 1974, world demand and low production of that grain drove the price of soybeans to a record $275 per ton (Figure 1.8), but soon thereafter the major agricultural producers were able to satisfy the market and the price went down. Up to 1973, the United States had produced nearly two-thirds of the soybeans in the world, but since then it has been challenged by other extensive cultivating countries, such as Brazil, which today is the second largest soybean producer (Figure 1.9). The recent recovery of western South America's fisheries has not curbed world soybean demand and production, since equal amounts of that legume are now used for human consumption. This example illustrates how an ecological disaster such as El Niño can determine an evolutionary trend in world agriculture.

The Damage to Marine Ecosystems

Having been monitored during its early development along the equator in the southern spring of 1972 by a battery of oceanographic and meteorological devices, the devastation wrought by El Niño 1972–73 during its

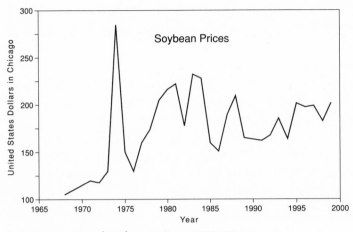

1.8. Progression of soybean prices, 1970–99

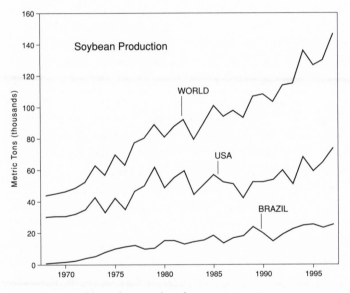

1.9. Major world producers of soybeans, 1968–97

eastward progression was well documented. Torrential rains on the otherwise dry equatorial islands of Jarvis, Fanning, Christmas, and Malden dismantled the nests of seabirds, and in December 1972, the Galapagos Islands reported high mortality rates of seabirds, iguanas, and turtles. In arid northern Peru, the rains practically washed away cultivated fields of corn, beans, cotton, coffee, and sugarcane, depositing loads of sand and silt in fields that had escaped river erosion. Houses on riverbanks, bridges, waterworks, and roads were erased when normally insignificant trickles of water swelled into wild rivers. The clogging of sewer systems caused waste waters to spill over into rivers and creeks, contaminating wells and causing cholera and typhoid outbreaks in the populated river oases of southern Ecuador and northern Peru, thus compounding the general misery attributable to El Niño.

Tropical pests from the lowlands bordering northern Peru and the eastern Andean rain forests made their way into the arid oases. Particularly feared were the *latigazo* (the whip), an otherwise rare tropical centipede that causes painful skin lacerations, and the outbreaks of Leishmaniasis, a serious skin infection transmitted by sand flies. At the height of El Niño 1983, starving bullfrogs from the humid lowlands of Ecuador and eastern Peru littered the flooded streets and parks of towns in northern Peru. In 1972–73, 1982–83, and 1997–98, egrets and herons camped in the newly created swamps and lakes that were normally barren lands.

The alterations caused by warm oceanic conditions in marine ecosystems are no less dramatic. Warm water invasions along the coast that lies under the influence of the Peru Current bring unexpected visitors to offshore waters. The number of sharks, tuna, albacore, and other species from warmer waters increase noticeably during El Niño years. Among the exotic species that can be caught in the coastal waters are the prickly globe-fish (*Diodon hystrix*) (Plate 1), the big-scale pomfret (*Taractichthys steindachneri*) common in the warm waters of the Kuro Shio Current off Japan, and the humped *jorobado* (*Selene* sp.). Particularly welcomed by Peru's artisanal fishermen are the guitarfish (*Coryphaena hippurus*), which, like the dolphin, or mahimahi, of north-hemispheric tropical waters, is coveted for its exquisite white, firm flesh, and the *pez guitarra* (*Rhinobatus planicep*), an edible ray often sun-dried (Plate 2). Other fish normally occurring only at the interface of warm tropical waters and the northern edge of the cold Peru Current, such as tropical perch (*mero*) and skipjack (*Katsuwonus pelamis*), move to cooler waters farther south.

Also observable is the unusual southward migration of coastal mollusks and crustaceans. The *ostion*, or Pacific scallop, a tasty shellfish normally sheltered in protected bays, experiences explosive population growth during El Niño years, so that millions of scallops litter Peru's beaches during warm water episodes (Arntz and Fahrbach 1991). On the shallow, silty shores of Ecuador and Colombia also affected by the waters of El Niño, crabs and shrimp—otherwise confined to propitious coastal locations—multiply in large numbers. Following El Niños of 1972–73 and 1982–83, a new industry started in the shallow bays of Ecuador: shrimp nurseries were established in huge ponds (Plate 3), the product destined for export, particularly to North America and Europe. The competition with small scale shrimpers and the pollution of coastal waters by artificial feed had environmentalists up in arms, so today this industry is operating in a low-key mode.

El Niño also causes alterations in marine ecosystems along the Pacific coast of North America. During the 1982–83 and 1997–98 events, the California coast experienced visible modification in sea life between San Diego and San Francisco, and even up to Cape Mendocino. Not far off the coast, commercial fishermen were able to catch exotic yellowfin tuna, mahimahi, skipjack, marlin, albacore, and yellowtail during those years. The black durgeon (*Melichtys niger*) and similar species were sighted as far north as Queen Charlotte Islands, Canada (lat. 53 °N), while other Californian species, such as the lizardfish (*Synodious lucioceps*) and tonguefish (*Symphurius atricauda*), advanced far north of their habitual temperate grounds, and crabs (*Nyctiphanes simplex*) expanded to the northern sector of Vancouver Island. Inversely, there was a marked contraction in salmon all the way from northern California to British Columbia.

A particularly damaging El Niño effect besets the coral populations in the Pacific basin. The colonies of these invertebrate organisms are very sensitive to environmental change. Since their survival depends on clear water, good circulation, and a narrow range of temperatures, a slight change in these conditions stunts their development or causes death. Thus oceanic fluctuations of El Niño or La Niña signature obviously have an enormous and immediate effect on corals of the Pacific Ocean, the Indian Ocean, and the tropical Atlantic. One of the main effects of ocean warming is coral bleaching—whitening of the coral surfaces due to the loss of a microorganism called zooxanthellae, which has a symbiotic relationship with growing corals. The absence of the temperature-sensitive zooxanthellae precipitates coral mortality and hampers the rapid rebuilding of young colonies. In addition, unusual warming of the waters leads to the disappearance of assorted crustaceans that feed on sea snails and sea urchins, the common predators of growing coral sprouts. Above all, coastal waters are polluted by abnormally high discharges of clays and silts from the copious runoffs of islands and continental margins, so that the resulting turbidity accelerates coral destruction. Glyn and Colgan (1992) estimate that the ENSO event of 1982–83 caused the extermination of nearly 95 percent of the Galapagos Islands' corals and resulted in a 70 to 95 percent reduction in the corals on the coasts of Costa Rica, Panama, Colombia, and Ecuador, all of them in the eastern Pacific Ocean. Fortunately, corals have a remarkable regenerative ability by recruiting larvae from nearby sound colonies; however, when disturbed marine conditions persist—as they did during the prolonged but mild El Niño of 1991–94—the regeneration process can be dangerously retarded.

Of the organisms living in tropical waters, corals are also the most prone to reflect environmental alterations in their biological development. The body of an individual coral grows radially by means of carbonate secretion, the growth phases being indicated in the latticed skeletal structures in the form of annual bands. The carbonate compound that constitutes the coral skeleton is aragonite, a mineral that incorporates into the calcium some trace metals such as cadmium, barium, and manganese, as well as oxygen isotopes ($\delta18$ oxygen). Cadmium and barium are regarded as indicators of cool upwelling water conditions, with barium being very sensitive to sea temperature changes. Manganese, which indicates fine sediments of continental origin, also tends to decrease during warm ENSO episodes due to increases of coarse particles. The $\delta18$ oxygen component of coral skeletal aragonite is precipitated by seawater and diminishes as water temperature and rainfall increase during El Niño episodes (Cole, Shen, Fairbanks, and Moore 1992). By analyzing thin coral sections, marine biologists and sediment geologists have established that deficits in $\delta18$ oxygen, calcium/cadmium, barium/calcium, and manganese/calcium are caused by warm ENSO phases (Evans, Fairbanks, and Rubenstone 1998). Today, chemical analyses of contemporary and fossil corals offer insights into climatic variations that neither instrumental nor historical series are able to provide and are considered one of the key tools for verifying disturbed oceanic conditions of El Niño signature in the past.

Bugs and Mice of Humid Years

Some astounding ecological responses to El Niño occur on land in various corners of the world. For example, in the forests of the Amazon, the German zoologist Arim Adis noticed that spiders and other insects seem to possess a sensorial mechanism that detects rising environmental humidity and prompts them to start crawling up tree trunks well before the onset of the rainy season or to move higher as the rains arrive. The vast expanses of the Amazon lowlands are crisscrossed by streams and side channels of the Amazon River, which at the height of the rainy season— March through August—are extensively flooded. Not only insects, but terrestrial reptiles and rodents as well, are forced to move to higher grounds. Early studies of precipitation in the South American continent showed that El Niño is coupled with reduced rains in the central Amazon basin and that the rainy season—if not failing altogether—is shortened to April, May, and June. Over the course of years of observation, Adis noted that the upward movement of insects started later than usual and did not go as high during years with lowered precipitation, or El Niño years, establishing a startling "distant ecological connection" with that anomaly in the Pacific Ocean.

Another fascinating connection between a biological crisis and El Niño gained notoriety in 1993, when in the Four Corners region of the United States (New Mexico, Colorado, Arizona, and Utah) the aggressive Hanta virus broke out in the Navajo reservation with that name. The virus— harboring in the desiccated feces of the deer mouse, a small rodent that lives in abandoned dwellings—attacks the respiratory tract and leads to death within a few days. As it happened, the deer mouse population (as well as the number of rodents that feed on grasses and succulents) had exploded in 1993, in the wake of the El Niño rains that fell over the southwest part of the United States during the 1992–93 winter. Thereafter, the fatal disease—also associated with rainy winters—surfaced in other parts of the nation and even made its way into South America in the aftermath of El Niño 1997–98. Hanta pulmonary deaths were recorded in northern Chile, the highlands of southern Bolivia, and northwestern Argentina, all of them arid regions like the Four Corners where rodents might multiply twentyfold during rainy El Niño years. The Hanta virus, whose sole transmitter is mice, has been known in eastern Europe and also in the cold steppes of Asia since the Middle Ages, but the strains that developed in North and South America are new and probably unrelated to those of the Old World. The outbreak of the Hanta virus in the Americas appears to be a case of biological convergence triggered by this climatic variability that we call El Niño.

2
~

Searching for Past El Niños

Humans are said to have a short memory. Innovations are taken for granted soon after their introduction, and it does not take long to adapt to the new technologies that are thrust upon us, seemingly overnight. Thus we all have become accustomed to the way in which weather information is passed on to us in terms of temperatures, air humidity, precipitation, wind direction and velocity, pressure, and cloud cover. At any time of the day or night, audiences watch weather reports and forecasts based on real time measurements of these different indicators and are able to make sense of the ways in which the atmosphere is changing.

The measurements of the different weather elements are taken with meteorological instruments at conventional intervals (hours, days) and then averaged over weeks, months, triads (groups of three months), semesters, or years. A long sequence of observations constitutes a *time series,* and when it is based on instrumental observations, it is called an *instrumental series.* These series are a fairly recent development. A need for temporally spaced weather observations was recognized by the scientists of the eighteenth century, "the century of Enlightenment," but since they used a variety of instruments and criteria to measure the state of the atmosphere, different record scales evolved. Temperatures, for example, were measured in Réaumur, Fahrenheit, Celsius, or Kelvin, and rainfall amounts in inches, centimeters, or ounces. Congruent instrumental weather observations became available in the first decades of the nineteenth century, and only in the most advanced countries of Europe, which means that even the longest instrumental series covers barely two centuries. There are, of course, observations from earlier times conducted by men who were curious about the vagaries of weather and who wanted to leave testimony of the climate episodes that affected their societies.

This chapter surveys the different modalities in which climate and its variations have been expressed and explores the sources of indirect information that can be used to extend backward the contemporary climatical time series. Combining historical commentary and instrumental records allows us to ascertain when and how climate crises came about and the ways in which they affected humankind.

What Instrumental Series Do Not Show

In the first chapter, the altered conditions of the atmosphere and the sea during El Niño and La Niña episodes were identified using objective and reliable indicators of precipitation, barometric pressures, sea-surface temperatures, ocean salinity, and water density. Reliance on these indicators, however, imposes a time limit on the recognition and documentation of these episodes on the west coast of South America. In fact, continuous and reliable measurements of air temperatures and rainfall in Peru, Ecuador, and Chile seldom go back to the first half of the nineteenth century, thus allowing the meteorological identification of the wetter El Niño years only after 1850. Pinpointing La Niña years on the west coast of South America is even more difficult because the cold and dry conditions associated with this phenomenon are hard to differentiate from normal dry conditions on the desertic or semiarid coasts of northern Chile, Peru, and southern Ecuador. With these limitations imposed by the nature of the climatological records, the only sure way to identify La Niña episodes is by matching dry years with occurrences of cold sea-surface temperatures.

This raises a question about the extent and accuracy of sea-surface temperature measurements along the west coast of South America. The earliest Spaniards who came to central Peru were astonished at the coldness of the ocean water considering the tropical location. Joseph de Acosta, a Jesuit priest who wrote a perceptive account of the natural singularities of the New World in 1582, remarked that the ocean in the Bay of Callao—the port of Lima—at latitude 10°S was so much cooler than the air above that sailors would cool their bottles of wine by immersing them. The German naturalist Alexander von Humboldt, who visited coastal Peru in 1802–3, was also intrigued by this singularity in the South American tropics as he made sporadic measurements of ocean temperatures and commented on the speed of the Peru Current. Successive naturalists and scientists measured sea temperatures at different times during their travels, but these data lack the continuity necessary to establish valid time series.

Continuous measurements of sea-surface temperatures did not start before the late 1920s, when stations were installed in Puerto Chicama and Callao, Peru; in Valparaiso and Iquique, Chile; and in La Libertad, Ecuador. In the open seas off these countries, oceanographic expeditions, such as those of Carnegie (1928–29) and William Scoresby (1931), collected circumstantial ocean and air data, but again, these were not continuous. Reliable and sequential sea-surface temperature records do not go back more than eighty years, and cold oceanic episodes in the eastern Pacific cannot be documented before the 1920s.

Given such reduced data sequences—a climatological series of no more than 150 years and oceanic records no longer than eighty years—it is necessary to seek proxy data, that is, records or information from other sources (in this case, historical, anecdotal, or archival) that indicate abnormal climatic and oceanic conditions and to use geophysical evidence as recorded in geological history. This means going beyond the temporal limits imposed by instrumental series and searching for clues about environmental crises identical in character to those experienced and well documented during contemporary El Niño/La Niña episodes. References to the hardships suffered by societies as a result of heavy rains, flooding, or droughts—such as crop failures, loss of life and property, pests, and disease—may be found in early documents, revealing environmental disturbances related to El Niño or La Niña long before the advent of instrumental time series.

On the Lookout for Indirect Evidence

In 1928 archeological excavations in Ur, the ancient Chaldean city of southern Iraq (origin of the patriarch Abraham), conducted by the British Museum and the Museum of the University of Pennsylvania, struck the oldest foundations of that city beneath a thick layer of river depositions. This was the first indirect evidence that a Great Flood, as recounted in the first book of Genesis, did actually occur. Thus, what had been regarded as a legend—told by the early people to try to explain the sudden erasure of Sumarian settlements along the banks of the Euphrates—turned out to have been a natural catastrophe, as is likely to occur in arid environments where erratic precipitation can lead to disastrous river flooding.

Along the same lines runs the search for indirect evidence of past climatic crises caused by El Niño/La Niña and their worldwide sequels. As noted in the previous section, our knowledge of the effects of such altered oceanic and atmospheric conditions is based on sound scientific observations and reliable instrumental readings, but these do not go back beyond the first half of the nineteenth century. It is therefore necessary to scrutinize all available indirect sources to create a sequence of abnormal years that is long enough to yield certain clues about their frequency and cause.

In so-called climatic reconstructions of past environmental conditions, European climatologists and environmentalists have drawn remarkable inferences from old chronicles, archives, notarized documents, prices and volumes of harvested crops, entries on settlement abandonments, and other official records in order to determine "lean years" and "years of plenty." On this side of the ocean, a fascinating book titled *Climates of Hunger* by meteorologists Reid Bryson and T. J. Murray traces climatic variabilities all over the world and particularly in North America, using several indirect evidences of climate change. The authors show how ancillary information extracted from historical sources and from "nature's notebook," such as sediment sequences, pollen spectra, tree rings, and other indicators of climate anomalies, can be used to extend backward the all-too-short instrumental series.

Let us now turn to the ways in which the time of occurrence and the intensity of past El Niños can be identified with the help of indirect evidence.

It is not clear when the term *El Niño* was first used in coastal Peru to refer to the warming of the coastal waters that was accompanied by torrential rains at the beginning of the southern summer. I have queried several Peruvian historians, who were unable to verify the use of the term in colonial times. The first written mention of El Niño appears in semi-scientific reports from the second half of the nineteenth century in reference to the seasonal invasion off northernmost Peru of waters from the Gulf of Guayaquil. The first time the term appears in the national scientific literature is in Luis Carranza's (1891) and Victor Eguiguren's (1894) and Camilo Carrillo's (1892) works about the oceanic warming and the devastating rains and floods that accompanied the mighty El Niño of 1891. The search for the term *El Niño* in historical sources published before 1891 has yielded no results. That does not mean, however, that this oceanic/climatic phenomenon did not occur earlier, only that references to its effects on the environment and human affairs did not expressly employ the name El Niño.

Based on the premise that El Niño events of great magnitude affect normally dry northern Peru and raise the temperatures of the coastal waters—thus inducing high mortality rates among fish, marine mammals, and seabirds—scientists have attempted since the 1980s to create a timetable of past El Niño occurrences. They combed historical and archival sources for indications of environmental changes that resemble the known manifestations of contemporary El Niños, such as torrential rains and devastating floods, loss of fields and crops due to river inundations, and destruction of roads, bridges, dwellings, and irrigation canals. They even checked petitions from regional farmers and plantation owners (sugar, cotton, and cacao) to the authorities in Lima for the deferral or waiving of taxes due to natural disasters. So although the word *El Niño* was not actually used in the historical sources, occurrences of past El Niños could be identified with great accuracy.

Combining this compilation with a thorough analysis of the existing bibliography on El Niño, the late William H. Quinn, an oceanographer at Oregon State University, his assistant Victor T. Neal, and the Peruvian historian Santiago E. Antúnez de Mayolo composed a list of El Niño occurrences from 1541 to 1983. The Quinn chronology is considered the yardstick against which the effects of past El Niños on the entire Pacific basin as well as on distant continents are gauged. With small modifications, this list is informative and authoritative for as far back as the time of the arrival of the Spaniards in Peru in 1531. The Quinn chronology also integrates a list of rainy years in central Chile that was compiled by Emilio Taulis in 1934, for central Chile experiences copious winter rains the year before or during the same year that El Niño occurs in northern Peru. It is noteworthy that this is the temperate zone of South America, more than 3,000 kilometers south of northern Peru where the phenomenon shows up with maximum intensity; Taulis's list proves that the events cited by Quinn also affected regions far from the "prime El Niño" areas.

In the following chapters, occurrences of severe climatic anomalies in other parts of the world will be examined insofar as they correspond to El Niño episodes included in the Quinn chronology as well as other updated chronologies, such as the one that I produced with P. R. Waylen in 1991. The latter chronology also includes La Niña years, which we identified by using the premise that they are characterized by droughts in coastal Peru and central Chile.

This book also considers the historical impacts of El Niño events, a subject that brings us to a branch of history known as environmental history.

A Case for Environmental History

Preoccupied as we are with the political and economic events of contemporary life, that is, with the affairs shaped by politicians, militaries, and corporate executives worldwide, we tend to overlook other histories that had an equally determining power. Let us consider, for example, the consequence of the pervasive drought that ravaged the U.S. Midwest in the 1930s. During these "dust bowl" years, millions of people were forced to leave rural areas and migrate to cities. This movement ultimately sparked the urbanization of prewar America and destroyed much of the rural lifestyle in the agrarian Midwest. As weather conditions returned to normal, farming was taken up in larger units, and rural land-managing strategies, such as irrigation and soil conservation, were adopted. Not only did the natural disaster change the way in which Americans farmed, but it transformed the social fabric of the United States. Were one to analyze these events from a strictly political viewpoint without considering the environmental history of those years, the emerging picture would be inaccurate.

The decline and ultimate downfall of the Maya in the lowlands of Guatemala and Yucatan, whose advanced state of civilization was manifested in impressive architectural monuments and astounding social and scientific achievements, cannot be explained solely on the basis of political events or cultural bottlenecks. One has to look for other causes. It seems that their demise was precipitated by repeated cycles of dryness. Studies of lake sedimentation in Yucatan have uncovered sequences of wet and dry periods that, 1,000 years ago, had devastating consequences for this civilization. Likewise, the enigmatic disappearance of the Minoan culture—one of the early Greek cultures—also seems associated with a climatic crisis that occurred around 1450 B.C. and exacerbated the stress caused by invading Greek tribes.

Examples like these from Western, Asian, and pre-European American civilizations show that history has often been shaped by natural disasters and by progressive environmental modifications. Historians are painstakingly scrutinizing old documents for indications of such crises and climatic changes. At the same time, they are trying to evaluate the impact of past political decisions or economic policies on natural environments. This novel branch—environmental history—looks at the ways in which modifications in natural environments have influenced human behavior and also analyzes societies' attitudes toward their environments in the course of history.

In the pursuit of this research, direct and indirect evidence of such "hidden" variabilities is interpreted according to the molds and criteria that apply to the study of contemporary interrelations between humans and environments under stress. This "actualistic approach" tries to evaluate past climate effects using contemporary explanatory models.

If climate is understood as the average condition of the atmosphere, which shows variations year after year (*inter-annual variations*), then—from a perspective that emphasizes food production, an essential prerequisite for human survival—copious rains (as long as they do not result in devastating floods) must be equated with "years of plenty," while droughts, scorching heat, or killing frosts are indicators of "lean years." If such variations from the norm persist over several years or are the precursors of a fundamental modification in weather patterns, then *inter-decadal variations* are said to occur. So, for example, following El Niño 1972–73 and the subsequent droughts in central Africa, there has been a marked tendency toward an increase in frequency and intensity of El Niño and La Niña occurrences. The same can be said—and all of it under the common denominator of a patent global warming—about the increased frequency of hurricanes in the tropical Pacific and Atlantic. Some geophysicists predict that if this trend continues and melting polar ice masses cause ocean levels to rise, winter storms and fall hurricanes will cause disastrous flooding in Miami, New York, and low-lying areas of New Jersey by the first quarter of the twenty-first century.

Having personally witnessed within our lifetime how serious a threat climatic fluctuations can be to densely populated areas in an advanced country like the United States, we can appreciate how technologically less advanced societies, present or past, can be overwhelmed by the effects of such fluctuations. The actualistic approach to past catastrophes has been successfully applied to the investigation of cyclical cooling periods in western Europe that led to the abandonment of settlements on the arctic fringe of Scandinavia or near the alpine snowline, and to climate-induced crop failures that caused famine, social dislocation, and mass migration, as the case of Ireland in the mid-1800s illustrates.

Historical-environmental investigations into the social, political, cultural, or economic implications of past El Niño episodes are sparse, and the findings are scattered in various publications. This book brings together information about environmental crises that seem to have been provoked by climatic/oceanic changes of El Niño character to illustrate the frequency, widespread impact, and intensity of these phenomena in the past. Readers are invited to keep their eyes open for "hidden indicators" of possible ancient ENSO events while reading formal histories. Along these lines, most of the examples in the upcoming chapters are intended to make the case for the relevance of El Niño studies in the context of environmental history.

Natural Crises and Human Tragedies

The Black Death in Europe is calculated to have killed 25 million people between 1347 and 1353. At the end of World War II, the total number of casualties in Europe and Asia amounted to nearly 60 million. The famines in India of 1685–88, 1770, 1789–91, 1802–3, 1832–33, 1837–38, 1853, 1896–99, and 1899–1900 are estimated to have taken the lives of more than 70 million. In China alone, the prolonged drought of 1876–79 caused 9 to 13 million deaths. In the northeast of Brazil, droughts in 1809–10, 1824–25, 1844–45, 1888–89, 1891–92, 1899–1900, 1915, 1919, 1931–33, 1951–53, and 1958 brought millions of people to the brink of starvation; towns and cities were looted by hungry mobs. The first of these disasters was the consequence of a biological hazard spread by infected rats, and the second was a human-inflicted tragedy. The others, however, resulted from climate variabilities that reduced the rain needed for agricultural production and precipitated famine, death, and social dislocation.

The reason for the droughts in India was the failure of the moisture-laden winds from the southeast to arrive at the onset of summer, which ruined the summer crops in the most populous areas, while the droughts in Brazil happened because the summer rains associated with the Inter-Tropical Covergence Zone's southward shift did not occur. We know now that both failures relate to anomalies in the general circulation of the tropical belt that are brought on by El Niño. But in those days hardly anybody suspected that such environmental crises were related to abnormal warming or cooling of the distant Pacific Ocean and that the atmosphere above reacted to these changes by taking humidity from the sea in some regions—western South America, for example—and withholding it in other regions, such as India, sub-Saharan Africa, and northeastern Brazil.

From our vantage point, and assisted by plenty of historical references and indirect clues, we can now make sense of the connectedness of these calamities and explain them as the result of periodical anomalies of the Southern Oscillation. We can also construct a global history of El Niño occurrences by linking seemingly unrelated environmental crises to documented human disasters. By using an explanatory diagram (Figure 2.1), we are able to visualize the impact of natural crises on several spheres of human affairs. The columns represent symptoms and effects of El Niño, while along the rows one follows the interactions between altered natural systems and human activities and the consequences of anomalous climatic and oceanic conditions in the Pacific Ocean for contiguous countries and distant regions. The model applies primarily to the experiences of countries on the eastern Pacific rim during El Niño years, and it cannot be applied directly to systematize the effects of El Niño on Asia, Africa, and Europe. In all cases, however, not only is the environment affected, but humans and their activities suffer as well.

One must be aware that not every El Niño entails all the interactions presented in Figure 2.1. During some occurrences certain effects appear muffled, while others are maximized; commonly, though, the impact on natural environments and on human habitation and production systems follows the patterns depicted in the diagram.

As explained in chapter 1, and displayed in the first column, every El Niño entails an oceanic aspect (the superficial warming of the Pacific

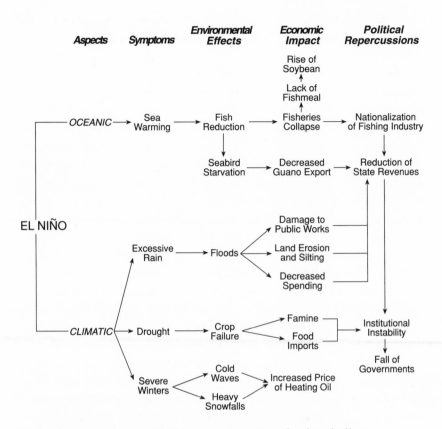

2.1. Implications of recent El Niños on economic and political affairs

Ocean) and an atmospheric or climatic aspect (the weakening of the high pressures and the temporary replacement of the dominating easterly winds by westerlies). While the easterly winds are usually dry and steady, the westerlies are warm, humid, and burst into stormy surges. As oceanic and climatic disruptions spread across the Pacific basin, global circulation flows transmit the anomalies of humidity and heat within the tropical belt. Certain regions experience copious rains fueled by moisture release from the overheated ocean, while others endure droughts of varying degrees of severity. Outside the tropics, El Niño produces either mild winters or severe winters marked by excessive snowfall and chilling temperatures. The oceanic and meteorological anomalies that begin to show in the Pacific basin at the onset of an El Niño episode are transferred over long distances by flows operating in the upper layers of the troposphere, such as the subtropical and polar jet streams, the upper-level westerlies, and the resulting Rossby waves (sinuousities in the polar jet stream that trigger bad weather spells in middle latitudes). Because the ocean and climate spheres interact closely with one another, on the surface of the earth all biological, economic, and human systems are also affected by atmospheric and oceanic anomalies.

The oceanic El Niño phenomenon causes alterations in water conditions that disrupt the thermal and biological balances of the ocean. Increases in sea temperature and decreases in oxygen and carbon content cause breakdowns in the marine food chain by dramatically reducing the production of microorganisms. Fish die or fail to reproduce as a consequence of these changes. As shown in the column illustrating the economic impact, coastal communities that depend on these sea resources then enter periods of contraction and impoverishment, as has happened in fishing communities in Peru and northern Chile during El Niño episodes. Apart from the fish, the survival of other creatures that depend on food from the sea is threatened. In the waters of the eastern Pacific, there are massive die-offs of sea mammals, including seals, whales, and otters, their carcasses littering the beaches of western South America and the Galapagos Islands. Also affected are the large populations of seabirds that have been supported since time immemorial by the bountiful fish of the eastern Pacific. They nest in the cliffs along the coast or on offshore islets, and their accumulated droppings (guano) were sold to Europe and North America as a coveted fertilizer before the advent of artificial fertilizers. Even today, guano is selectively used to grow ornamental flowers and delicate fruits. So when a dwindling fish supply causes high mortality rates for these birds, the small-scale guano export economies of coastal Peru are also depressed.

Other disturbing sequels triggered by these variations include their destabilizing effects on regional and national economies and political systems, outlined in the final column. Severe recessions in Peru's fishing industry, at both the artisanal and industrial level, wrought havoc in the wake of the El Niño episodes of 1971–73 and 1982–83. The effects of these events on the fisheries in the Pacific off South America were discussed in chapter 1. Up to 1972, fishing and the processing of fish into fish meal and fish oil in Peru were owned by private investors, providing work for the people and a sizable income for the government through diverse taxation and export fees. When in 1973, fish dwindled due to overfishing and unemployment became rampant in Peruvian coastal towns, the government of General Velasco-Alvarado bought up all the industrial fishing establishments in order to "protect the Peruvian sea resources"—at a moment when there were few resources to protect. In a poor country like Peru, this move added a financial burden that precipitated a state of insolvency and institutional malaise lasting well into the early 1990s. In retrospect, one might even say the chaotic sociopolitical climate that allowed the rise of violent movements, such as Shining Path, was a consequence of the over-exertion of the national budget in 1973. This is but one example of the impact a natural anomaly such as El Niño can have on national politics. At the international level, the political implications of the droughts and famines associated with this phenomenon were strongly felt in Ethiopia, the Sahel countries, India, and the former Soviet Union.

Another development associated with the 1972–73 disruption of the ocean's ecological balance was the transition from reliance on fish meal to soybean meal as animal feed. The switch to soybeans stimulated the production of this commodity for the international markets, and today it is one of the most largely produced after wheat, rice, and corn. Had it not been for the El Niño–induced ecological crisis in the Pacific off Peru, very likely the soybean would not have achieved such prominence.

The climatic aspects of El Niño (bottom half of figure 2.1) are exemplified by the torrential rains in Peru, Ecuador, and central Chile and by the stormy episodes on the coasts of California, Oregon, and Washington during the southern winters. Excessive rains have three major environmental consequences. The first consequence is river swelling and flooding in low-lying areas, as experienced in Peru, Ecuador, Chile, California, Louisiana, and northern Florida, with corresponding damage to public works (such as roads and bridges) and water management facilities. The various administrative units hit by these disasters incur vast debts trying to cope with and mitigate the effects. Flooding in normally rainless valleys can lead to sewage spilling into the rivers. During the El Niño occurrences of 1972–73, 1982–83, and 1997–98, epidemics of typhus, dysentery, hepatitis, and intestinal infections ravaged the northern oases of Peru because of contaminated water.

The second consequence of heavy rains is soil erosion and silting of croplands that have been inundated by sediment-laden rivers (Plate 4). In

Peru's coastal region, fertile soils dedicated to the production of sugar-cane, cotton, or maize may disappear under layers of initially infertile silts; it takes years before they can be put to agricultural use again.

A third consequence is landslides. Known as *huaicos* in Peru, the land-slides add to the general misery by destroying rural roads, thus isolating communities already hard hit by the torrential rains. During El Niño 1997–98, roads from the lowlands of western Ecuador into the densely populated areas of the Andean interior were washed out, so that long and costly detours had to be improvised in order to bring help from the heart-land to the afflicted coastal communities. No less frequent were *huaicos* in northern and central Peru, where vital connections between the coast and the interior sierra were disrupted.

Nature provides trade-offs. The abundant rainfall during El Niño years also has positive aspects. The water supply in most of the river oases of Peru and northern Chile consists of runoff from the high Andes, where precipitation, scant as it may be, falls in the form of snow or rain that feeds montane rivulets and then infiltrates the groundwater storage to be gradually released into the life-sustaining rivers. In these desert areas, the rains of El Niño years replenish the chronically low underground re-serves for several years. They are also a bonus for the cattle ranches and dairy farms, which enjoy the temporary addition of natural grassland to their normally irrigated pastures.

The implications of El Niño phenomena are more complex for the glo-bal circulation than for the regional winds closer to the core area of the oceanic and climatic El Niños. Global atmospheric circulation involves air flows that are not restricted to particular regions but, like the westerlies of high latitudes, blow across vast latitudes and longitudes. Within the natu-ral order of our planet, these inter-regional flows serve a balancing func-tion within the various atmospheric pressure centers. Thus, if one region experiences excessive inputs of heat and humidity, other parts of the world respond with cooler and drier air through this "self-compensating" mechanism, which is more pronounced during the altered states of the atmosphere caused by El Niño or La Niña (see chapter 7) than in climato-logically normal years.

This interaction was not clearly perceived until the early 1970s, when scientists working on the climatic variabilities induced by El Niño real-ized that during those same years or shortly before or after, severe droughts affected certain regions outside the classical circum-Pacific El

Niño realm. Included in these regions are the high plateaus of southern Peru and Bolivia (altiplano), the "dry hump" of South America in northeastern Brazil, the center of Australia, the islands of Indonesia, the peninsula of India, the Sahel region of Africa (comprising primarily Ethiopia, Somalia, Sudan, and Chad), South Africa, and the central lowlands of eastern Europe. In these places the lack of water, particularly during the spring and summer planting season, prompts crop failures and food shortages. In all of them the rural economy hinges on animal husbandry so that the losses inflicted by the droughts are enormous and, in many cases, threaten the very existence of pastoral communities. Famine has been the tragic outcome of catastrophic droughts in these regions. During El Niños in the 1960s and 1970s, crops failed in Russia because the early summer rains did not arrive or snow reserves had dwindled during dry winters and made it necessary for the Soviets to purchase grain from Western countries such as Canada, the United States, or Argentina. The disastrous Sahel droughts of 1973–75 had political repercussions: as thousands crossed the diffuse borders of sub-Saharan states, emerging warlords demanded ransoms from the hunger-refugees or else sold them as slaves to warring factions, or they rebelled against distant or debilitated (and often corrupt) central governments. The fall of the Ethiopian emperor Haile Selassie, engineered by his army under the guise of a communist liberation movement, illustrates how an environmental crisis generated by a distant El Niño event destabilized this African nation until the end of the twentieth century.

Droughts in southern Asia during El Niño years also opened the eyes of many scientists to the relationship between those episodes in the Pacific off South America and famines in India. In past centuries these catastrophes had been lethal for millions. Dams and irrigation networks constructed during the last decades of British rule and first years of the Indian republic averted further tragedies of that scope, but even today the lack of rains in El Niño years continues to severely tax the resilience of that overpopulated country. More recently, El Niño–induced droughts in 1997–98 sparked so many wildfires in Indonesia that for weeks the air was unbreathable on Java, Sumatra, and Timor, and even an air crash on Kalimantan was attributed to poor visibility from the smoke of forest fires.

Another way in which the global atmosphere compensates for the heat and humidity excesses in the tropical belt during El Niño years is by activating the mechanisms that produce mild but snow-rich winters in the northern latitudes of North America and western Europe, and extremely cold winters with isolated but intense snowfall periods in eastern Europe and the buffer zone of the Euro-Asiatic plains. In both regions, humans have to endure prolonged winters with all the extra costs that this entails. The prediction in the fall of 1997 of an extreme winter for the Central Plains and the Midwest in view of the El Niño that was brewing in the South Pacific led to a surge in fuel oil and kerosene prices, while along the coast of California price increases were registered in storm repair and hazard prevention materials, such as plywood, nails, bags for sand, and plastic sheets, in anticipation of a stormy winter.

These examples, drawn from different places near and far from the cradle of El Niño, demonstrate how a natural crisis that once appeared to be restricted to a remote region of South America actually involves almost the entire world. We now turn to the past to see how earlier societies in the Americas were affected by El Niño and La Niña episodes.

3
~

Tracing Early Occurrences

When we look for climatic anomalies known today as El Niño or La Niña, one of the difficulties we encounter is that they were not described as such in the past. The concept of El Niño originated in northern Peru very likely during colonial times when coastal native communities were christian-ized. As mentioned in the previous chapter, the anomaly must also have existed in pre-Hispanic times, but no references to torrential rains or cata-strophic flooding are made in Indian accounts or oral traditions. There is sufficient geological evidence, though, to prove that they did occur, and the search for the hidden clues of El Niño constitutes a fascinating piece of detective work in contemporary science.

This chapter focuses on natural oddities mentioned in early narratives that seem to correspond to El Niño manifestations along the coast of South America. Putting a name on these events will provide first clues concerning their continual presence within the eastern confines of the Pacific Ocean. From there we will proceed to incorporate similar events from other maritime regions.

Did El Niño Help Pizarro Conquer Peru?

In the history of the conquest of the New World by the Spaniards, two episodes have amazed the world because of the temerity involved: the conquest of the Aztec empire of Mexico by Hernán Cortéz in 1519, and the swift takeover of the Inca empire of Peru by Francisco Pizarro in 1532. Without detracting from the boldness and endurance displayed by Cortéz and his men, it can be said that Pizarro's feat was more outstanding considering the natural obstacles and climatic adversities he had to overcome when venturing far from the Spanish main in the Caribbean. Starting in 1524, Pizarro made three attempts to reach the mythical land of Birú—which the Indians said was rich in silver and gold—by sailing south from Panama along the west coast of South America. During the first two, equatorial gales, contrary winds, and the oppressive dampness off the coast of Colombia and northern Ecuador prevented him from reaching his goal. Only the third attempt was successful, and in 1531, his party finally stood at the gates of the Inca empire (Figure 3.1).

Considerable research and heated debates have revolved around the question whether Pizarro's advance into the heart of the Inca empire was made easier because of humid weather conditions in a region that is usually bone-dry, or whether those references to rains and swollen rivers made by the early chroniclers may have been incorrect since they were written years after the undertaking.

As early as 1895, the American geologist A. E. Sears, noting the impact of El Niño 1891 on the nature of northern Peru, suggested that Pizarro's voyage along the Colombian/Ecuadorean coast in 1525–26, and his final thrust into Inca land in 1531–32, were facilitated by changes in climate due to what we today call El Niño conditions. The idea was adopted by successive researchers, and the dates of these episodes were included in the Quinn chronology as the first historical occurrences of El Niño.

The suggestion that 1525–26 and 1531–32 might have been El Niño years has been strongly rejected by the French scholars Anne-Marie Hocquenghem and Luc Ortlieb who claim that the remarks of some chroniclers denoting humid years were misinterpreted. It is therefore appropriate to review carefully the original events to ascertain whether El Niño contributed to the fall of the second richest New World empire into the Spaniards' hands.

In 1524, in their first attempt to find Birú, Pizarro and his men sailed along the coast for months before reaching the San Juan River in Colom-

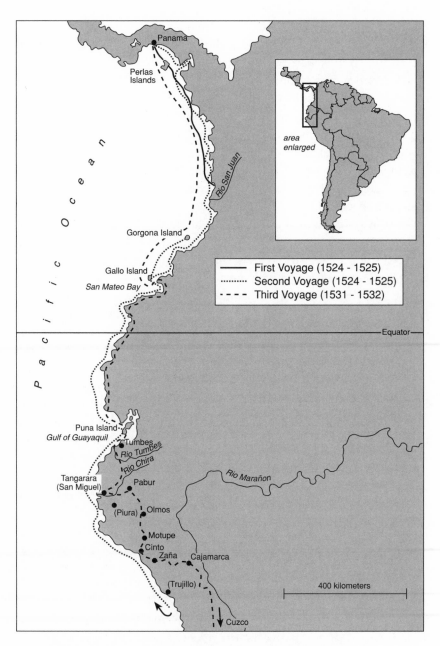

Panama

Perlas
Islands

Pacific Ocean

Rio San Juan

area
enlarged

Gorgona Island

Gallo Island
San Mateo Bay

First Voyage (1524 - 1525)
Second Voyage (1524 - 1525)
Third Voyage (1531 - 1532)

Equator

Puna Island
Gulf of Guayaquil
Tumbes
Rio Tumbes
Rio Chira

Tangarara
(San Miguel)
Pabur

(Piura) Olmos

Motupe
Cinto
Zaña Cajamarca

(Trujillo)

Rio Marañon

400 kilometers

Cuzco

3.1. Routes of Francisco Pizarro's three voyages from Panama to northern Peru,
1524–32. Adapted from Hocquenghem and Ortlieb 1990.

bia, from where they had to return to Panama empty-handed (Figure 3.1). Difficulties with sailing south along this coast are usually associated with the strong southeasterly winds that blow in the equatorial Pacific off South America. The second attempt, in 1525–26, took them past the Gulf of San Mateo—today the province of Esmeraldas in Ecuador—at 1 °N, to the Gulf of Guayaquil, and from there to the Indian town of Tumbes (in northern Peru). The fact that this time the sailing vessels made it so far south suggests that they were impelled by northeast winds from the Caribbean; such winds will cross the Isthmus of Panama when attracted by the low pressures that establish themselves over the warm waters of the equatorial Pacific during El Niño years.

The third expedition departed from Panama in 1531 and this time kept a good distance from the coast. In only thirteen days Pizarro and his men covered some 500 miles and arrived in the Gulf of San Mateo, an indication that they were sailing with the northeast wind in their back and that 1531 was a year of anomalous wind conditions in the equatorial Pacific. From San Mateo, they journeyed overland and reached the Gulf of Guayaquil early in 1532. On Puná Island the exhausted Spaniards had to rest and send for reinforcement from Panama. Probably due to unusual rains, the swollen rivers prevented a more expedient advance to the south, and even the normally wadeable Tumbes River had to be crossed on rafts. From Tumbes, the party continued south, avoiding the extreme dryness of the coastal fringe and keeping close to the green Andean foothills, the usual route taken by Inca couriers and troops. Thus they came upon the Indian town of Tangarara, on the Chira River—later San Miguel de Piura, the first Spanish settlement in Peru—where only the inhospitable Sechura Desert separated them from Cajamarca, the northern residence of the Inca emperor Atahualpa.

At this point of the account, the route followed by Pizarro from Piura to Cajamarca becomes crucial for the contention that the march was conducted under unusually humid circumstances (Figure 3.2). The chroniclers report that the expedition departed from Piura at the end of September 1532, and that the rivers over the next 250 miles were so in spate that the expeditioners had to swim or use rafts to cross them and that several men drowned. In normal years, the rivers of northern Peru experience high waters from December through April, the prime time of El Niño. In this case, the Spaniards were en route at the height of the dry season in October and November, when—had 1532 been a normal year—the rivers should have been at their lowest level. Adding these circumstances to the fact that the stay on Puná Island was prompted by exhaustion from advancing through rain-sodden territory, is a fair indication that the year when the Spaniards made their way through southern Ecuador and northern Peru was an extraordinary humid one.

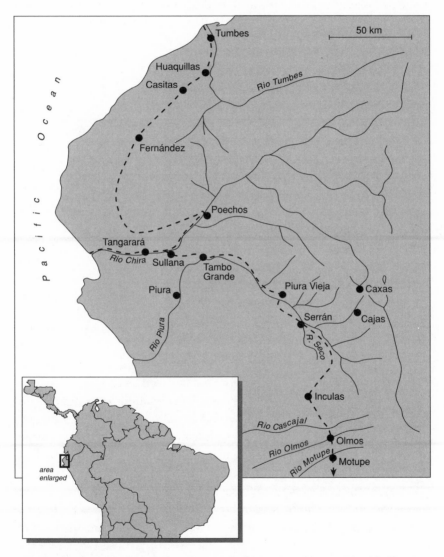

3.2. Overland route of Francisco Pizarro on his way to Lima, 1531–32. From an original chart in Hocquenghem 1994.

The first leg of the journey from Piura to Cajamarca required the conquerors to make a difficult decision: they could either take the direct route south through the Sechura Desert—definitely not advisable in normal, that is, dry, years—or follow the route at the foot of the Andes (Figure 3.2). The latter was preferred by the Inca because, although it meant crossing some pre-Andean ranges, it was dotted with Indian settlements and way stations that the coastal route lacked. The French historian Anne-Marie Hocquenghem made a thorough study of this part of Peru, and her investigations have helped clarify which route Pizarro took in 1532. The network of roads and way stations that she established favors the interior route, which went from San Miguel de Piura, then located on the Chira River, up the well-watered Piura Valley, and from there across a wide Andean spur to the green Motupe Valley (Plate 5). From there on, the journey was probably less difficult since there were Indian settlements and extended grasslands, and enough water for man and beast. Still, several natural obstacles had to be overcome. The water courses in the semi-arid area between the Motupe and Zaña river valleys are fed by springs and whatever precipitation falls on the western slopes of the Andes during the summer. The increase in rains with elevation keeps these rivers running even during the dry periods of the southern winter. However, during El Niño years, the slopes of the Andes are drenched, and the runoff in the rivers that collect those waters can reach impressive amounts. One of these rivers is called La Leche because, as the local people say, when it rains during an El Niño summer, this river spills over its banks, just like milk boiling over in a pot.

The chroniclers' reports of Pizarro's expedition encountering swollen rivers at the end of 1532 should not be dismissed as erroneous recollections recorded by uncritical chroniclers. During an El Niño summer, the rivers of northern Peru do swell with the heavy rains and are especially difficult to negotiate within the first Andean ranges—which the conquerors were crossing. For Hocquenghem and Ortlieb to maintain that the years 1531–32 did not include weather phenomena indicative of an El Niño occurrence, they have to disregard the early chroniclers' numerous references to floods and unbearable humidity, which are definitely not normal features of the north Peruvian climate. Furthermore, there are indications of abnormalities in other places during those two years that point to global climate anomalies. In a helpful list of storms in the seas of western Europe compiled by Hubert Lamb, 1530 and 1532 figure prominently as years in which the British Isles and continental Europe, from the Netherlands to Denmark, were battered by violent storms. As will be seen in the following chapter, stormy weather over western Europe is a conspicuous distant reflection of upset conditions in the tropical Pacific. Moreover, historical climatologists like Lamb have indicated that the summers of the 1530s were very erratic, in correspondence with major alterations in the world's climate. In the twentieth century, unusual weather conditions similar to those encountered by the Pizarro expedition were observed in the wake of El Niños 1972–73, 1982–83, and 1992–94, so why could they not have been operating also during 1531–32? This would explain why Pizarro—after two previous failures—reached in a rather easy manner the heart of the Inca empire in 1532.

Floods and Misery in the Far Spanish Colonies

The unusually wet conditions experienced by Pizarro and his men in northern Peru were, in retrospect, manifestations of a climatic variation in the Pacific basin that was ingrained in the natural rhythm long before the Spaniards arrived in western South America, as surely as it continued for centuries to come.

While the conquerors of Peru and their followers were intent on acquiring wealth and surrounding themselves with glory in the shortest possible time, the main goal was to gain control of the gold and silver mines in southern Peru, which had attracted them to this part of the world in the first place. Thus the thrust of the Spanish conquest was directed at Lima, Cuzco, and several mining centers in Alto Peru (today Bolivia). The northern part of Peru that Pizarro had crossed during his third voyage never amounted to more than a transit area. In the river oases that he had traversed at great risk, incipient agricultural centers languished throughout colonial times, supplying maize, cotton, sugarcane, potatoes, and horticultural produce to Indian pueblos and the early Spanish colonists. The largest towns of the region, Trujillo and San Miguel de Piura, were presided over by the representatives of Crown and Church, who were directly answerable to the viceroy of Peru in Lima.

The colonial structure needs to be mentioned here, because whenever natural disasters struck in this part of the viceroyalty, regional authorities and local clergy turned to Lima for help and with requests for the remission of taxes. Since the Spanish empire overseas was highly formalized and bureaucratic, any political or military event was dutifully recorded, as were natural catastrophes such as earthquakes, volcanic eruptions, tidal waves, hurricanes, floods, and excessive rains or droughts. Today this wealth of information can be examined for indications of El Niño episodes during colonial times. By contrast, only scattered references exist about especially rainy or dry years on the eastern seaboard of North America, while reliable records of rains and floods that might be indicative of the influence of an El Niño–type event in California start only after the Gold Rush of 1849.

As already stated, the coasts of central Peru and most of northern Peru are dry all year around. In late summer there may be sporadic rainfall whenever equatorial air masses break through the barrier imposed by the cold Peru Current and the stabilizing air above. For this reason, it can be assumed that any records of heavy rains and devastating floods found in the colonial archives are indicative of El Niño phenomena very similar to those of today.

In 1552, not long after the initial conquest, there are reports of torrential downpours and the destruction of roads and settlements that point to an El Niño occurrence in Peru. On the other side of the continent, 1552 and 1553 were recorded as unusually dry years by the Portuguese, who were trying to establish the first settlements in northeastern Brazil. According to Lamb's list, January 1552 also brought inclement weather to Europe. These coincidences are very interesting because the relationship between droughts in northeast Brazil and El Niño in the tropical Pacific was recognized only in the 1970s, and the global implications of El Niño became apparent even more recently.

In 1578, heavy rains wrought havoc throughout northern Peru and destroyed the nascent settlement of Santiago de Miraflores on the notoriously erratic Zaña River. This was the very same river that had given serious problems to the advancing hosts of Pizarro in 1532.

Among the climatic disasters of the 1500s, El Niño of 1591–92 had worldwide repercussions if calamities in other continents are added to the copious rain fallen on northern Peru. In fact, Denmark was battered by severe storms in 1592, and, according to early Portuguese reports, the usually dry country of Mali in western Africa was devastated by floods.

In 1607, northern Peru and central Chile had another bout of concentrated rains and widespread flooding, while northeast Brazil experienced lower than usual precipitation. For that year and the following, there are reports of severe winters in Maine, North America, as well as brutal cold and big squalls in the British Isles. Other incidences of torrential rains, not all of them indications of El Niño conditions, occurred in the northern oases of Peru in 1624, 1634, 1681, 1687–88, and 1696: true El Niños were those of 1624, 1686, and 1696. Northwestern Europe also experienced sequences of bad weather during several of the mentioned years, lending further support to the established notion that the seventeenth century was exceptionally cool and wet in the climatic history of the western hemisphere. This so-called Little Ice Age surely had negative effects on the colonization efforts in the newly discovered South American continent as it did also in North America.

During the eighteenth century the global cooling continued, and the frequency of Pacific sea-warming episodes decreased. Still, rains and floods in western South America and inclement weather in Europe and North America indicate that climate anomalies occurred whenever outbursts of solar energy interrupted the pervasive cold period. During that century official reports on calamities became more frequent and accurate, making it easier for us to reconstruct anomalous climate conditions. Among the worst years were 1720, when the flood-prone town of Santiago de Miraflores on the Zaña River was practically swept off its foundations and had to be relocated at its present site. In 1728, the colonial city of Trujillo was wiped out, and in 1791, several river oases in northern Peru were flooded. Most of these events can be linked with climatic crises in other parts of the world, such as cold and stormy winters in Europe and droughts and famines in India, where colonial administrators kept meticulous records and European travelers conscientiously filled the pages of their diaries.

All of this—plus comparisons with rainy years in central Chile, with droughts in northeastern Brazil in 1721, 1727, and 1791–92, and with shipwrecks on the coast of South Africa in 1722, 1728, and 1790—paints a picture of "altered conditions" in the key regions of the world that experience climate anomalies during contemporary El Niño episodes. Our cursory examination of the wet years in northern Peru indicates that these occurrences figured large in the rather uneventful lives of the Spanish and Portuguese colonies, on a par with the pirate onslaughts and earthquakes that episodically tormented those distant outposts of Western civilization.

Of Fish, Birds, and Men

Among the most attractive and graceful figurative motifs on ancient Greek vases are those that depict sea creatures, particularly playful dolphins and streamlined tuna. Having been exposed mainly to the beauty of these masterworks of classical Western civilization, we tend to underrate the artistical merits of early maritime cultures in the New World. Fine Moche ceramics in northern Peru and delicately woven Nazca textiles in southern Peru are also decorated with sea motifs whose strange beauty touches even those unfamiliar with non-Western aesthetic canons.

Such works of art testify to these peoples' close relationship with the sea and dependence on its resources. Their watercraft utilized a variety of ingenious designs, ranging from inflated sealskins or bundles of reeds tied together and packed in a way that allowed a fisherman to sit on these *caballitos* (little horses)—much as today's sports kayakers do (Plate 6)—to large rafts fitted with cloth sails. Early Spanish travelers reported seeing huge rafts sailing along the coasts of Peru and Ecuador, and Peruvian archeologists like Luis Lumbreras (1981) cite evidence of trade contacts between Moche merchants and not only coastal communities in Ecuador but probably even Mesoamerica, involving precious stones from the Andes and pottery or textiles from the Peruvian coast on one side, and nacreous shells and colored feathers from the tropical coast of Colombia and Central America, on the other.

In 1947, impressed by the nautical feats accomplished in such simple watercrafts, the Norwegian archeologist Thor Heyerdahl built a raft with the same balsa-wood from Guayaquil available to pre-Columbian Indians and undertook a voyage from Callao to the Marquesas Islands in the tropical Pacific. He named his craft after the Tiwanaku god Kon Tiki, since the daring adventure was intended to prove that the stone-carving peoples of Polynesia originated from the Andes of South America and not from the western Pacific, as biological makeup and linguistic affinities suggested.

The pre-Hispanic cultures' close rapport with the sea is manifested all along the Peruvian coastal desert. Edible fish still bear Indian names, although the Spaniards gave many local fish the names of similar-looking species from the Mediterranean Sea and the Atlantic Ocean. Then there are the excrements of the *guanay* seabird, a species of cormorant which—

in the course of time—has covered entire rocky islets off the dry coast with the deposit called guano. The usefulness of this urea-, nitrogen-, and phosphate-rich material was already known to the Inca, who used it to improve soil conditions in the valley oases where many of the crops that sustained the empire were cultivated.

As noted in the previous section, the early conquerors were less interested in exploiting the land than in finding gold or silver as the most expedient way to ascend in the rigidly stratified society of colonial Spain. Agricultural production was pursued only to the extent that it was necessary to support the meager populations of the villages, towns, and few major cities, which rarely counted more than 25,000 souls—and not as a means to quick wealth. Thus guano fell into disuse during colonial times, while the Peruvian economy hinged mainly on silver and gold mining in the high Andes, where the larger cities of Cuzco and Potosí developed. The halcyon period of these precious metals was already on the decline before Spanish colonial rule came to an end in the early 1800s, but by then the descendants of the early settlers had discovered that cultivating land and maintaining large livestock holdings (*estancias*) could also bring financial rewards and lead to social distinction.

When, after decades of warfare and internecine struggles, Peru emerged as an independent state in 1824, agricultural production turned progressively toward export commodities, such as cotton, sugarcane, and grain, and the agriculturists in the coastal oases rediscovered the virtues of guano as a cheap and very accessible fertilizer. The guano-extracting operations of local entrepreneurs on the off-shore islets soon attracted the attention of the Europeans. Sensing the potential for large profits, British entrepreneurs were the first to try to secure for themselves a monopoly, but ultimately, it was the manipulative Frenchman Auguste Dreyfus who bribed Peruvian politicians into granting him the exclusive rights in guano export. During the nineteenth century, the income generated from these exports paid Peru's external debts and made Dreyfus richer by 3 million sterling pounds within ten years. Sir Robert Marret, a historian and ambassador to Peru, speaks of this time when entire fortunes were made from guano as the "second cycle in the rich-making history of Peru"—the first being the mining cycle of the colonial period. Marret also reports that in 1859, $16 million of Peru's total state revenues of $22 million came from the guano exports.

Since the guano deposits are replenished by the droppings of the *guanay* seabirds, severe contractions in earnings and state revenues occurred each time El Niño struck in the nineteenth and early part of the twentieth centuries. With the disappearance of the cold water fish, widespread mortality among seabirds set in, and guano deposits were partially dissolved by the torrential rains. This occurred during the El Niño episodes of 1844, 1861, and 1864, demonstrating the vulnerability of a country so heavily dependent on a product derived from resources of the sea. By 1877—as historian Paul Gootenberg remarks in *Between Silver and Guano*—the guano bonanza was over, and two years later Peru lost the war against Chile, little aware that this defeat was the ultimate consequence of a dismal state of affairs precipitated by the severe El Niño of 1877–78.

After decades of prostration, Peru's economy received a boost when British and American companies started to extract oil in the north of the country and to deep-mine copper and silver in the Andes. The export of crude oil and strategic minerals assured the Peruvian state a comfortable buoyancy through both world wars and was sufficient to satisfy the modest aspirations of the country's reduced middle class. With the lower social strata—mostly small farmers and landless peasants—caught up in the daily struggle for survival, it was the privileged few who profited most from Peru's "third rich-making cycle."

For eighty years after the collapse of the guano-supported economy, Peruvian and foreign investors turned away from the sea. This was to change in the 1950s. Despite the great variety and abundance of edible fish in the Peruvian waters, catches were minimal up to that time due to an extremely rudimentary system of distribution that seldom went beyond the small urban centers along the coast to the densely populated highlands, known as the Sierra. Then, following the pioneering example of Norway and South Africa in producing animal feed from fish meal, European entrepreneurs seized this opportunity to make a quick fortune and established the first elementary plants for producing fish meal. Due to the lack of rain along Peru's coast, heaters, crushers, and driers could be installed in the open behind simple prefabricated walls, and installation costs were kept to a minimum. So was investment in the first fishing fleets: they consisted of wooden launches that only later were replaced by metal trawlers built according to a model developed by a Seattle firm. Fishing crews and workers in fish meal plants were recruited from among the local unemployed, but as business expanded, additional labor was required. Indians from the Sierra flocked to the coast. To satisfy the minimum requirements for being allowed on the ships, the newcomers from the mountains were often thrown into the water with tires around their waists to demonstrate their swimming ability. Within a short time, these traditional highland dwellers turned into an industrial proletariat that changed Peru's social fabric forever.

The mainstay of this rapidly growing fishing industry was the anchovy, a fish about twelve inches long that lives in dense shoals in the cold coastal waters, and whose only predators up to that time had been cormorants, seagulls, pelicans, and seals. Amazingly fertile and quick to mature, the anchovy withstood both animal and human onslaughts for quite a while. Fishermen working for the fish meal plants mentioned that during the early years of the industry, there was no need for nets since the tanks on the trawlers could be filled within hours merely by introducing a suction hose into a *mancha* (dense shoal) of anchovies.

At the fish meal plants, the anchovies were pumped out of the tanks into huge boilers, and the extracted mass was then dried and crushed into meal. The fish-oil by-product could be used in paints and emulsifiers. The fish meal was poured into plastic bags and sent to one of the export harbors nearby that had emerged to serve the new industry. Storage facilities were not necessary since a steady line of cargo ships transported the product to Europe, South Africa, and North America.

It was not long before the early European and North American financiers were joined by nationals. Wealthy landowners and industrialists entered into the competition by opening their own plants, but it was actually a shrewd member of the Peruvian bourgeoisie, Luis Banchero, who became the "Peruvian Auguste Dreyfus" of the fisheries boom. Like his predecessor, Banchero was an obscure businessman and had never stood out in Lima's business circles. But then, through cunning and clever use of personal connections, he erected a fishing empire that included the nine largest plants in the country located in five of the major fishing ports. As his wealth grew, so did his influence in venal administrative circles, which he exploited to out-bribe national and foreign industrialists when it came to speeding up the processing of his own shipments.

Whereas Peru's total fish landings had been a mere 45,300 metric tons in 1949–50, they had risen to 483,000 in 1957, and by 1960 had surged to 3.5 million metric tons. Sixty-seven fish-processing plants operated in twenty-two ports during the early 1970s, with the largest concentration in

Chimbote, 250 miles north of Lima. Chimbote had grown from an insignificant village of 4,000 in 1940 to a town of 64,000 in 1965, and it became Peru's fourth-largest city—with 240,000 inhabitants—in 1976.

The exploitation of the fish resources went on continuously and irresponsibly. For the sake of filling their fiscal coffers with export taxes and providing scores of jobs, civilian governments and military regimes alike set no limits on the extraction of anchovies and other fish that happened to be caught in the trawlers' huge nets. Two times, in 1965 and 1969, when moderate sea warming affected the coastal waters of Peru, the anchovy landings showed a sensible contraction (see Figure 1.7), but these early signals that the system was being overtaxed were not heeded by industrialists and governments unwilling to tighten the reins on an activity that ensured quick enrichment.

When El Niño 1972–73 struck, the anchovies did not respond to the regeneration pressures resulting from a quarter century of relentless exploitation and the brisk changes in their aquatic environment. The anchovy-based fisheries collapsed, and the main profiteers of this "third cycle of enrichment" fell into an abyss. The military ruler, Juan Velasco-Alvarado, stayed on only a few years, and thereafter the impoverished country sank deeper into chaos and social dysfunction as incapable and corrupt politicians or military men seized power. Luis Banchero, secluded in a splendid mansion that was an offense to the poor, was murdered by a male lover in 1977.

It had taken an El Niño event to bring Peru to its senses concerning stewardship of the resources of the sea. This country, so richly blessed with natural goods, has been struggling to extricate itself from the clutches of poverty ever since. Peruvians in record numbers (second only to Mexicans) have been applying for admission visas at the U.S. embassy, and in 1998 Peru was allocated the largest number of visas of all Latin American countries through the INS's diversity visa lottery program.

Accounts of Early El Niño Occurrences

The preceding sections reviewed the ways in which the oceanic and meteorological El Niño has influenced historical developments in Peru, from its discovery by the Spaniards to the most recent sociopolitical events. It remains to be seen how the phenomenon began to be perceived as a recurrent variability of the marine environment even before it received the name it now bears. To recognize this distinctive deviation from the norm, inhabitants of and visitors to Peru first had to become aware of the fact that this phenomena was not normal for a country bathed by cold coastal waters and accustomed to being enveloped in a constant fog. Needless to say, it did not take long before these deviations were, indeed, noted by observant members of the army, clergy, and administrative corps.

Among the first chroniclers of the landscapes, exotic plants and animals, and strange peoples of the New World is Joseph de Acosta, a Jesuit priest who spent several years in Peru and Bolivia, and whose *Natural and Moral History of the Indies* was published in 1581 in Seville. He not only described with great precision but attempted to explain the many natural novelties that awaited the Europeans as they advanced into these uncharted lands. He is the first to remark that the waters of the Peru Current were abnormally cold considering the tropical latitudes through which they flow and even noticed that there were certain years when the water was warmer than usual—a sure recognition of what today we call El Niño. Further, he made the first references to an alleged relationship between rainy years on the west coast of South America and an usually high occurrence of seismic movements, a connection that was also mentioned by Charles Darwin when, during his travel in northern Peru in 1835, he heard from the locals that in years of extraordinary raininess earthquakes were also more frequent. This illustrates how a "new discovery" may not be new after all.

In two articles published in 1988 and 1994, Daniel A. Walker, a geophysicist at the University of Hawaii, advanced an explanation for the remarkable coincidence between the temporal variations of the Southern Oscillation and high numbers of seismic events. He contends that tectonic activity in the Pacific basin and submarine volcanic eruptions along the East Pacific Rise (an ocean floor spine that marks the boundary between the Pacific and the Nazca tectonic plates) tend to precede or coincide with the oceanic warmings typical of El Niño phenomena due to the escape of glowing magma through vents on the ocean floor that heat by contact the waters above. What Acosta had noticed some 400 years earlier and Darwin had pointed out almost 300 years later—without any knowledge of the complexities of plate tectonics and pressure cell interactions in the Southern Oscillation—seemed to be confirmed by Walker at the end of the twentieth century.

For centuries, there had hardly been any mention in the scientific literature on the origin of the cold conditions of the Peru Current or the temperature variations in these waters, much less an attempt to explain the
former or link the latter with the episodic torrential rains in the area. In
1802, while sailing from Lima to Guayaquil, Alexander von Humboldt
took measurements of sea-surface temperatures and commented on the
unusual frigidity of these waters in his travelog, but he made no mention
of the warming episodes. More useful for the purpose of digging out past
El Niños is a reference in his writings to a galleon that, in 1791, had sailed
from Manila to Lima in a matter of ninety days! These vessels had to make
the long and dreaded eastward voyage across the Pacific *against* the normal winds from the east and, in the process of crossing from the northern
to the southern hemisphere, risked being becalmed for weeks in the equatorial lows. Thus a crossing that was accomplished in as little as three
months was an exception that caught the attention of the great naturalist,
who commented that this rapid voyage could be explained only by winds
abaft. And sure enough, 1791 was one of the major El Niño years of the
eighteenth century, which means that this particular galleon had been
driven eastward by unusual winds blowing from west to east.

In May of 1804, Captain Alexei J. Krusenstern, commander of the Russian ship *Nadjejda*, was en route from the Marquesas Islands to Hawaii
when, at longitude 146° W, he ran into winds blowing from the west and
a strong current from the same direction that would not let him advance
farther and made his ship drift helplessly back to the east. The amazed
captain recorded this inconvenience in the diaries of his four-year tour
around the world, totally unaware, of course, that he had had an encounter with the effects of the strong El Niño episode of 1803–4.

Similar events occurred in the eastern Pacific before El Niño was recognized as a recurrent phenomenon. It is not clear whether, in 1822, M.
Lartigue, commander of the French explorer *La Chlorinde*, was driven
southward along the coast of central Peru by conditions that today we
would call El Niño. Since 1822 does not figure in the Peruvian chronicles
as an El Niño year, it is more likely that his vessel was caught by localized
eddies that are generated by upwelling at different points along the Peruvian coast in normal years. More pertinent is a remark made by Captain
Robert Fitz-Roy, commander of the *Beagle*, on which Charles Darwin took
his voyage around the world. Fitz-Roy mentioned in his memoirs the
appearance—at undetermined intervals—of a "countercurrent" close to

the coast, which he himself, however, did not encounter when sailing up the coast of Peru in 1835.

There are no known reports of the oceanic anomalies during the mighty El Niño episode of 1877–78, although entries of irregularities may be contained in the navigation logs of the numerous ships that, around that time, trafficked along the South American west coast in the direction of Panama and California. Fortunately, descriptions of the damage caused on land by the torrential downpours of those years are contained in Peruvian historical sources, and the records of shipwrecks in Chile and New Zealand indicate that the effects were severe in the subtropical eastern Pacific. By comparison, the event that started in the southern summer of 1891 was one of the most powerful El Niños of the nineteenth century, and the coverage it received was remarkable, even according to the scientific norms of our day. By the end of that century, communications had become more practicable, and Mother Nature's behavior was being monitored by scientific expeditions with proper means and methods of observation. The American naturalist Alexander Aggasiz, for instance, who visited the Galapagos Islands aboard the *Albatross* in April of 1891, reports on the extraordinary greening he saw on the islands that Charles Darwin had found barren and dry. Surely, Aggasiz had witnessed the aftereffects of the heavy rains El Niño had dumped on the archipelago a few months earlier.

In 1814, 1828, 1844–45, 1864, 1871, 1877–78, and 1884, there were other warm and humid ENSO events, whose manifestations as torrential rains and floods in northern Peru were found worth mentioning in the country's chronicles of that time. Such historical evidence allows us to pinpoint other nineteenth-century El Niños and establish a relationship between these occurrences and climatic anomalies in distant regions.

It is admitted that 1891 was the first time that travelers and scientists really became aware of the singular phenomenon, but that does not take into account the earlier references by Humboldt, Fitz-Roy, and Krusenstern. It is true, though, that the intense rains over northern Peru prompted Luis Carrillo, president of the Geographical Society of Lima, to write an article in 1892 in which he related the anomalous weather to the appearance of a "current that ran counter" to the Peru Current. A year later, Captain Camilo Carranza described in more detail the characteristics of that flow, which he called *El Niño countercurrent*, adding that this was the name used by the fishermen of Paita (in northern Peru) to refer to the warm waters. Actually, he is credited with introducing the term that was increasingly finding its way into the Peruvian scientific literature. In 1894, Victor Eguiguren reported on the torrential rains and the damage caused in the province of Piura by El Niño 1891, and after reviewing the historical sources available to him, he produced the first list of El Niño years to serve as a base for comparative studies with climate variations elsewhere. The credit for defining the concept and linking the excessive rains with the "countercurrent of El Niño" goes to these pioneers, and not to a certain Federico Pezet, who, at the International Congress of Geography held in London in the year 1895, merely summarized the findings of the aforementioned scientists.

After the memorable El Niño of 1891, the recurrences of the phenomenon in 1899–1900 and in 1911 were rather weak. Only casual allusions can be found to cormorants migrating south during those years and to heavy rains in the northern provinces of Peru. More dramatic in its effects was El Niño 1925–26. By then, the means of communication had further improved, and observations were becoming more numerous and accurate. Special mention goes to Robert C. Murphy, a naturalist from the American Museum of Natural History who, since the early 1920s, had been journeying along the west coast of South America. He was fortunate to be in Peru in 1925–26 and experience firsthand the effects of El Niño; his exhaustive documentation of the damage inflicted on nature and humans by the floods of those years is among the most enlightening on a phenomenon that was still not within the public domain.

El Niño 1932 elicited no comments in northern Peru or southern Ecuador and is known only through indirect references. Somewhat better coverage was accorded to El Niño 1940–41, which actually started with heavy rains in northern Peru at the end of 1939. The naturalist Eliot G. Mears offered a sketchy report of the damage occasioned by the downpours of 1940 and 1941, while M. J. Lobell touched briefly on the nature of the phenomenon in general. This is understandable because the attention of the world and the resources of the Western industrialized nations were directed toward the war in Europe. Nevertheless, the effects of those El Niño events did not go unnoticed by Erwin Schweigger, the German biologist at the Guano Company in Lima mentioned in chapter 1, who wrote several articles and reports about the altered ocean conditions and the damage sustained by marine and coastal life forms during these episodes.

The next El Niño—in 1953—was of moderate intensity, but its effects were vividly described by the marine biologist Daniel Merriman, who happened to be on expedition in northern Peru during that southern summer. He observed the rise in river levels, the invasion of tropical fish, and the mortality of common cold water fish.

The more severe El Niño of 1957–58 was monitored in an organized manner, and its ramifications beyond regional boundaries were becoming more obvious. Ever since that event, as each subsequent El Niño occurrence revealed new connections, the rising number of scientists fascinated by this natural phenomenon were able to add more pieces to this global puzzle. After presenting in this chapter historical evidence of past El Niños in the waters of the eastern tropical Pacific and in contiguous Peru, we will turn our attention, in the next chapter, to the effects of this global event in other oceans of the world.

4

~

Raging Seas of El Niño

The review of the basic mechanisms of El Niño revealed that when this phenomenon occurs during abnormal years, the oceans—particularly the tropical Pacific—are the breeding grounds for fierce storms and tropical cyclones that have been fueled by the enormous caloric energy transfer from the warm seas into the atmosphere above. Over the oceans of middle latitudes, the exported energy and humidity bolstered by El Niño meet air masses that are cooler and drier. In these encounter zones, large fronts that stir up the seas add a new component to the upset ocean and atmosphere conditions.

More than three decades ago, while searching for documentary sources containing references to bad weather spells in central Chile, I came across a book listing all shipping disasters along the extended South Pacific coast of that country since 1535. What struck me was that in years known to have had an El Niño, there were also comparatively larger numbers of shipwrecks than in years termed "normal." (Obviously, in the days of navigation by sail, when ships were at the mercy of waves and winds with no engines to propel them, the possibilities for disaster were much greater than they have been since the introduction of engine-propelled vessels.) Intrigued by this discovery, I started to look for records of shipwrecks in other regions of the southern seas that would allow me to test the thesis that during El Niño years, shipwrecks had been more frequent than in normal years. Indeed, I did find bibliographic sources about shipwrecks on the coasts of South Africa, New Zealand, and Australia that lent themselves to this kind of study. Later, when I examined historical accounts for references to storms and sea disasters on the west coast of the United States—which, as we know, is battered by storms and heavy seas during El Niño years—and also in the North Atlantic and in the North Sea, I found further evidence of increases in maritime accidents during El Niño years.

When carefully conducted, a study of historical series on shipwrecks can provide additional clues for identifying past El Niño occurrences beyond those indicated by instrumental series. This chapter reviews these historical maritime sea disasters to corroborate their usefulness for identifying distant ENSO effects in regions that only recently have been associated with them.

Several precautions were taken in order not to influence the search with the personal desire of finding what one is hoping to find. First, among midlatitudinal shipwrecks were considered only those for which the cited causes were storms, gales, or strong gusts associated with frontal passages. Unless expressly stated that the accident was weather induced, capsizings were not considered because in the past, freight misalignments and overloading were common causes for the overturning of a ship. Nor were vessels included that had been thrown against the rocks by longshore currents, unless bad weather conditions were expressly cited. Second, for the coasts of Chile, New Zealand, Capetown, California, and the North Atlantic, only shipwrecks that occurred in the winter months were counted, for it is known today that most of the ENSO-related bad weather manifestations happen during that season. Third, the association between frequent ship losses and El Niño events was based on qualitative, not quantitative, assessments, since the higher number of shipwrecks in the nineteenth century is not an indication of worse weather conditions but of greater maritime traffic than in previous centuries. Even as sails were starting to be replaced by steam engines in the latter part of

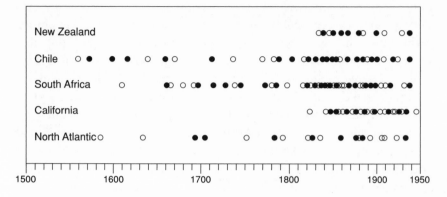

4.1. Years with numerous shipwrecks and severe storms during El Niño (dark circles) and non–El Niño (open circles) years

that century, there were still years with heavy losses, such as 1887, 1888, and 1891, which correspond to globally altered oceanic conditions.

Characterizations of particular years as "stormy" or "rich in shipwrecks," and their comparison with similar occurrences on other coasts or continents, are difficult to quantify due to the dissimilar degree of detail offered in the various compilations that served as bases for this survey. Nevertheless, these qualifications are mostly categorical, and the relationships established with El Niño phenomena in the Pacific are not at all arbitrary. Figure 4.1 indicates whether or not the years that appear in the sources as "stormy" or "rich in shipwrecks" are in phase with El Niño occurrences.

Warm Seas and Mighty Storms in the Tropics

In 1984, in the wake of the major El Niño 1982–83, the French meteorologist Jean-François Dupon characterized the unusual occurrence of nine tropical cyclones that hit the Society Islands, Tuamotu archipelago, and Marquesas Islands as "the exception that confirmed the rule," meaning that they were the manifestation of a climatic oscillation in the South Pacific of a magnitude not known since 1906, the last time a powerful cyclone had swept through the islands. Also interesting in this context is Dupon's reference to the devastation wrought by the cyclone of February 8, 1878, on the flat islands of the Tuamotu archipelago, for that cyclone was an expression of the oceanic alterations in the South Pacific at the height of the powerful 1877–78 El Niño. Other cyclones of note were reported on the islands of French Polynesia on January 16, 1903; March 25, 1905; and February 9, 1906—years *not* cataloged as El Niños in the Quinn chronology, but which exhibit negative values in the Southern Oscillation Index if one consults SOI series. Implied by this is that in those years the low pressure over Indonesia was stronger than the high pressure center over Tahiti, a situation that increased the flow of warm and humid westerlies over the tropical Pacific and furthered the development of tropical cyclones.

Between December 1982 and April 1983—summer in the southern hemisphere—cyclones Lisa, Nano, Orama, Reva, Veena, and Williams battered French Polynesia, causing fifteen deaths, erasing coastal villages, wharf installations, and public works, and destroying coconut groves and pearl farming grounds. As illustrated in Figure 4.2, these cyclones originated over warm equatorial waters and then moved westward, veering to the east near latitude 15 °S. This change in direction was probably due to the cyclones' gaining strength and being impelled eastward by the dominating westerlies. The implications of such episodic changes in wind di-

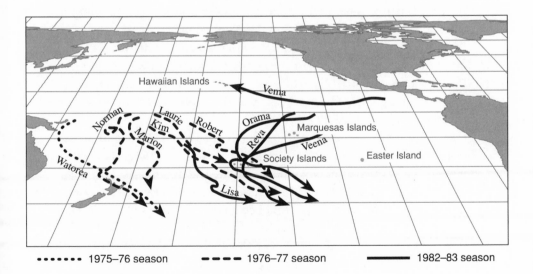

4.2. Track of tropical cyclones in Polynesia during El Niño years of diverse intensity

rection for the discovery and colonization of Easter Island will be dealt with at length in chapter 8.

Not even the Polynesian islands north of the equatorial line—in particular the Hawaiian archipelago—were spared by the cyclones the overheated Pacific Ocean had spawned in the southern summer of 1982–83. Long observation series have established that most northern winters during El Niño years are low in precipitation due to the collapse of the trade winds. In fact, during El Niños 1941–42, 1957–58, and 1972–73, the Hawaiian islands suffered severe dryness for this reason. It may also happen that the islands received heavy rains from cyclonic vortices (isolated low-pressure centers) during such years. For example, rains were registered at the onset of El Niño 1982–83, when several vortices formed over the hot and humid water pool in the central equatorial Pacific. Then, on November 23, 1982, an extremely strong cyclone coming from the southwest caused $200 million in damage on the west coast of the archipelago. This was a rare event, though, because from December through March of 1983, the islands experienced the very severe dryness that was to be expected in an El Niño year.

Colin Ramage, a meteorologist at the University of Hawaii well acquainted with these phenomena, advanced the startling hypothesis that, instead of being generated by the ocean warming during El Niño, the tropical cyclones were the elicitors of El Niño episodes. He postulated that early-season typhoons over the western Pacific begin to develop out of season during the northern spring (that is, almost nine months before the appearance of an El Niño off shore of Peru) and that they activate the eastward-traveling Kelvin waves and the equatorial westerlies. The ocean warming induced by these early cyclones tends to persist through the northern summer and autumn, which explains the prolongation of the tropical cyclone season in the western Pacific well into the early northern winter as it happened in November of 1982. The hypothesis does not account, however, for the tropical cyclone occurrences between October and December of El Niño episodes: four between longitudes 140°E and 160°W during El Niño 1957–58, eight during El Niño 1972–73, and five during El Niño 1982–83. But—while proven neither right nor wrong—the hypothesis is based on the premise that oceanic warmings of El Niño character are definitely associated with a high frequency of this type of cyclones in the overheated waters of the tropical Pacific.

The following section will expose the havoc these storms have wrought on the maritime traffic along the coasts of New Zealand, the landmass closest to the place of origin of the tropical cyclones mentioned above.

Sailing the Rough Seas of New Zealand

Discovered in 1643 by the Dutch navigator Abel Tasman, these "Islands of the Antipodes" were to the Europeans one of the remotest corners of the world. For the British navigators, who sailed the route of the Cape of Good Hope, the islands were even "farther down" than Australia. Their remoteness and difficult access were aggravated by sudden storms and briskly changing winds, treacherous reefs, and the strong currents around the tortuous perimeter of the islands.

No wonder, then, that maritime traffic in these remote parts was minimal, as were records of shipwrecks and instrumental data. So what justifies beginning the examination of shipwrecks caused by El Niño in distant seas with a review of these islands? There are four reasons for starting here.

First, the islands of New Zealand are located in the immediate vicinity of the western Pacific, where frequent tropical cyclones and mighty fronts are generated during warm ENSO episodes. If stormy weather development is exacerbated by oceanic warming in the South Pacific, the islands usually bear the brunt of these variabilities.

A preliminary question should be answered before proceeding any farther: do variations of the Southern Oscillation have an impact on New Zealand? Neil D. Gordon (1986) investigated this relationship and found that, indeed, the islands' weather depends closely on the variations of the Southern Oscillation. When El Niño is in progress in the tropical Pacific, precipitation tends to increase up to one year after the event has subsided.

Second, the overall shape of the islands—an open V with its apex toward the central Pacific—leaves North Island wide-open to the storms from the northwest that might develop during an abnormal year. Also, the east coast of South Island is exposed to the influences of the open sea and the weather generated in the central South Pacific. In the times of sailing navigation, the largest numbers of sea disasters were caused by storms from the northeast spawned by cyclonic depressions and by gusts and squalls associated with the passage of fronts.

Third, under normal oceanic and atmospheric conditions, the prevalent winds over New Zealand, especially over South Island, are the high-latitude westerlies (blowing over the Pacific between Australia and New Zealand), which batter the west coast, while the east coast is protected from the wind.

The latter explains why most settlements on South Island were founded along the east coast and why this coast, open to the Pacific, is most affected by the storms of El Niño.

Charles W. N. Ingram published in 1972 a collection of shipwreck data from that part of the world titled *New Zealand Shipwrecks, 1795–1970*. A comparison between years with high numbers of maritime accidents in that collection and the Quinn chronology shows certain coincidences with El Niño occurrences along the west coast of South America, but also some discrepancies. For instance, not all years listed as "major El Niños" in western South America or the eastern Pacific correspond to years of larger incidence of shipwrecks in the waters of New Zealand, while ENSO events qualified as moderate by Quinn seem to have caused more storms and ship losses in the western Pacific. Moreover, there is a tendency for storm-induced sea disasters to occur during southern winters *preceding* El Niños, and not in the following winter. These solely shipwreck-based results are further corroborated by Gordon's finding that temperatures in New Zealand tend to be higher in the year preceding an El Niño event, suggesting that the ocean warming has already started. A particularly high number of shipwrecks (around fifty-four) occurred in 1866—actually a record in New Zealand's history—perhaps heralding the moderate El Niño of 1867–68. Also interesting is the fact that the sea disasters are especially frequent near Hokitika, a port on the west coast of South Island that is well protected from the bad weather onslaughts out of the northeast or southeast.

Other El Niño occurrences of rather strong intensity in the tropical Pacific during the nineteenth century caused ship losses such as those of 1845, 1850, and 1857–58. It should also be noted that during the moderate ENSO episodes of 1837, 1874, 1880, 1887–88, and 1896, the number of ship losses in the waters of New Zealand was not especially high. After the 1880s, a decade of abundant sea disasters, there was a sharp contraction in shipwrecks during El Niño events of both high and moderate intensities, a fact that might be explained by the increased numbers of steamships, which were easier to maneuver in rough seas than sailing ships and which could navigate against winds and currents.

The El Niño episode of 1877–78—an event of severe global repercussions—affected New Zealand with more than twenty ship losses during those two years, and about another twenty in 1879. Inversely, during the strong event of 1891—notorious in the environmental histories of Peru and Chile—the losses were as low as three or four. Subsequent El Niño events in 1911, 1935, 1940, and 1957 are not reflected at all in shipwrecks off New Zealand.

Reviewing the shipwreck series for New Zealand, one notices years with comparatively high numbers of ship losses, such as 1839, 1841, 1843, 1849, 1851, 1852, 1863, 1883, and 1886, that do not correspond to warm ENSO episodes in the Pacific. During those years, the west coast, open to the westerlies, was most affected by gales and storms and suffered ship losses, while the east coast experienced fewer fronts and cyclones. This is due to the constantly blowing westerlies, which can induce rough seas and fierce gales as they approach the islands from the west but which spare the east coast, the coast that is more prone to get storms during El Niño years. What is of value in the historical series available for New Zealand, particularly during the time of sailing navigation, is that El Niño years stand out as having repeated spells of bad weather.

The reader may wonder about the shipwreck history of Australia, the next landmass to the west, particularly since some storms during ENSO are brewed in the sea between Australia and New Zealand. Shipwrecks off the eastern Australian coast from 1837 to 1956 have been listed in Jack Kenneth Loney's *Victorian Shipwrecks*. In that book, the prominent El Niño years of 1844, 1850, 1864, 1877–78, 1911, and 1940–41 all show a conspicuous absence or low number of sea disasters, while other ENSOs, such as 1837, 1854, 1858, 1860, and 1891, have their good share of shipwrecks. Particularly 1891 is referred to by Loney as "a year of many sea catastrophes," thus reflecting the upset oceanic and atmospheric conditions in the eastern Pacific. As in the case of New Zealand, the moderate El Niños of 1866, 1867, and 1868 also wrought havoc on the sailing traffic off the east coast of Australia. Interestingly, most of the ship losses were caused by wind gusts and gales coming from the southeast, that is, the same direction from which the New Zealand storms came, indicating cyclonic depressions and fronts generated over an overheated tropical Pacific as their common source.

Australia falls within the eastern hemisphere of the Southern Oscillation, which means that during major El Niño episodes pressures are higher and instead of copious rains or tropical storms, the continent is beset by droughts.

Another interesting observation arising from the consideration of shipwrecks as surrogate indicators of El Niño is that such episodes are not equally intense across the Pacific. El Niños that proved to be powerful off the coasts of Peru and Ecuador appear attenuated in the western Pacific, whereas episodes of medium intensity off the coast of South America proved devastating on the other side of the Pacific. This spatial inconsistency has to do with the peculiar way in which the warm waters tend to make their appearance in the western or central tropical Pacific. During certain episodes, they fail to invade the realm of the cold Peru Current—resulting in moderate El Niños off South America—while in the western Pacific the pooled equatorial waters tend to descend toward New Zealand and Australia and generate strong ocean warmings there. In other instances, when the onslaught of warm waters on the west coast of South America has been precipitous—as in 1877–78, 1924–25, 1957–58, 1982–83, and 1997–98—the western Pacific was spared the storms that brew over heated ocean surfaces.

The Dangerous Waters of Chile

On the west coast of South America lies Chile, the longest country in the world. The entire 2,650-mile coast—which equals in length the distance from Acapulco, Mexico, to Juneau, Alaska—lies wide-open to the influences of the Pacific Ocean, and the country's climate depends on weather systems that have originated there. This is why Chile is an important place to look for global effects of El Niño, present and past.

However, a long extension also makes for significant climate differences that account for nonhomogeneous responses to El Niño. The northern desert region lies under the influence of the drying winds from the South Pacific high-pressure cell and the cold Peru Current. That stretch of the coast is spared bad weather spells and storms, but a steady flow of winds from the southwest and heavy swells can drag vessels toward the rocky littoral.

The coast of central Chile underlies the same influences, but in addition, powerful winter storms roll in whenever depressions or fronts are generated over the central Pacific. Most Spanish settlements were founded in this part of the country, and through republican times, they were mainly connected by water routes. The southern coast is the most dangerous, owing to its exposure to the constantly blowing westerlies and the ragged shoreline, full of fjords, channels, and dead-end sounds that made navigation a nightmare. Before the Panama Canal was opened in 1912, maritime traffic between Europe or North America and the west coast of South America had to be conducted through the Strait of Magellan or via Cape Horn. The strait was fraught with dangers, due to numerous narrow passages where both sailing vessels and steamships were cast upon the rocky shores by the westerlies or suddenly arising gales. The route into the Pacific around the cape was equally dangerous because, after descending as far as 57 °S along the Atlantic coast, ships had to turn west and head into the "roaring westerlies," a venture that took weeks. Seafaring in the opposite direction was no less hazardous because of the northward-flowing Peru Current and the steadily blowing southwest winds. To dodge these contrary forces, ships sailed south as far west off the coast as possible, but then had to turn east at the right latitude so as to take advantage of the westerlies in order to pass into the Atlantic Ocean, keeping a prudent distance from the dangerous Cape Horn.

For the sailboats that maintained the rather infrequent communication between Lima and the colonial ports of Chile, there was still another danger. Particularly during the winter, traveling cyclones and fronts from the central Pacific caused violent storms in central Chile that would force them to weather the storms in the open sea. The Chilean historian Francisco A. Encina offers insights into the hazards of maritime circulation between Lima and Chile during colonial times in his monumental *Historia de Chile*. On the average, no more than nine ships per year made the trip between Lima and Chile, or vice versa, revealing the tenuous contacts between the viceroyalty and the colonial outpost. Losing a ship was always a major disaster in the years of colonial rule since—apart from the loss of lives—the cargo was vital for those awaiting it, and vessels were extremely costly to replace. Pilots and crews were not the most proficient. Many crew members were actually individuals working off their fares who had to bring their own provisions, and sailors often would take along up to five black slaves, because they fetched good prices in the far colony. Frequently, vessels were loaded beyond capacity, making them prone to capsizing or flooding even in slightly choppy seas. The ships themselves were not of the best quality either. Sailing ships were mostly built in Guayaquil from fast-rotting tropical timber. In the absence of nails and bolts, wooden wedges commonly held the planks together, which resulted in additional shipwrecks due to the development of leaks.

The combination of poor equipment, inexperienced crews, and powerful winter storms made seafaring along the coast of Chile so dangerous that in 1673, the governor of the colony forbade navigation to or from Lima between May 15 and August 15—an implicit recognition that, as far as the weather was concerned, these were the worst months to sail the waters of Chile. This historical note points to a recognition of the link between winter storms and increased numbers of ship losses.

I conducted a survey of the years with the highest numbers of shipwrecks using Francisco Vidal-Gormaz's compilation *Algunos naufragios ocurridos en las costas de Chile desde su descubrimiento hasta nuestros dias* (1901). Since that compilation stops in 1900, I consulted works by other Chilean historians for references to shipwrecks and memorable winter storms during the twentieth century. The main premise underlying this search was that since, according to contemporary climatology, El Niño years exhibit the highest frequency of severe winter storms, heavier than usual ship losses along central Chile corresponded with El Niño-like circumstances.

Pairing the years of the Quinn chronology with the shipwrecks listed by Vidal-Gormaz reveals an interesting coincidence between maritime accidents and El Niño events in 1634, 1660, and 1720. A large number of ships was also lost during the winters of 1787, 1788, and 1789, which were not precisely El Niño years but preceded the 1791 episode, the most intense of the eighteenth century. There is another way in which connections between stormy winters and increased shipwrecks can be confirmed: since rainy winters in central Chile go along with frequent spells of bad weather generated over a warm South Pacific, the occurrence of a high number of winter storms there before the mighty 1791 El Niño struck northern Peru suggests that the warming process started before El Niño became evident in the equatorial Pacific.

During the nineteenth century, sources of information are more abundant and the reports more accurate. El Niños in 1804, 1814, 1828, and 1884 had no serious effects on coastal navigation, but those of 1844, 1864, 1871, 1877–78, and 1891 caused numerous shipwrecks along the Chilean coast. It should be noted that during the century the major Chilean ports were the stops for the ships that had made the dangerous passage through the Strait of Magellan or around the cape. This increased traffic along the coast meant more opportunities for disasters to happen, even after the introduction of steamships in the 1860s, that is vessels with improved maneuverability and greater independence from winds and currents.

It is an interesting coincidence that in both Chile and New Zealand a relatively high number of ship losses occurred in 1866, 1867, and 1868, which according to Quinn were "moderate" El Niño years but of broad implications in the whole Pacific basin. Yet the powerful 1877–78 and 1891 episodes, which did not cause many maritime accidents in New Zealand, led to conspicuous above-average incidences in Chile. This reflects the fact that El Niño conditions were more favorable to the genesis of storms and fronts in the eastern than in the western Pacific—a demonstration that El Niños need not show equal magnitude at both extremes of the ocean. With losses of eight and seven ships respectively, the winters of 1877 and 1878 were particularly violent on the coast of central Chile. Even worse was the winter of 1888, with seventeen shipwrecks (eight of them during a storm on August 7 and 8) and the winter following El Niño 1891, when twelve ships went down (five of them during the furious storm that pounded Valparaiso on July 7 and 8). It is highly suggestive that these disasters and the active cyclogenesis in the southeastern Pacific coincide with the early signs of the end of the Little Ice Age over the whole earth (see page 206).

The twentieth century was inaugurated by an El Niño that started during the southern summer of 1899 and continued into the winter of 1900; seven ships were lost, five of them in the second half of July. During subsequent ENSO episodes shipwrecks diminished, except for those caused by winter storms in 1925, 1940, and 1965, all of them conspicuous El Niño years along the west coast of South America. No further ENSO episodes are reflected in the number of ship losses, surely because steam and diesel ships were safer and because traffic in Chilean waters was drastically reduced after the opening of the Panama Canal.

Once the era of instrumental record keeping began, accurate precipitation data became available. These data show that the moderate El Niños of 1914, 1919, 1930, and 1953, as well as the major events of 1972–73 and 1982–83, brought heavy rainfalls to central Chile, which were probably caused by the passing of cyclonic depressions and unusual large fronts in the southeast Pacific. What is the connection between repeated spells of bad weather in winter and El Niño? It is an established fact that the abnormal warming of the South Pacific results in the transfer of large quantities of moisture into the atmosphere. When heat and humidity are exported into extratropical latitudes, they meet with colder water and air masses, thereby generating fronts. Satellite images of the South Pacific during El Niños 1982–83, 1992, and 1997–98 show cyclonic depressions, identifiable as clockwise-rotating swirls, progressing from northwest to southeast toward the South American coast. The long, white plumes being trailed by most of these swirls are huge associated fronts (Plate 7). Both the depressions and the fronts attest to the advance of warm air masses into domains of cool air and water, thereby generating periods of winter storms. Upon reaching the coast of central Chile, fronts and depressions drop part of their humidity, but on the Argentine side of the Andes, there is still enough left to cause heavy snowfall and torrential rains. For this reason, the eastern flank of the Andes in Argentina belongs to the main areas affected by the winter manifestations of El Niño.

After reviewing weather maps and satellite imagery of the southeast Pacific, Chilean climatologists Hugo Romero and Orlando Peña charted the common tracks of these cyclonic depressions and associated fronts. One route, running from west to east between latitudes 30° and 40°S, is the path taken by cyclones developing over the moderately warm waters of the central tropical Pacific in normal years. Depressions along this track are strongly energized during El Niño events. (This point will come into play when we consider, in chapter 8, the possibility of Easter Islanders having reached the coast of southern Chile in the past.) A second route, which touches the continent south of 45°S, brings to southern Chile constant rains and storms that are not associated, however, with ENSO episodes. The third and most southerly route starts in the south-central Pacific and runs obliquely into the Sea of Drake, the sea expanse between Cape Horn and the Antarctic Peninsula. This transition zone between Atlantic and Pacific offers an interesting peculiarity during El Niño events. It is an active route for depressions and extended fronts that, once they have broken through this bottleneck, continue with renewed vigor east toward the southern tip of Africa. Depending on the strength and size of these disturbances, bad weather is experienced in Capetown and surroundings (Plate 7). The dynamics of the constant eastward progression of sub-Antarctic depressions in these southern waters lends support to my thesis that rainy winters and high incidences of shipwrecks in southernmost Africa correspond to El Niño years (Caviedes 1980).

To dispel the suspicion that this author also included years that are not indicated as El Niño years in the Quinn chronology, an explanation is necessary. In several cases, high numbers of shipwrecks occurred in the winter *before* conspicuous El Niño years, a fact that does not seem consistent with the notion that El Niño arises in equatorial latitudes and then its effects are exported into higher latitudes. How can one explain the appearance of these effects in middle Chile before the phenomenon emerges in the central equatorial Pacific? To understand this, one has to realize that the actual manifestation of El Niño events at the onset of the southern summer is preceded by a "preparatory phase" in winter and spring, during which the South Pacific high pressure weakens and the related trade winds slacken. This was precisely the situation during El Niño 1997–98 when the first oceanic symptoms were detected in May of 1997—that is, before the start of the southern winter—and produced copious winter rains in Chile before El Niño showed up in Peru and Ecuador in the subsequent summer.

Another point pertains to the higher frequency of depressions and fronts circulating between latitudes 30° and 40°S in connection with El Niño events. In preparation for a warm and humid ENSO episode, an expansion of warm waters in the south of the western Pacific seems necessary, as evinced by seasonal warmings of the sea between New Zealand and Samoa: this condition increases the possibilities for cyclonic depressions to develop. There is remarkable concurrence between this finding and a statement made by Romero and Peña concerning the cyclones that reach Chile as originating from an area of the South Pacific near longitudes 150° to 160°E,—which is precisely to the north of New Zealand. In this way, a plausible explanation is given for the remarkable coincidence of years with frequent spells of bad weather and shipwrecks in central Chile and New Zealand.

During El Niño years, depressions and fronts rotate like a carousel from west to east in the southern oceans, propelling weather systems across the South Pacific. Eventually, the perturbances "aboard" these carousels will arrive in the South Atlantic and affect the west coast of South Africa, causing the disasters detailed in the next section.

Shipwrecks around Capetown

In 1976 I was amazed to discover that during the years when the eastern tropical Pacific experienced El Niño phenomena and historical sources indicated abnormally high numbers of ship losses in central Chile, the southwestern tip of Africa also exhibited frequent shipwrecks. Considering the fact that the rest of South Africa suffers extreme dryness during ENSO events, this was quite a deviant but suggestive case.

To establish parallels between ship losses in central Chile and southwestern Africa, I utilized the historical information in J. Rawe and A. Crabtree's *Shipwrecks of the Southern Cape* (1978) and José Burman's *Great Shipwrecks off the Coast of Southern Africa* (1967). At this point, it is pertinent to mention that there are two types of researchers who study shipwrecks in historical sequences. Among the first type are maritime historians like Francisco Vidal-Gormaz, a chief hydrographer of the Chilean navy in charge of disasters at sea during the nineteenth century who became so excited by the subject that he scrutinized all historical documents at his disposal in search of lesser-known shipwrecks, and the South African José Burman, who collected details about the circumstances and historical background of such accidents in the waters of South Africa. The motivations of the second type of researchers are less academic and more practical, as their interest lies in treasure hunting and deep-sea diving. For example, the information about shipwrecks in Rawe and Crabtree's compilation was gathered in order to provide destinations for adventurous scuba divers, while Don B. Marshall's list of shipwrecks along the coast of California—which will be examined in the next section—was primarily geared to identify and locate salvageable ship remains. Whatever the motivation, these works represent valuable sources for tracing disastrous effects of past El Niños in that they furnish information about place, time, and, in many cases, weather conditions under which the accidents occurred.

The South Atlantic route past the Cape of Good Hope was taken by Portuguese, Dutch, and British navigators to reach their colonial outposts in India and Southeast Asia. Later, when British colonies were established in Australia and New Zealand, ships with those destinations used the same route. While rounding the cape was not as dangerous as the South American passages through the Strait of Magellan or past Cape Horn, it was not devoid of danger either, because once the cape was cleared, the Aguhlas Current, which flows from north to south—that is, against the oncoming ships—had to be fought. In the year 1500, Bartoloméu Díaz, the Portuguese navigator who had been the first to sail around the cape in 1487, paid with his and his shipmates' lives for daring these dangerous waters at the beginning of the southern winter.

Initially under Dutch dominion and then as a strategic stronghold for the British, Capetown became the port where ships stopped before venturing into the Indian Ocean. The city is located on Table Bay, a beautiful, large bay open to the northwest, girdled by reefs, shoals, and low-lying islands that made for a hazardous entry, especially in the days of sail. The opening toward the northwest exposes Table Bay to gusts, swales, and heavy seas coming in from that direction—the most frequently mentioned causes for shipwrecks. When cyclonic depressions and fronts approach in winter, gales from the northwest batter the bay, and in the past, these gales pitched ships that were not properly anchored against the rocky shores of Capetown.

An examination of the shipwrecks listed by Rawe and Crabtree and by Burman allows us to pinpoint bad weather episodes that occurred in phase with moderate or strong El Niños. In the seventeenth century, ship losses in 1660, 1668, and 1696 correlate with strong El Niño episodes in the southern Pacific, but there were also elevated numbers of shipwrecks in "normal" years, such as 1611 and 1692. During the eighteenth century, above-average numbers of ships were lost due to storms near Capetown in 1728, 1747, 1776, and 1785–86, all of them conspicuous El Niño years. However, serious maritime accidents, such as the loss of eleven ships and 600 lives in the storm of June 17, 1722, and shipwrecks in 1788 and 1789, are not associated with ENSO developments in the South Pacific. Other El Niños to which there are references in Peru, such as those of 1701, 1720, 1775, and particularly the very strong episode of 1791, appear not to have had serious repercussions in that corner of South Africa.

These discrepancies demand an objective test to determine whether, in

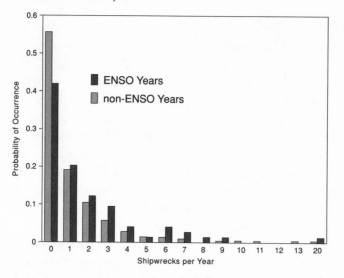

4.3. Probabilities of ship losses in Capetown during ENSO and non-ENSO years

reality, shipwrecks were more frequent in El Niño years or whether that contention springs from an overeager researcher's bias. To resolve this question in the most appropriate manner, I matched all the years for which there are references to ship losses in South Africa with proven El Niño and non–El Niño years along the west coast of South America (Caviedes 1980). The validity test demonstrated that in Capetown the probability of having no shipwrecks was larger in non–El Niño years (55 percent) than in El Niño years (43 percent). Such an outcome was optimal, for—as expected during years without El Niño in the South Pacific—the probability of having storms associated with large weather systems generated in the Pacific was less. But the test also showed a 43 percent probability of having *no* shipwrecks during El Niño years, which indicated that not all shipwrecks around Capetown were linked to warming conditions in the Pacific. This proves that other local and regional climate controls have engendered big storms and caused ship losses in the past as well as in the present. When considering one ship loss per year, the probability percentages are almost equal for ENSO and non-ENSO years; but when it comes to two or more losses, the probabilities of their occurring during ENSO years are always higher (Figure 4.3).

I conducted another statistical test to ascertain whether the storms corresponded to above-average winter rains around Capetown. I grouped the years for which rainfall has been recorded in Capetown into those that correlate with an El Niño and those that do not. As already mentioned, the rest of South Africa experiences severe droughts during El Niño episodes in the South Pacific, so that rainy winters in Capetown during El Niño represent an anomaly within the regional climatology of South Africa. Of the 146 years available for statistical verification, 26 of the rainiest years in Capetown corresponded with El Niño in the Pacific. Only during one ENSO event was the rainfall amount lower than during normal years. Conversely, years with La Niña conditions in the Pacific were the driest in Capetown, which means fewer cyclonic depressions and rain-dumping fronts, and by inference, lesser numbers of shipwrecks. The results of this second test confirmed that my personal expectations did not bias the outcome.

For the nineteenth century, the Capetown series are as extensive and reliable as those for New Zealand and central Chile, allowing more accurate comparisons of El Niños in the Pacific Ocean with ship losses in South Africa than for previous centuries. Also very helpful for establishing whether El Niño years resulted in copious rains in Capetown—a good indication of abundant winter storms—is the chronology compiled from historical sources by Coleen Vogel (1989) for the years 1820 to 1900 (Figure 4.4). This work shows clearly that strong El Niño events in the tropical Pacific had their repercussions in extraordinarily wet years in the southern Cape Province, but only in the western part because the eastern segment of this region undergoes dryness during the same years.

There were higher numbers of ship losses in years of strong El Niño events like 1828–29, 1844–45, 1877–78, 1889, and 1899–1900, as well as in 1821, 1850–51, 1857–58, and 1880, which were moderate El Niño years. Only in six non–El Niño years—1822, 1840, 1842, 1847, 1856, and 1865— did the numbers of sea tragedies equal or surpass those of ENSO years. In fact, José Burman calls 1840 a "grim year," and 1865, with twenty-five shipwrecks, stands out as the worst in the maritime history of Capetown. Twenty of these occurred during the "great gale of 1865" on May 17. During that year, so disastrous for South Africa, no ENSO episode was recorded in the Pacific, but inclement weather caused an unusually high number of shipwrecks in the waters of New Zealand and central Chile during the following year. Perhaps an anomaly in the regional winds of the southern hemisphere was brewing in those years.

More clearly than in central Chile and New Zealand, the El Niño episodes of the twentieth century are marked by frequent sea disasters in

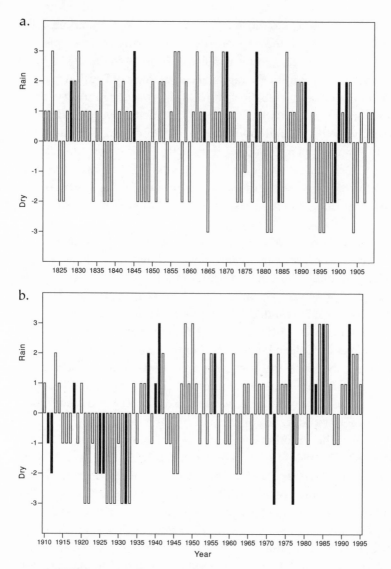

4.4. Rainfall intensity in Capetown during El Niño (dark bars) and non–El Niño (open bars) years. (a) Adapted from Vogel 1989; (b) Caviedes.

South Africa. In fact, the moderate 1902 episode was conspicuously bad: twenty-one ships were lost in Algoa Bay near Port Elizabeth during the tempestuous days of August 31 and September 1. These accidents hap-pened on the east side of South Africa's southern tip, but since the cause given for the shipwrecks was strong winds from the southeast, one can assume that these were gusty winds at the rear of a strong depression which was coasting eastward a few hundred miles south of the Cape of Good Hope. As demonstrated by climatologist Peter Tyson, this sort of midlatitudinal cyclone is consistent with disturbances induced by troughs in the ocean expanse between the South Atlantic and the southern Indian Ocean during moderate El Niños, such as that of 1902 (Tyson 1988).

El Niño occurrences of 1911–12, 1917, 1939, 1965, and 1976–77 are also reflected in higher numbers of shipwrecks, although by then actual losses were significantly less than during the nineteenth century. Exceptional years without notable shipwrecks are 1925–26, 1940–41, 1957, and 1972, all of them El Niños of large magnitude in the South Pacific. This deviation from the established rule is further evidence that ENSO episodes during the twentieth century have varied in time of inception, size of the warm water expanse in the southern Pacific, and magnitude of the associated fronts and storms.

Bringing to the forefront the scarcely known link between stormy winters and high numbers of ship losses in the Cape Province and El Niño episodes in the tropical Pacific, not only in present times but also in the historical past, contributes valuable evidence in favor of the existence of teleconnections between oceans and places as distant from each other as New Zealand and South Africa.

Expanding these connections even farther, can shipwrecks reported on the coast of California also be linked with El Niño episodes in the South Pacific since we know that El Niño creates mayhem in the Golden State? The next section attempts to answer this question.

The Treacherous Currents of California

It was not until the transition from 1982 to 1983 that those living on the West Coast of the United States experienced firsthand the effects of an El Niño. That winter arrived with gales and heavy seas off the coast of southern California and drenching rains in the interior. The appearance in December 1982 of 64°F (18°C) waters in the bight of Los Angeles, where the seasonal mean is 58°F (15°C), was also unusual. Californians—and by extension, all Americans—had known El Niño only as an exotic freak of nature, if they knew of it at all. After a prolonged episode in 1992–94, and the big one of 1997–98, most North Americans became aware of that phenomenon, and henceforth it has become the favorite culprit for any environmental mishap associated with excessive rains and stormy weather. During the 1982–83, 1992–94, and 1997–98 events, powerful winter storms battered Santa Monica, Malibu, Santa Barbara, San Mateo, and San Francisco, demolishing coastal frontages and eating up beachside properties. Recreational watercraft were lost in the marinas along the coast between San Diego and Point Reyes. The citizens of the Golden State learned to fear the rough seas, furious gales, and torrential rains that were visited upon them when the tropical Pacific was affected by an El Niño occurrence.

It is therefore assumed that ship losses during past El Niños were very frequent. Verifying the association of higher numbers of winter storms and shipwrecks in California with El Niños in the South Pacific proved to be more difficult than making the connection with New Zealand, Chile, and South Africa. High traffic along the coast began only with the Gold Rush, and after 1850, maritime accidents occurred not only during winter storms but also in other months when ships were thrown against rocky shores by powerful swells and strong west winds. These circumstances make it hard to single out those accidents that might have been associated with El Niño–induced weather. The difficulty is compounded by the fact that records of shipwrecks along the coasts of California, Oregon, and Washington are sparse and hard to come by. The following analysis is based on Don B. Marshall's *California Shipwrecks: Footsteps in the Sea* (1978) in which—unfortunately for this research—the emphasis is more on the ships' build, monetary value, and cargo than on the weather conditions under which the disasters occurred. Marshall presents numerous cases of vessels' capsizing without clarifying whether the cause was faulty cargo loading or heavy seas, gales, or stormy weather, and of ships' wrecking, but he does not indicate whether this happened from natural causes or from lack of skills and negligence. For these reasons, our identification of shipwrecks as being caused by El Niño-related weather is only tentative, pending more thorough investigations in the future.

The available list of California shipwrecks, especially before the Gold Rush, is less continuous and detailed than the lists for Chile, New Zealand, Australia, and South Africa. This has to do with California's colonial history as a distant dependency of the Viceroyalty of Mexico. Even right up to the time of its takeover by the United States, the Mexican Republic showed little concern for this outlier in the northwest, and communications were poor. Only an occasional ship would leave Acapulco for San Diego, Los Angeles, Monterrey, or San Francisco. The Spaniards also had little interest in that remote coast, making just a few official trips to check for points where galleons to and from the Philippines could find anchorage and replenish their water supply in case of emergency. Equally neglected were the isolated enclaves of Russian pioneers on the coast of northern California. Thus references to sea disasters from the sixteenth to the eighteenth century are too sparse to establish a sensible time series for this segment of the Pacific rim. Considering the meticulousness of the Spanish administration in general, somewhere in the colonial archives in Seville or Mexico City one should be able to unearth references to the torrential rains, destructions of dwellings, and coastal storms that *must* have accompanied El Niño occurrences of those centuries. Finding references to the effects of storms on the early Russian settlers on California's northern coast is another subject awaiting research.

As was to be expected, the discovery of gold in the hinterland of San Francisco Bay in 1849 prompted an unprecedented movement of people, beasts of burden, and implements from the East Coast to the vast uninhabited territories on the West Coast, which greatly enhanced maritime traffic via the Strait of Magellan and Cape Horn. The poorly charted coast of California, inept captains and pilots, adventurers-turned-sailors, and indiscriminate use of vessels regardless of age or condition—all of this resulted in a disproportionate increase in the number of sea disasters. The stretch between Point Santa Cruz and the Golden Gate proved particularly hazardous: strong currents from the west, rocky shoals masked by dense kelp, and long shore drafts could mean the end for ships coming close to the coast to duck a sudden gale or limping because of engine malfunction. As for sailing vessels, the entrance into San Francisco Bay was extremely dangerous in itself. Water entering and leaving the bay creates such strong currents that—especially when some tightfisted skipper had dismissed the services of pilots and tugboats—these ships were frequently cast against the rocky flanks of the Golden Gate or dragged shoreward by drift if the winds slackened.

This difficult coastal environment is still dangerous for crippled vessels or ships caught in the swiftly developing storms during contemporary El Niño events. The above-mentioned vagueness pertaining to the weather conditions during which ship losses occurred during the nineteenth and early twentieth centuries does not allow for a quantitative analysis; only a qualitative assessment of the shipwrecks, with resulting limitations in terms of absolute accuracy, can be undertaken.

According to the tally presented by Marshall, the winters of 1862 and 1863, as well as 1875 and 1876, had the most shipwrecks in the nineteenth century. None of these winters correspond to El Niño years, although their occurrence in pairs suggests prolonged oceanic and climatic variabilities. Several ship losses in 1867–68, however, coincide with a moderate El Niño in the tropical Pacific and are very close to the notorious 1866, when shipwreck numbers in the waters of New Zealand and central Chile were very high. Next come, in descending order of disaster frequency, the years 1854, 1887, and 1914, which also appear in the Quinn chronology as moderate El Niño years. A comparatively high number of accidents occurred in 1879, conspicuously following the very strong ENSO event of 1877–78 in the South Pacific. Major El Niño occurrences in 1844–45, 1870, 1891, 1914, 1930, 1932, and 1939–40 did not noticeably raise the numbers of sea disasters, which may indicate a low frequency of winter storms in Californian waters. The year 1926—in phase with El Niño 1925–26— stands out with a relatively large number of shipwrecks in the twentieth century. Not at all in keeping with the general rule of higher numbers of storms and sea disasters in winters with El Niño development in the South Seas are the years 1884, 1899–1900, 1911, 1940, 1957, 1965, and 1972. This confirms that not all El Niños necessarily result in strengthened storm activity along the coast of California, although some of these years exhibited above-average winter precipitation as an indication that there was a high frequency of passing fronts and depressions.

A review of high incidences of bad winter weather and related sea disasters in California yields good results in some ENSO years but remains inconclusive in others. To quote meteorologists Eugene M. Rasmusson and John M. Wallace (1983): "Not all the major climate anomalies of the 1982–1983 winter can be unambiguously interpreted as interlocking pieces of the ENSO jigsaw puzzle. Wet, stormy winters over California and other parts of the Southwest have occurred during warm episodes in the equatorial Pacific (such as 1977–1978), but there have also been abnormally dry winters during warm episodes (such as 1976–1977). So when the entire historical record is taken into account the correlations between various indices of the ENSO phenomenon and California rainfall are not very impressive." This assessment by two respected specialists in the climatology of El Niño is consistent with the results of our preliminary survey of storms and shipwrecks on the West Coast of California.

From the California coast, we now travel to another part of the northern hemisphere to examine the possible association of storms in the North Sea and off western Europe with ocean warming in the Pacific.

Storms of the North Sea

The El Niño occurrence of 1972–73 is credited for bringing into the open the interconnectedness of anomalies that prior to the early 1960s was suspected only by a select few who considered El Niño a catalyst for climate variability. One of these individuals was Jerome Namias, a climatologist at Scripps Institution in La Jolla, California. Trying to explain suspected teleconnections between air circulation anomalies in the northern Pacific and Atlantic, he sustained that oscillations in the Aleutian low pressure cell were somehow related to variations in the Iceland low pressure cell. Taking this even farther, he also noted that the recurring droughts in northeastern Brazil were associated (not precisely in their genesis, but in their time of occurrence) with pulsations of the Iceland low, which in turn were echoed by the high pressure cell in the southern Atlantic. If this assumption was correct, then what was the thread that connected the variabilities of the Aleutian low with the Iceland low, and ultimately with the pulsations of that distant high located between Africa and South America? Definitely, the air circuits of the Pacific and Atlantic had a connection that ran across the vast North American continent, and not across South America or through the narrow bridge of Central America.

In higher latitudes, the weather situations associated with the variations in the Aleutian low are propelled eastward by means of the Rossby waves. These meanders in the trajectory of the polar jet stream determine the development of winter weather over Canada and the United States. When the trajectory runs almost linearly from west to east, cold air stays in the north, and warm air remains confined to southern latitudes; when, however, the jet stream adopts a wavy or meandering trajectory, this leads to active exchanges between the cold air from the north and the warm air from the south, with resulting alternations between bad and fair weather conditions over North America.

The previous examples of shipwrecks occurring in defined yearly clusters may persuade the reader that connections exist among the major winter weather conditions in the North Pacific, continental North America, the North Atlantic, and, ultimately, western Europe. Further, since the large pressure cells over the oceans tend to interact freely, variations in intensity of the South Pacific high pressure cell can be felt in the North Pacific and transmitted from there to the North Atlantic or Iceland low.

How, then, can researchers verify whether—notwithstanding the enormous distances—climate alterations in the tropical Pacific are also reflected in the overall weather patterns over the North Atlantic and western Europe? Winter weather conditions over Europe are dictated by a constant succession of cyclonic depressions, fronts, and wandering high pressure cells, interspersed with periods when the dominating westerly winds prevail, especially over Scandinavia. This explains the day-to-day variability that characterizes weather over the British Isles and continental western Europe. The situation is different when strong high pressure cells from Eurasia move into western Europe, causing extremely cold weather spells. German meteorologists call these major weather clusters that process each year across Europe *Grosswetterlagen,* which loosely translates as "generalized weather situations."

In western Europe, one of the most unpleasant weather situations is brought about when extended depressions tracking down from Greenland or Iceland across the North Atlantic make a frontal assault on Scandinavia, the Jutland Peninsula, the British Isles, Holland, and Germany. These depressions, which rotate counterclockwise, advance very fast over the open ocean, and winds reach velocities of up to 100 miles per hour, which translates into heavy seas as well as flooding and erosion of low-lying coastal lands. Wind direction depends on the track followed by the cyclonic storms: when depressions cut across Scandinavia, the gusts arrive from the west and northwest; when they pass over the northern tip of the British Isles, they blow from the west and southwest. In both cases, the coastal areas exposed to the west receive the brunt of the storms, which are particularly destructive and costly, in terms of lives and materials lost, for the low-lying coasts of Holland, Belgium, Denmark, and Germany, especially ever since the reclamation of coastal flats for habitation and agricultural use. Because of their particular vulnerability, these countries have kept fairly accurate records of storms and their damaging effects since the sixteenth century.

One of the most exhaustive compilations of storms in western Europe was produced by the climatologist Hubert H. Lamb, whose *Historic Storms of the North Sea, British Isles and Northwest Europe* (1991) critically examines 166 storm occurrences between 1500 and 1989. Dates, regions affected, damages incurred, and intensities are thoroughly documented, making this list a most valuable tool for ascertaining whether storm development in the North Atlantic has been related to climatic variations elsewhere and—in keeping with our goal—for examining whether these storms were more frequent and more devastating during periods when El Niños developed in the tropical Pacific.

The Quinn chronology that starts in 1525 and Lamb's list that begins in 1500 are the longest series in the Western world registering altered states of oceans and atmosphere. Based on the information given in these series, of the three earliest stormy winters documented in the northern hemisphere—1509, 1530, and 1532—only the latter two can be paired with climatic irregularities in the tropical regions of the New World. Also a major storm in January of 1552 that affected all of Europe coincides with one of the earliest El Niño occurrences in Peru after the conquest. The infamous "All Saints Flood" of early November 1570, which took the lives of an estimated 100,000 to 400,000 coastal inhabitants of Germany and Holland, comes close to a well-documented El Niño episode in 1567–68. Unforgettable in history is the fate of Spain's Invincible Armada as it attempted to invade England in August of 1588. The storms rolling in out of the northwest hit after the northern summer had peaked, thus representing an isolated singularity. Or do they? In another of his books, *Climate, History and the Modern World* (1995), Lamb notes that 1588 is the year when the Indian city of Fatepur Sikri had to be abandoned due to an extreme drought (possibly caused by monsoon failure), which suggests that this year was marked by variabilities worldwide, though not precisely of El Niño signature. The century closes with a big storm in November of 1592, which concurred with the El Niño of 1591–92.

In the early 1600s, there were several stormy winters in northwestern Europe that do not correlate with ENSO developments in the Pacific, but the severe winter of 1613–14 occurred in close proximity to the 1614 El Niño. A bad weather spell over the North Sea in March of 1625 coincided with the decaying phase of El Niño 1624, and a big storm at the end of October 1634 in the North Sea that claimed more than 6,000 lives can be paired with that year's El Niño in northern Peru. The stormy winters of the following three decades were not in phase with ENSO events, but nonetheless seem to indicate a period of serious climatic deterioration in the North Atlantic. The last three ENSO episodes of the century, in 1681, 1687–88, and 1696, were mirrored by winter storms in the North Atlantic. A great storm in September 1695 killed 1,000, and the storm of early December 1694 is ranked among the four most severe during the five-century period under consideration.

The eighteenth century was inaugurated by a strong El Niño in 1701 that can be matched with big storms over southern England during the winter of 1700–1701. However, the December 1703 storms that took some 10,000 lives in the vastness of the North Sea and the Baltic Sea do not correspond to any reported El Niño development off Peru. The same is true of the infamous "Christmas Storm" that claimed 11,000 lives all over western Europe in December of 1717. The winters of 1735, 1737, 1739, 1741, 1751, and 1773 were also exceptionally stormy in western Europe, but there is no correlation with anomalies in the eastern Pacific. Then again, El Niños 1761 and 1786 reveal a certain correspondence with winter storms in the North Sea and over the British Isles, particularly in 1786, which took a heavy toll on ships and structures in coastal communities. The last El Niño episode of the eighteenth century, in 1791, was that century's most intense in South America. In Europe, 1791 was a year of climatic extremes, and March brought the most powerful storm of the century. The year 1792 is equally memorable, in Lamb's eyes, for its high frequency of big storms. These telltale occurrences strengthen the point made throughout this book, that the transfer of energy and humidity from the tropical Pacific into the global atmospheric system during El Niño events has distant repercussions.

The nineteenth century opened with a prolonged period of global sea and atmospheric anomalies, judging from the occurrence of a strong El Niño in 1803, stormy Mid-Atlantic seas in October of 1805, the early arrival of a mild but snowy winter in 1805–6—which made it so difficult for the Lewis and Clark expedition to cross the Bitteroot Range and the northern Cascades—and ultimately the onset of a moderate El Niño in the South Pacific during 1806. Almost half a century of mixed signals followed, with stormy winters (for example, in 1818, 1822, and 1825) in close proximity to El Niño episodes, and other anomalies (such as the infamous storm on January 6 and 7, 1839, that killed 8,000 coastal dwellers) showing no relationship with special events in the Pacific.

A series of brisk climatic fluctuations around 1850 marks a plunge toward colder temperatures that bottomed out in the 1880s. A close succession of ENSO events in 1850, 1854, 1857–58, 1860, 1864, and 1866, paralleled by stormy winters in Europe in 1855, 1859, and 1861, is followed by the explosive 1870s, which began with El Niño 1871 (without significant effects in Europe) and ended with the major El Niño of 1877–78. In western Europe, March 1878 was marked by a storm that caused a large number of shipwrecks off the British coast, and December 1879 is remembered for the tragic accident that sent a train into the river when the Tay Bridge collapsed under the onslaught of gale-force winds. A moderate El Niño that developed in the tropical Pacific in 1880 was mirrored by the October storm of 1881 that swept through the North Sea into Denmark, causing numerous shipwrecks. While 1883 was also a very stormy and fatal year in the North Atlantic, 1884 stands out as a strong El Niño year in the Pacific, and in January of that year, what may be the largest storm ever was churning in the North Atlantic between latitudes 45°N and 60°N. In 1891, the last major El Niño of the nineteenth century was echoed in the North Atlantic by a furious storm in the English Channel in March of that year. There followed the moderate El Niño of 1896 and the 1899–1900 event, which did not substantially impact the northern seas.

The parallel between warm and humid ENSO events in the tropical Pacific and strong storms in the North Atlantic continued in the twentieth century. The El Niño of 1911 was echoed by a storm surge of more than twenty-seven feet on the west coast of the British Isles in November of that year. However, the ENSO occurrences of 1917 and 1925–26 are not in phase with severe storm developments in the North Atlantic, unless one considers the relative increase in spells of bad weather and substantial number of shipwrecks in the winters of 1927 and 1928 to be a delayed sequal to global stimulations by El Niño 1925–26. While the moderate 1932 El Niño can be paired with the very stormy 1933 winter, the subsequent ENSO in 1940–41 shows no catastrophic consequences in the nordic seas, but its aftermath greatly influenced the defeat of Hitler at Stalingrad.

The first ENSO episode of the second half of the twentieth century, in 1953, is qualified as "moderate" in the Pacific. Nevertheless, the storms of January and February of that year claimed more than 2,000 lives and numerous ships in the North Sea, and one storm at the end of January was among the most intense of the century up to that time. Storm activity was also heavy in 1954 and 1956, but seemingly unrelated to any anomaly of global extent. Another isolated incidence was the storm of February 1962, which caused extensive damage and the loss of 300 lives—an elevated toll considering the technological advances in catastrophe prevention and early warning procedures that had been achieved during the post-war years. The next major El Niño, in 1972–73, had a global impact and hit northern Europe with storms in November 1972, April 1973, and December 1973, and a serious stormy spell in January of 1974 may be correlated with the decaying phase of the 1972–73 ENSO event, which was particularly notorious for its association with droughts in the Sahel and central India. The "aborted" El Niño of 1976 can be linked with an extensive January storm of unusual severity in the North Sea. Then, during the 1982–83 El Niño event—the most powerful of the twentieth century—the distant relations with stormy winters in the North Atlantic again became patent with a severe storm in the North Sea at the end of 1981—the beginning of the ENSO development—and two major storms in January and February of 1983 during the maturing phase. Nineteen eighty-six, which some analysts consider a moderate El Niño year, is notable for the December 15 storm during which, in the words of Lamb, "the deepest cyclone ever observed over the North Atlantic" was registered. Whether that storm was a distant echo of sea and air anomalies in the tropics has yet to be determined by meteorologists. What can be safely ascribed to ENSO-like variabilities, however, are the series of cyclones that crossed the North Atlantic in January of 1990, heralding the onset of the sustained, yet mild, El Niño period of 1991–94.

5

~

Droughts in the Tropics

Within the established order of nature, the outburst of energy and humidity that characterizes an El Niño event in many regions around the Pacific Ocean is coupled with rain shortages in other parts of the world. However, not until the occurrence of the 1972–73 El Niño did this reality become patent to meteorologists who were trying to link globally scattered climatic anomalies. Climatic variations previously considered as disconnected freak occurrences began to make more sense when placed within the context of major climatic fluctuations. What did come as a surprise was the realization that deviations from the norm in some regions showed positive signs—higher temperatures and/or increased precipitation—while in other regions they carried opposite signs—cold and/or dry weather conditions (Figure 5.1). Having dealt with the former (torrential rains, cyclones, floods, and winter storms that are common during ENSO events), we now turn to the historically documented droughts that have occurred in phase with El Niño and, where possible, to past climatic fluctuations bearing that signature as inferred from archeological or sedimentary evidence.

Drying Winds of El Niño

The coincidence of excess precipitation in some areas and absence of precipitation in others calls for an explanation of the mechanisms that underlie this duality. As in the case of many alterations in regional precipitation and temperatures caused by ENSO events, anomalies in the circulation of seasonal winds during periods of oceanic warming lie at the root of these changes. The term *seasonal* is emphasized because the failure of humid winds to occur "when they should" is the determining factor in the development of dry spells or outright droughts. During those periods the major pressure centers that rule the circulation of ocean currents and major wind systems are deeply altered, so that regions next to weakened high pressure centers experience a higher likelihood of rain-bringing cyclones and fronts, whereas those in the vicinity of strengthened pressure centers experience dry air and desiccating winds. At the same time, there are radical alterations in the meanderings of the tropical and polar jet streams that affect the exchange of air masses between tropical and temperate regions.

Three major situations lead to humidity deficits in critical regions during El Niño events: (1) the ups and downs of the pressure centers in the tropical belt due to variations in the location and intensity of the Walker circulation (discussed in chapter 1); (2) blocking situations arising from the strengthening of high pressure centers in the subtropics; and (3) the weakening or total failure of humid seasonal winds. Each of these situations inhibits precipitation and prevents the timely onset of seasonal rains in tropical and subtropical latitudes, particularly during summer.

As explained in connection with the treatment of the Walker circulation in chapter 1, the displacement of warm waters west or east from their usual location within the equatorial belt during anomalous years also causes the area of rising warm air to change position. Thus, if this source of heat and humidity moves from its usual position over Indonesia and the Philippines into the central equatorial Pacific, the corresponding dry descending branch will be displaced toward equatorial Australasia, causing conditions of aridity there. In addition to this major Walker circulation over the equatorial Pacific, there are subcircuits over the Indian Ocean

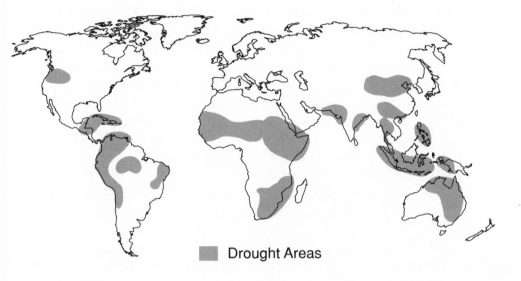

Drought Areas

5.1. Droughts in the world during El Niño years

and the Atlantic Ocean, which affect the bordering continents (Figure 5.2). In these cases, the rising branch is located over the warmer continents and the descending limb over the comparatively cooler oceans. This usual pattern changes drastically when climatic conditions in the tropical belt are upset by El Niño developments. Consistent with this generalized model, descending branches of the Walker subcircuits move toward India, tropical Africa, and the lowlands of South America east of the Andes, where the descending dry air causes generalized droughts.

Blocking occurs when high pressure centers increase in strength to a degree that impedes (blocks) the incursions of transient cyclones and fronts, which are the major rain sources in summer and in winter. These blocking situations often arise in association with cool ocean waters or over cold continental masses in winter. Australia commonly has a blocking situation during El Niño episodes that prevents precipitation and leads to drought. Another type of blocking tends to develop over the tropical Atlantic shortly before or during the onset of an El Niño when the South Atlantic high pressure cell is fortified to such an extent that it prevents the southward shift of the rains associated with the Inter-Tropical Convergence Zone—the reason for the droughts in northeastern Brazil.

The third situation conducive to generalized droughts is the failure of humid summer winds to occur, the classic example being the monsoons of Southeast Asia, India, and eastern Africa. Monsoon was the name given by Arab navigators in the Indian Ocean during the Middle Ages to the winds that propelled their sailing vessels from the east coast of Africa toward India and the Spice Islands (eastern Indonesia) during the summer season, and back again in winter. These seasonal winds blow from northeast to southwest in the wintertime, and from southwest to northeast in summer. In the winter they blow from the continent toward the sea, and since the Asian continent is cold and no sources of evaporation are available, a dry season results. In the summer the flow reverses: after traveling over the tepid waters of the Indian Ocean where they collect water vapor, the monsoons release precipitation over India, Burma, the Malayan Peninsula, Vietnam, and southern China, producing the rainy season in these countries. Should the summer winds fail to occur due to the falling air associated with a descending branch of the Walker circulation over the Indian Ocean, the dry conditions of winter extend into summer; as a result, subsistence crops cannot be planted, and food production is seriously curtailed. In the past, starvation and death were the inevitable consequences, but today, with water reservoirs in place and the ability to predict these weather anomalies, the worst outcomes can be averted in most cases.

The mechanisms that cause the failure of the rain-bringing winds are

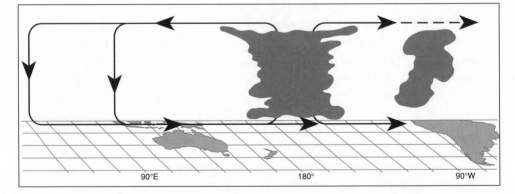

5.2. Altered Walker circulation in the equatorial Pacific. Heavy rains are caused by rising air over the warm waters of El Niño and on the western slopes of the Andes. Notice the descending branch over Australasia.

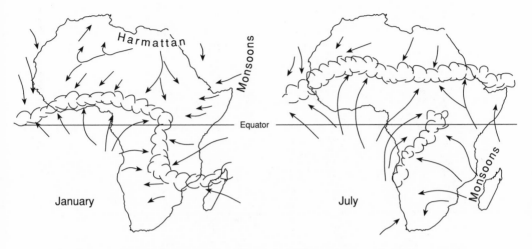

5.3. Rains and winds over Africa in January and July. Clouds indicate the relative location of the Inter-Tropical Convergence Zone.

somewhat different over central and western Africa. Dry spells and rainy periods on that continent are controlled by three major situations (Figure 5.3): Over northern Africa and the Saharan region, dryness is caused by the *harmattan* winds blowing from the northeast during the winter. The eastern tier of the continent receives rain in the summer months through the monsoon winds coming in from the Indian Ocean. In west-central Africa, winter dryness is determined by the strength of the harmattan, while the summer rains depend on the northward advance of humid winds from the tropical Atlantic and on the location of the Inter-Tropical Convergence Zone (ITCZ). In years when the ITCZ that attracts humid winds from the sea does not move far enough north and the inland-blowing winds are weak, Africa's semiarid belt experiences its most severe droughts. Likewise, when the humid winds from the Indian Ocean do not penetrate deep enough into eastern Africa, that region suffers a severe lack of rain. Since the strength of the seasonal winds depends on several factors, such as the meanderings of the tropical jet stream over Asia and Africa, the cooling or warming of the surface waters of the southeast Atlantic and Indian Ocean, or the relative positions of the Walker subcircuits during years of ENSO, it is very difficult to disassociate droughts from El Niño in many tropical locations.

The sea-air interactions that result in catastrophic droughts for sub-

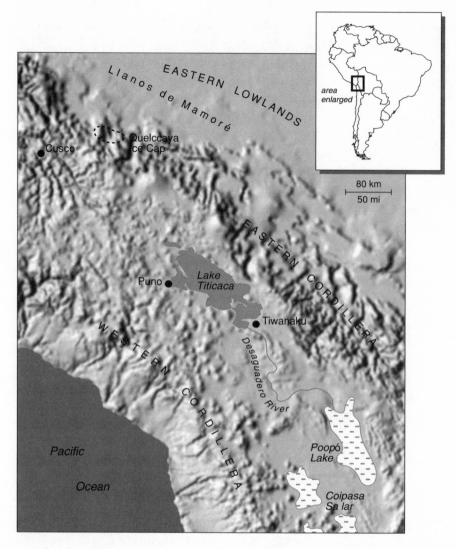

5.4. Lakes and mountain ranges of the Bolivian altiplano

Saharan west Africa and the arid countries of Sudan, Chad, Ethiopia, and Somalia will be examined in a later section, but first we will look at the equally devastating droughts in certain South American regions, such as the altiplano of Peru and Bolivia, and the northeast corner of Brazil, because, after all, South America is the continent assailed first and foremost by the effects of the disruptive El Niño.

Disaster for the Shepherds of the Altiplano

Between two majestic ranges of the Andes extends the high plateau of the altiplano. Cooled by the altitude (13,000 feet above sea level) and eternally exposed to the sun under a clear blue sky, this region of southern Peru and western Bolivia exudes an air of mysticism, which is enhanced by the silence and the rigors of the altitude climate. At the northern edge of the altiplano lies Lake Titicaca, the highest mountain lake on earth and the last remnant of an extended system of inland waters that accumulated between the two ranges after the last glacial period in South America (Figure 5.4). A few kilometers away from the shores of Lake Titicaca, in a sleepy locality known today as Tiahuanaco, arose two millennia ago the grandiose Tiwanaku civilization, the predecessors of the Inca.

Continued desiccation of the altiplano and evaporation of secondary lakes in the course of the last 12,000 years forced upon the communities living in this space a frugal lifestyle based on potatoes and quinoa (a grain rich in protein) and herding. The latter focused on llamas in early times and was complemented with sheep after the arrival of the Spaniards. Indian families usually keep two or three cows for milk and meat and a few donkeys as pack animals. Hard yellow grasses, renewed only during the short-lived periods of precipitation in the southern summer, allow the persistence of a pastoral livelihood complemented by the agricultural products mentioned above. This harsh environment is home to native herdsmen who, except for the fairly populated shores of Lake Titicaca, live in dispersed villages and hamlets.

Cold and dryness are the marked characteristics of this place: from May through September (southern winter), temperatures drop below freezing every night and by noontime reach 60 °F (16 °C). Due to the elevation of the altiplano and its distance from sources of humidity in the tropical lowlands to the east and the Pacific Ocean to the west, the air is extremely dry and evaporation strong. During the summer the pervasive cold diminishes somewhat, and the dryness can be temporarily alleviated by rains. Summer rains occur when the sun declines to its southernmost position and air masses from the eastern lowlands make their periodical incursions across the Eastern Cordillera into the altiplano. Short-lived downpours from November to March account for three-quarters of the altiplano's annual precipitation, which averages twenty-four inches (600 millimeters) and varies greatly from year to year. When the summer rains fail or fall in a few concentrated episodes, the chronic dryness of these highlands is intensified, and water becomes dangerously scarce for crops and animals.

The summer rain peak also affects the high mountains of the Peruvian Andes, known as the Sierra, so both altiplano and the southern Sierra of Peru can be considered as a unit as far as the influence of El Niños on precipitation is concerned. Since the summer rains are the primary providers of humidity for the altiplano—snowmelt being a minor contributor—it follows that the largest body of water in this part of the Andes, Lake Titicaca, reflects accurately the inter-annual fluctuations of precipitation. These year-to-year changes offer interesting insights into the climatic oscillations of the Central Andes that are ruled by the temperature and humidity fluctuations of the Pacific Ocean.

In the early 1970s, curious about the effects of warm anomalies in the Pacific Ocean on the South American continent, I reviewed long precipitation series from key stations and discovered that sierra and altiplano showed consistently low amounts of precipitation during El Niño years. At that time, several other researchers became aware of the pronounced variations of annual precipitation over the altiplano and detected similar fluctuations in the water levels of Lake Titicaca, but none related these to the water temperatures in the eastern Pacific. That was to change with the occurrences of El Niños 1972–73 and 1982–83. A detailed analysis of reliable long-term records for sierra and altiplano stations conducted by the French glaciologist Bernard Francou confirmed the general finding, but he also discovered that the signals of El Niño were not always consistent. Although some severe ENSO episodes, such as those of 1925, 1940–41, and 1982–83, resulted in remarkable reductions in summer rainfall totals (or even their total absence), other moderate episodes had negligible effects. That very realization had thrown off balance the German hydrologist Felix Monheim, who two decades before, after studying the fluctuations of Lake Titicaca, went so far as to state that sea warmings in the eastern Pacific Ocean were coupled with heavy rainfall in the altiplano.

What Monheim did find out in the course of his investigations was that the fluctuations in the lake level stretched over several years, including those in which ENSO episodes were conspicuous, such as the drastic low levels in the wake of El Niños 1940–41, 1932, and 1919. It also seemed to him that only recent ENSO episodes were associated with severe droughts in the altiplano, a point made by Francou as well. There has been, indeed, an increase in El Niño–induced drying effects on the altiplano and the sierra during the second half of the twentieth century. Low levels in Lake Titicaca were first reported around 1845—probably a consequence of El Niño 1844—and later in the 1870s, which were deeply impacted by ENSOs in 1866 and 1877. In the 1890s, C. Nussert-Asport, a German who lived for a while on the shores of Lake Titicaca, observed that the lake level was so low that large tracts of shoreland could be reclaimed—probably a consequence of the strong 1891 El Niño. The French geographer M. Neveu-Lemaire remarks that around 1903 he himself still saw the signs, as well as heard from local residents, that the level of the lake had been very low, a point that is consistent with the fact that 1902 had been a moderate El Niño year.

The scarcity of reliable meteorological stations in the region and the short duration of rainfall records make Lake Titicaca's water levels an appropriate surrogate measure for the general climatic fluctuations of the whole drainage region. Continuous level measurements exist only since 1912. Prior to that, the sole recourse is indirect historical references, which are often distorted or contradictory. A balancing factor is that the fluctuations usually spread over several years, which allows the identification of prolonged responses to varying humidity coming from the tropical Pacific and from the wetter lowlands of central South America.

After the establishment of the lake-gauging station in the town of Puno (Peru), the effects of ENSO events during the first half of the twentieth century could be accurately documented. Based on these data, the hydrometeorologist Albrecht Kessler continued Monheim's work, producing a time series that offers clues to the relation between El Niño in the eastern tropical Pacific and receding lake levels (Figure 5.5). The series begins with a lowering tendency from 1913 through 1916, which can be interpreted as delayed responses to the El Niños of 1912 and 1914. A rising trend that peaked in 1925, another El Niño year, was followed by low levels between 1926 and 1929. From 1930 to 1935, the lake level rose again, notwithstanding a strong ENSO event in 1932. A sustained lowering of the lake level from 1935 to 1943–44 seems to have been the response to the prolonged drought that ensued after the very strong 1940–41 El Niño. Conspicuously enough, a record low lake level of 4.3 meters (thirteen feet) below the official water mark was registered in Puno in the dry winter of 1943 in the aftermath of that severe episode.

The prolonged drought of the early 1940s had catastrophic conse-

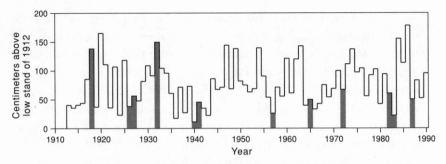

5.5. Levels of Lake Titicaca, 1912–90. El Niño years are darkened.

quences for the Urus, an Indian tribe of lakeshore dwellers that derive their livelihood from fishing, *totora* reed weaving, and cattle that feed mainly on aquatic plants. Communities broke apart as families and individuals left to seek temporary relief among befriended Aymara or Quechua Indians in other areas. When the drought finally subsided in 1947, some returned, but for many the cultural ties with their communities and environment had been permanently severed.

The drought that followed El Niño 1972–73 was not as devastating on the lakeshores as it was for the pastoral communities of the southern Peruvian sierra and the Bolivian altiplano. Precipitation deficits in the summers from 1970 to 1973 reduced staples, such as maize, potatoes, the native grain quinoa (*Chenopodium quinoa*), and the tuber oca (*Oxalis tuberosa*), but with the return of the rains in the summer of 1973–74, the shortages of previous years were recovered, and life resumed as normal.

The drought that began at the end of 1981 and persisted until November of 1983 had more serious effects. This response to the strong ENSO episode of 1982–83 was felt throughout the Peruvian Andes, the Bolivian altiplano and neighboring territories in northern Chile. Absence of rains for nearly two years had depleted the scarce water reserves of this huge area, and the natural grasses were unable to recover during the scant rains of the summer months. Herds of llama and sheep died for lack of fodder, and their carcasses lay strewn around dried-up watering holes. In towns and villages Indians held on to their emaciated cattle for as long as they gave milk, but then slaughtered them and sold the meat. This time many Indians from remote pastoral hamlets could not seek refuge among friends and relatives because all were equally affected. Reports circulated about desperate families selling their daughters and sons as servants to better-off families in the cities. Many more native families than in the 1940s emigrated to the major cities of La Paz, Cuzco, Arequipa, and Lima. These developments illustrate the ways in which climatic crises in the altiplano associated with El Niño events have changed the makeup of the urban populations in southern Peru. Today Aymara-speaking natives—the largest group in the altiplano region and Lake Titicaca basin—outnumber the Quechua-speaking Indians, who used to be the predominant ethnic element in many cities of southern Peru (Sallnow 1987).

Hunger and Deprivation in Northeastern Brazil

In the realm of distant connections a decisive discovery was made in the early 1970s, when researchers noticed that the droughts of northeastern Brazil had a conspicuous tendency to occur during or just before years when El Niño appeared in the waters of northern Peru. With northeastern Brazil some 3,000 miles away and separated by the imposing barrier of the Andes Mountains and the vast Amazon basin, how was it possible for anomalies in the tropical Pacific to traverse the widest part of the continent and cause dryness on the Atlantic side of South America?

The northeast "hump" of Brazil, the easternmost extremity of South America, is separated by a mere 1,800 miles from the African continent. That this part of South America was so close to Africa was unknown to the Spanish emissaries to the Holy See when they negotiated with their Portuguese counterparts in 1494 and asked the pope to draw a line that would separate Spanish from Portuguese territories in the Atlantic. A line running from north to south at 370 leagues (1,480 miles) from the Cape Verde Islands was declared satisfactory by both parties.

Since 1450, the Portuguese had been sailing down the coast of western Africa, setting up outposts where they traded gold and purchased African slaves from Arab raiders or warring native parties. These "commodities" were carried to the western European markets, where they fetched good prices. Hence it was in the interest of the Portuguese to acquire exclusive navigation and trading rights in the eastern half of the Atlantic. By 1489, they had reached the southern tip of Africa, and the way to India and the Spice Islands (eastern Indonesia) lay open to them. In 1498, Vasco da

Gama landed on the west coast of India, and Portugal was the first European nation to build an overseas commercial empire based on its outposts in Africa and southern Asia.

In 1501, en route to India, the Portuguese navigator Alvares Cabral, attempting to avoid contrary winds and ocean currents, deviated too much to the west and accidentally touched land in northeastern Brazil, which, according to the treaty of 1494, Portugal could now rightfully claim. This new land provided the Portuguese with the much needed opportunity to replenish water and repair vessels on their way to India, and with a stronghold of great strategic value because, already in the early 1500s, aggressive traders and navigators from the Netherlands were trying to break Portugal's monopoly on the slave and spice traffic. Faced with that threat, the Portuguese pursued an active policy of establishing fortified enclaves along the coast of northeastern Brazil and later farther south.

The coastal fringe of northeastern Brazil is directly in the path of the humid winds from the Atlantic, which deliver the rains that sustain the green forest (*agreste*) and sugar and cotton plantations. As the winds advance inland after having shed their humidity, the drying effects lead to an arid landscape known as *sertão*, the bush (Figure 5.6). Rainfall comes during the southern winter, and if dryness extends into the subsequent summer a drought ensues. Rains released by humid air masses from the equatorial Atlantic and the southward shift of the Inter-Tropical Convergence Zone (ITCZ) bring relief to the parched land only during the southern summer (October through March).

In this severely arid landscape, Indians from coastal northern Brazil sought refuge from the Portuguese. During subsequent centuries of racial contact, a mixed breed of Indians and Portuguese—the *sertanejos* (bush dwellers)—emerged who were adept at coping with the climatic extremes. When this pioneer land turned into the most populated region of the whole country, the devastating effects of episodic drought became patent. Newly plowed land would turn rock-hard under the scorching sun of a rainless summer; cattle and goats would starve around dried-out rivers and water holes, and the normally green *sertão* would change to grayish brown, denying its benefits to human and beast. Driven by the specter of starvation, thousands of *sertanejos* would converge on villages, towns, and cities, hoping to survive the lean times. Brazil's colonial history is dotted with episodes of violence, pillage, and death in the wake

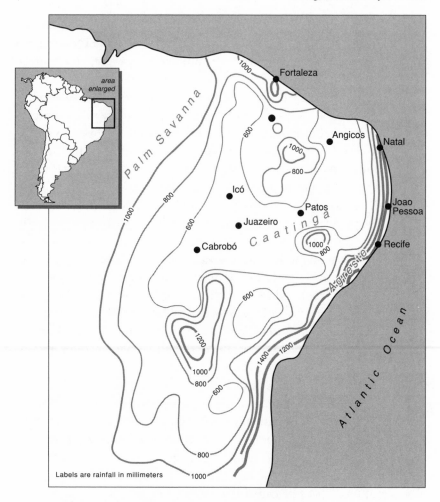

5.6. Annual rain and vegetation belts in northeastern Brazil

of the recurring droughts. To reconstruct a temporal series of these droughts, we have at our disposal a wealth of popular literature, as well as serious treatises addressing their sociocultural implications.

During the winter of 1971, I attended a lecture given by geographer Reuben Brooks in Milwaukee, Wisconsin, on the sociological implications of the northeastern Brazilian droughts and the ensuing population movements. As a missionary in that part of Brazil, Brooks had collected first-hand information on a rural society's perception of and adjustment to drought. When he produced a list of the drought years during the nineteenth and twentieth centuries I realized that those were roughly the years of increased winter precipitation in central Chile and El Niños in the South American Pacific! The striking simultaneity of events could not be dismissed as sheer coincidence.

Among the statistical tests for assessing relationships between events, "contingency tables" allow us to calculate the probability of an event occurring once another has taken place. Based on all the El Niño events known up to 1971 (the Quinn chronology was not published until 1987) and the numerous mentions of droughts in Brazilian sources, I calculated that there was a 61 percent probability that a drought would hit northeastern Brazil the same year or the year before an El Niño in the tropical Pacific. The probability of an El Niño event following a drought in northeastern Brazil, though, was only 38 percent. The 61 percent value is significant enough to suggest a more than accidental relationship between El Niños in northern Peru and droughts in northeastern Brazil. However, the much lower likelihood for droughts in northeastern Brazil to be predictors for the occurrence of El Niño in Peru, Chile, and Ecuador indicates that not all the climatic mechanisms that lead to drought are applicable to the inception of an El Niño. Thus, the door had been opened for investigating *how* stimuli generated in the tropical Pacific were able to make their way into the tropical Atlantic.

In the 1970s Jerome Namias, the perceptive meteorologist at Scripps Institution, turned his attention toward the problems of distant connections between climatic anomalies, which became more interesting as more information was made available. In one of his articles, Namias explored the interlocking of the low pressure center over "Greenland and New Foundland"—as he called the Iceland low—in the North Atlantic and the high pressure center off Brazil, which is directly responsible for the dry and the humid episodes over the Brazilian "hump." He noticed that when cyclonic activity (bad weather) in the North Atlantic is strong, the Azores high and the northeast trades that push the ITCZ southward during the southern summers are weak. At the same time, the South Atlantic high pressure cell is robust, the southeast trades are intensified, and drying conditions prevail over northeastern Brazil. Namias assumed that a deepening of the Greenland/Iceland low, caused by variations in the north-hemispheric westerlies, prompted changes in the pressures and winds of the whole Atlantic. He thus was the first to explain how a north-south relationship could be operating in the Atlantic Ocean.

A few years later, James C. Chung (1982) suggested that the relationship also worked in reverse. That is, the strengthened high in the South Atlantic and the intensified southeast trades "push" pressure centers and corresponding wind systems toward the north.

In 1973, I recognized and explained the "simultaneity" between El Niño occurrences off the South American west coast and droughts in northeastern Brazil as due to the failure of the ITCZ to move south of the equator in the Atlantic, while advancing farther south than usual in the tropical Pacific due to the presence of warm waters (oceanic El Niño) there. I detected a convincing counter-balance between the warm and humid ITCZ's moving south on the Pacific side of South America, and its being prevented from doing so on the Atlantic side. This was the first "seesaw" motion on opposite sides of a continent observed within the general modern-climatology framework provided by the Southern Oscillation and the Walker circulation. As the understanding of the relations between ocean and atmosphere has improved, so have the insights into the circulation mechanisms operating over the Atlantic under ENSO conditions.

The large number of simultaneous occurrences of droughts in Brazil and El Niños in the South Pacific during the past 100 years hints at a relationship between them, so the next step is to trace earlier dry periods in Brazil to see whether they match known El Niño sequences in the Pacific. The task is facilitated by the fact that the human misery engendered by the droughts is mentioned in numerous social and historical analyses and the droughts themselves also attracted the attention of noted meteorologists. One of those was Adalberto Serra, who wisely used the resources at his disposal at the Weather Service in Rio de Janeiro to determine intensities and periodicities in the drought outbreaks. Exhausting literary, anecdotal, and archival sources, he was able to create a year-by-year sequence of annual rains for the city of Fortaleza, in northeastern Brazil, spanning 1540 to 1970. This sequence complemented previous Brazilian drought lists and underscored the seriousness of this recurrent natural catastrophe. Historians and sociologists had classified them simply as *secas* (droughts) when they involved only one summer. Since the southern summer lasts from October to March, droughts—like El Niño events—usually spread over two calendar years. The more serious *grande secas* (big droughts) comprise two consecutive summers of insufficient rains which may span three calendar years. Table 5.1 lists the droughts

Table 5.1
Droughts in northeastern Brazil between the 1500s and 2000

1557–1558*	1804	1951
1574*	**1809–1810**	1953
1583*	1816	**1957–1958**
1587*	**1824–1825**	1971
1603	1827	1983
1614	1830	1992
1692	1833	
1710–1711	**1844–1845**	
1721	**1877–1879**	
1723–1727	**1888–1889**	
1736–1737	1891	
1744–1745	1893	
1754	1900	
1760	1902	
1772	1904	
1774	1907	
1777–1778	**1915**	
1784	**1919**	
1790–1793	**1931**	

Prolonged and severe droughts (*grandes sêcas*) are indicated in bold.
* Extracted from the list of annual rains at Fortaleza, by Serra 1973.
Sources: Andrade 1948; Martins Pinheiro 1960; Brooks (1982).

compiled for northeastern Brazil from the chronologies of Serra (1973), Alves de Andrade (1967), and Lopes de Andrade (1948) and reveals their associations with El Niño, as shown in Figure 5.7.

The 1500s were generally abundant in precipitation in many regions of the New World. Northeastern Brazil experienced short-lived periods of dryness in 1557–58, 1574, 1583, and 1587. For none of those years are El Niño conditions mentioned in the historical sources of Peru, nor are there any reports of serious climatic problems for the early settlements of northeastern Brazil, so they can be considered as independent events.

In the seventeenth century, 1603, 1614, and 1692–93 were "drought years," and 1633, 1645, 1652, 1654, and 1671 were "years of scant precipitation," to use Serra's classification. By comparison, in the Pacific basin, 1614, 1634, 1652, and 1692 correspond to historical El Niño years. Particularly the 1692 drought left a lasting memory among the few inhabitants of northeastern Brazil because bands of Indians displaced by the Portuguese expansion into the inhospitable ranges of the interior descended on incipient settlements and ranches, driving their inhabitants back to the fortified towns on the coast. Discouraged by the waywardness of the rains in the *sertão*, scores of families headed south to the region of Minas Gerais, where gold was being mined.

The eighteenth century was marked by dramatic climatic oscillations all over the world. Droughts in northeastern Brazil became more frequent and more devastating, and correlation with El Niño in the Pacific improved. The negative effects of these events are mentioned more frequently in the regional chronicles of the expanding network of rural settlements in northern Brazil. A major drought in 1710 seems to have been an isolated occurrence, but the drought of 1721 can be associated with El Niño 1720. Water was so scarce that even moving the herds to the banks of the drying rivers did not save them. The abandoned farms and settlements were again raided by armed bands, which were becoming more organized with each new drought.

An extended drought that lasted from 1723 to 1727 is considered the most severe of the entire colonial period: not only did starvation threaten the few who remained in the scorched countryside, but a plague of caterpillars devoured everything green. On larger estates near the coast, where sugarcane plantations were fairly well established, many slaves were set free because there was nothing to feed them, only to swell the ranks of the pillaging roving bands. The fact that the end of this prolonged drought coincides with El Niño 1728 makes the 1720s an important hallmark in tropical climatic history. The next two droughts, during 1736–38 and 1744–45, were severe but independent from ENSO events. Other major droughts during 1777 and 1790–92, and average ones during 1760, 1772–74, and 1783–86, occurred in close temporal proximity to reported El Niños in the Pacific. The drought of 1790–92 is significant because of its coincidence with the severe El Niño episode of 1792, considered one of the most serious of the eighteenth century, with implications even for the North Sea. In northeastern Brazil, ranching, which had recovered thanks to the demand for dried beef to feed the slaves on the sugar plantations, suffered a permanent setback. Cattle that could not be taken to neighboring palm-savanna regions died by the thousands on the banks of dried-up rivers and water holes; cattle that had survived elsewhere were not taken back to the Northeast afterward.

The first drought of the nineteenth century, in 1804, which coincided with a major El Niño, was followed by a major drought during 1809–10 that, although not connected with an ENSO event in the Pacific, seems to relate with climatic anomalies in other tropical regions. A drought in 1814 correlates with a major El Niño, and another in 1816–17, with a moderate El Niño in Peruvian waters. A prolonged drought in 1824–26 is in phase with an El Niño of moderate intensity in the tropical Pacific and with a devastating drought in the Deccan plateau, Bombay, and Madras. Again the rural population fled to the major population centers along the coast with bands of robbers at their heels, many dying from starvation along the road or falling prey to a raging epidemic of smallpox. Whether a drought that hit Bahia and Piauí in northern Brazil in 1827 is part of this prolonged tropical anomaly is debatable, but there is no doubt that a climatic oscillation similar to that of the 1720s was recurring. Other droughts between 1830 and 1833 can be related to a moderate El Niño in 1832 and correspond in time with the devastating 1832–33 drought in the Deccan and Andhra Pradesh. This calamity, added to that of 1824–26, reveals that, with increasing information about international affairs, linkages with drought disasters in distant regions could be established.

Another great drought was visited upon northeastern Brazil between 1844 and 1846, and its timely relation with the El Niño episode of 1844–45 is evident. Food was so scarce that rural populations resorted to eating cacti and wild plants and finally—as on previous occasions—fled to the major coastal towns. It is interesting that the ensuing thirty-two-year hiatus in the occurrence of this type of natural catastrophe coincides with the absence of major El Niño episodes on the Pacific side of South America. In fact, during that entire period, there were only two El Niños of medium intensity in 1864 and 1871. When the major El Niño 1877–78 struck, this global-scale anomaly showed in northeastern Brazil as a major drought that lasted from 1877 to 1879, in central and northern India, and in central China.

In the history and folklore of northeastern Brazil, this drought left the deepest imprints: dryness in the *sertão* killed animals, insects, and plants; the starving rural population again flocked to the coast. It is reported that Fortaleza, a coastal settlement of some 25,000 inhabitants before the drought, grew to as many as 114,000 in one year. The problems of overcrowding were compounded by a smallpox outbreak, which, added to the effects of beriberi, killed about half of the unfortunate refugees. In the face of such adversity, nearly 55,000 northeasterners left in search of more promising living conditions in the Amazon basin. It is to these *nordestinos* that Brazil owes the colonization drive into the forests of the Amazon.

After a pause of nine years, drought hit again in 1888–89, in the wake of the moderate El Niño of 1887, and returned with renewed vigor in 1891–92, in phase with one of that century's major ENSO developments. One more drought in 1898 preceded the 1899–1900 El Niño episode and anticipated yet another catastrophic drought in India. After the global crisis of 1877, the tendency of Brazilian droughts to anticipate ENSO occurrences in the tropical Pacific by one year began to emerge with more clarity, providing an indication that variations in pressures and wind systems started earlier in the South Atlantic than in the tropical Pacific.

The twentieth century opened with a widespread drought during 1902–4, coinciding with the moderate El Niño of 1902; another in 1907 that affected only the state of Rio Grande do Norte was clearly connected with the moderate ENSO of the same year. The rather intense El Niño episode of 1911–12 seems to have passed without serious consequences for northeastern Brazil, but the moderate El Niño of 1914 was followed by a great drought during 1914–15. As in past occurrences, the rural population flocked to towns and cities, or whatever greener patches they found along rivulets, and those who could afford it used the improving transportation systems to move south into the emerging urban-industrial centers of São Paulo and Rio de Janeiro.

It should be mentioned at this point that by the turn of the century, the droughts began receiving national attention, and concerned politicians were promising to do something about them. In 1909, a government agency, IFOCS, was entrusted with the task of constructing dams, irrigation canals, and other waterworks, but these initiatives could not keep pace with the rapid growth of the *nordestino* population that put more pressure on scarce water resources.

During the great drought of 1919, which follows El Niño 1917–18, cattle herds survived thanks to water available from newly constructed reservoirs. Reflecting weak responses in other world regions affected by ENSO events, El Niño of 1925–26, which hit the South American west coast with severity, went unnoticed in northeastern Brazil. The same cannot be said of the 1932 ENSO event, however; it started with an early drought in 1931 that became more acute in 1932 and persisted in many states until 1933. It seemed that all the government's preparations had been for naught as the cities were again swamped by close to a million drought refugees. Camps were opened near most major cities in the Northeast to prevent looting, and jobs were created in public projects. The Amazon basin also received a new wave of migrants. Nine years later, in

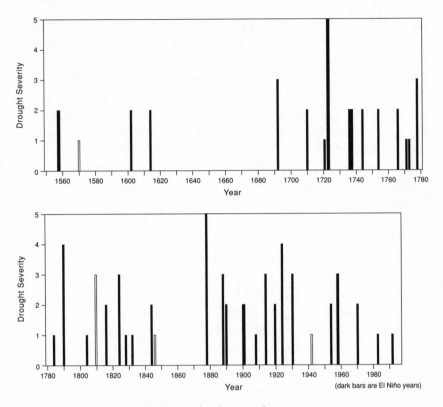

5.7. Droughts of northeastern Brazil in historical times

1942, drought conditions returned at the close of the prolonged ENSO episode that had begun in 1939. The mechanisms of spontaneous migration were again operating fast and efficiently: close to a million *nordestinos* moved to the industrial hub of São Paulo and pushed the colonization frontiers farther into the Amazon rain forest, Mato Grosso, and Acre in southwestern Brazil.

During the second half of the twentieth century, a prolonged drought during 1951–53 preceded the moderate El Niño of 1953, and a severe drought in 1958 followed the rather strong episode of 1957. The *nordestinos* could travel along recently constructed roads between their parched homeland and the new capital of Brasilia, Rio de Janeiro, and the emerging industrial centers in the south. To make it more attractive for the affected populations to stay in the northeast, a government agency, SUDENE, was created in 1959 whose task it was to improve and expand

the rural infrastructures, to offer alternative employment, to lend immediate assistance in the form of water pumps and the like, and to imple-
ment water storage and distribution projects.

The coping mechanisms were all in place when the 1971 drought arrived. Although this drought occurred a year before the major ENSO of
1972–73, it supported the scientists' contention that droughts in northeastern Brazil and El Niño occurrences in the Pacific Ocean were the two
faces of the ENSO fluctuations. Repetitions of simultaneous droughts and
El Niños in 1982, 1992, and 1997–98 strengthened this contention, now
based on a wealth of oceanic and atmospheric observations. Connections
that were previously considered spurious became central pieces in the
global anomalies puzzle. More useful than anything else for the understanding of modern climatology was the fact that the Atlantic Ocean had
been finally incorporated into the global ENSO mosaic.

Death and Unrest in Sub-Saharan Africa

Along with several other manifestations of ENSO, the droughts that befell
areas south of the Sahara Desert were placed into the context of global
variabilities only after the occurrence of El Niño 1972–73. During the preceding five years, insufficient rains had made life difficult for the nomadic

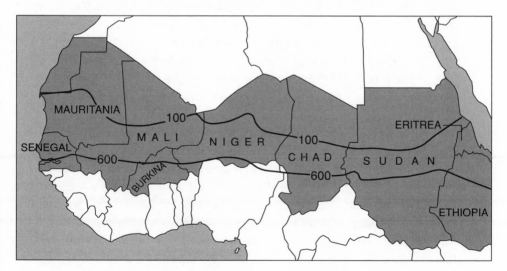

5.8. Countries of the Sahel limited by the 100- and 600-milimeter annual rainfall
lines

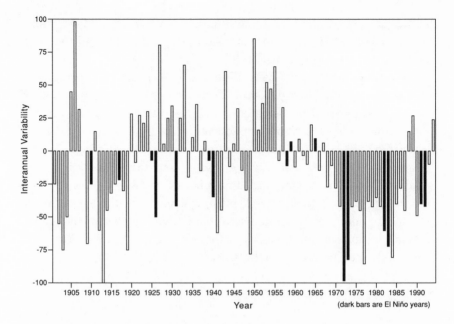

5.9. Variability of rain in the western Sahel, 1901–95

herders of the Sahel—the local name of the transition belt between the Sahara Desert and the tropical savannas of central Africa. When the summer of 1972–73 brought no rains at all, death and desolation among the tribal communities could no longer be warded off.

The Sahel—by no means known for its climatic regularity and even less for the political stability of the nations that lie in this region—occupies a belt where annual precipitation oscillates between ten and twenty inches, and year-to-year variations may amount to 40 percent of the total. This is the largest variability range of all semiarid regions (Figure 5.8). Early rains occur from April through July, when the sun is on its northward trajectory to the Tropic of Cancer and the northeasterly harmattan winds that cause the dryness of the Sahelian winters withdraw to the north. Humid winds from the Gulf of Guinea follow the sun's path as the continent heats up, and by July the rainy season is well under way and persists until October (Figure 5.3). These rains fall in sudden downpours that can evaporate quickly before penetrating the scorched soil, but if they do not, water holes, ephemeral ponds, and natural pastures come to life, allowing herders to move northward as summer progresses.

Like the altiplano in South America, this region has been undergoing progressive desiccation since the end of the last glaciation, some 12,000 years ago. Prior to that, most of what is now northern Mali, Niger, Chad, and Sudan and up to the massifs of the Sahara was covered by an extensive lake; present-day Lake Chad is a small remnant, with old beach lines up to sixty feet above the current lake level testifying to its past grandeur. Some 6,000 years ago, rainfall must have been twice what it is today; the region was covered by a humid savanna dotted with isolated trees, where prehistoric herders domesticated goats and wild cattle sometime after this had occurred in the Middle East. As the lands north of the lake started to dry out, these tribes adopted a more nomadic lifestyle, taking their herds south to the savannas during the dry winter months and returning during the rainy summer season.

In the course of the centuries, as the permanent aridity boundary shifted farther south, these nomadic tribes were forced into a zone where dysentery and the tsetse fly are endemic. In the words of Michael Glantz (1976), they were "sandwiched on increasingly marginal land on the southern edge of the Sahara, between the desert to the north and the cultivators (as well as the tsetse fly) to the south." Agricultural communities are viable around latitudes 15° to 13°N, where precipitation increases sufficiently to support rain-fed crops. Still, this area too depends on erratic summer rains, and drought in the Sahel causes hardship not only for the nomadic herders but also for these sedentary cultivators.

Drought means something different to each of these highly vulnerable populations. For the agricultural communities, a dry summer after a rainy planting season or an untimely dry spell in an otherwise reasonably wet summer can be as devastating as a protracted drought. For the nomadic herders, early arrival of the summer rains is less crucial as long as there is precipitation at the peak or toward the end of summer, because that will still awaken the fast-growing dormant grasses. Even a total lack of rains during one summer season is not disastrous as long as the wells and watering holes are not depleted. The situation becomes serious, however, when the water levels drop significantly or when not enough dormant grass is brought to life by the short downpours. A relatively humid summer season caught between a series of dry years is equally bad for the herders, because it may lead to a proliferation of the herds beyond the carrying capacity of the land. Unfortunately, dry years in the Sahel tend to occur in clusters and not as single events (Figure 5.9).

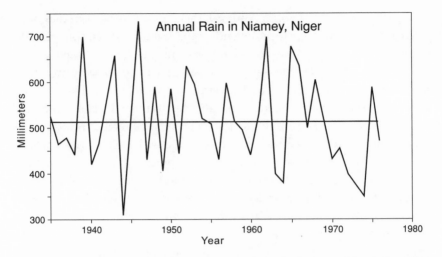

5.10. Annual rain in Niamey, Niger, western Sahel. The horizontal line is the 1935–80 average.

Since France and England had no interest in these colonies until the end of the nineteenth century, precipitation records begin only around 1900 for the western Sahel, while for the eastern Sahel (Ethiopia, Sudan, and northern Kenya), instrumental observations are available from the 1880s on.

In 1898 a prolonged drought started in the western Sahel and continued without interruption until 1904, probably a reflection of the ENSO episodes of the turn of the century and of 1903. This sequence of dry years—for which there is no casualty count—was followed by a sequence of rainy years that restored the herds and probably resulted in bumper crops at the northern margins of rain-fed agriculture. According to Michael Glantz, dry spells alternating with years of salutary rains are especially bad for the Sahel—as well as for other arid regions with large inter-annual variations—because they foster a false sense of security based on the assumption that lean years must always be followed by fat years. Also problematic is the herders' tendency, in response to the herds' multiplication during the good years, to rely on the newly sprouted grazing lands, forgetting that they will revert to their former barrenness once the water bonanza is over. This seems to have occurred during the sequence of dry years that extended from 1911 until 1919. The episode started in correspondence with El Niño 1911 and peaked during 1913–14, when herds shrank by two-thirds and the human death toll for the drought-stricken areas of Mali, Niger, and northern Nigeria was an estimated 80,000. Then the good years returned with their promise of a better future: 1921 was the first in a sequence of nearly eighteen years of adequate summer rains favoring the region. Still, two years of scarce precipitation—1926 and 1931—within that sequence coincided too close with El Niños 1925 and 1932 to be considered haphazard occurrences.

Another period of aridity began toward the end of the 1930s and lasted until 1942, mirroring almost perfectly the extended ENSO episode of 1940–41, which some analysts say was heralded by a moderate El Niño in 1939. The rains returned in the mid-1940s, with their corollaries of cattle multiplication and northward expansion of the boundary of rain-fed agriculture resulting in a steep increase in human population (Figure 5.10). The good years lasted through most of the 1950s, and not even the 1957 ENSO event had a negative impact. Thus, when many countries with territories in the Sahel gained independence in the 1960s, optimism reigned among these young African nations, and their faith in prosperity and population growth was strong.

By 1968, the incipient signs of a new period of dryness showed up in a sharp decline in seasonal precipitation from the optimal mid-1960s levels. The decline intensified during 1972–73—a very strong El Niño year in western South America—and continued until 1974. Rain-fed agriculture at the southern edge of the Sahel collapsed, the herds of the nomadic tribes farther north shrank to levels from which there has been no recovery, and a rampant famine ensued. Scenes of starvation and pictures of emaciated children and adults appeared in the Western media, while some African rulers—particularly the "emperor" of the Central African Republic—who in the previous decades had reveled in ostentation, pleaded with the industrialized countries for help. Aid did arrive, only to be embezzled by unscrupulous principals and government officials; the rural populations were left to fend for themselves as bands of robbers, led by local or regional warlords, viciously battled each other and supported their gangs by looting and selling hostages as slaves. As in northeastern Brazil, the impoverished rural masses flocked into the towns and sprawling cities, only to compound the serious problems plaguing these agglomerations. The system of exploitation, irresponsibility, and venality that had been put into operation during the fat postindependence years was revealing all its vices, and in the face of an abject inability to deal with emergencies, the young nations plunged into a crisis from which they are still trying to extricate themselves.

It is estimated that more than 200,000 individuals died in the whole Sahel, without counting those damaged for life by malnutrition and congenital illness. Over a million head of cattle were lost, an extraordinarily high number considering that animal husbandry is not concentrated in certain areas but spread over vast rangelands, and that it takes a minimum of five animals to support a pastoralist (Brown 1971). This ratio gives an approximate idea of the number of families affected. Among camels, goats, and mules, the losses stayed within the 5-to 20-percent range.

With the arrival of ENSO 1982–83, the effects of the extended drought of 1968–74 and the insufficient summer rains at the end of the 1970s became dramatically acute. By 1984, an estimated 250 million people suffered food shortages (*FAO Food Crops and Shortages,* Special Report No. 10). While in Niger, Chad, Sudan, Ethiopia, and Kenya, the problem was basically inadequate food production, in Mali, Upper Volta, Mauritania, and Senegal, it was the governments' mishandling of food distribution.

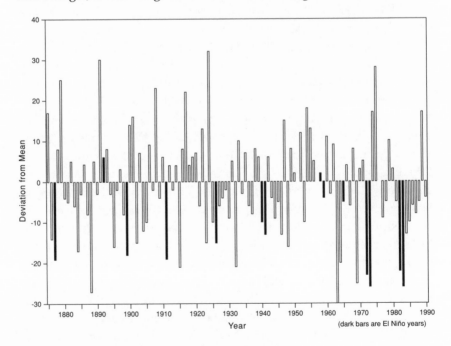

5.11. Variability of rain in eastern Africa, 1875–1990

1. Tropical fish caught in Pimentel at the height of El Niño, 1982–83

2. Guitarfish being dried on the shores of Paita

3. Shrimp harvested in northern Peru during El Niño, 1982–83

4. Siltage on riverine lands caused by flooding near Lambayeque, Peru

5. The green oasis of Motupe

6. *Caballitos* made of totora reeds in Santa Rosa

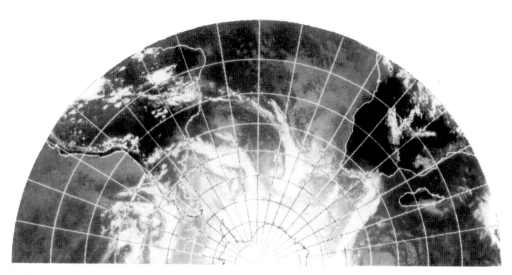

7. Sequence of subpolar depressions in the Southern Ocean. Extracted from ESSA satellite

8. *Huaca* in a river oasis of northern Peru

9. Temple of the Sun in Tiwanaku, Bolivia

10. Cloud pennant over Moorea, Society Islands

11. Stone statues of Easter Island

12. Beach of Anakena, Easter Island, where Hotu Matu'a and his colonists arrived

When summer precipation improved in 1988—after twelve years of insuf-
ficiency—most of the damage had been absorbed by the agrarian communities located at the northern margin of rain-fed agriculture, whereas
the once lively herding nomads of the Sahel huddled in camps in Sudan,
Ethiopia, and Chad.

The short respite of 1988 had barely started the region on the path to
recovery when a new period of deficit precipitation began in 1990, this
time associated with the inception of the protracted ENSO of 1991–94. The
post-1968 droughts in the Sahel are considered by most environmentalists
to be the worst crisis of this kind in the entire world; sociologists special-
izing in rural societies hold these droughts responsible for ending nomadic pastoralism as a form of livelihood in sub-Saharan Africa. In the
aftermath, most of the national structures in the region have collapsed,
rebellion and internecine tribal wars are widespread, and in many instances human nature has descended to its lowest levels.

The situation in the eastern part of the Sahel is not much better. On the
uplands of Ethiopia, western Somalia, and northern Kenya, summer precipitation is delivered by the summer monsoons coming across the Indian
Ocean. The calendar of subsistence agriculture in Ethiopia is divided into
three seasons: the planting season (February to May), which takes advantage of the short rainy season of spring (*belg*) that accompanies the northward migration of the sun; the growing season of summer (*kirmet*), from
June to September, when the monsoons bring the needed rain; and the
harvest season of winter (*bega*), from October through January, during
which any rainfall serves to replenish the water reserves needed for human consumption and the large herds. When a *bega* season has been very
dry, the subsequent planting season gets off to a bad start. The situation
gets worse when the rains of *kirmet* are insufficient to keep the planted
crops growing, which is what happens when, in response to ENSO occurrences in the Pacific Ocean, the monsoons fail.

The available instrumental series for eastern Africa, which begin in
1875 (Figure 5.11), show that as many as 80 percent of the dry periods
occur in a year that El Niño conditions develop in the tropical Pacific, the
year before, or the year after, which is acceptable evidence that the two
situations are associated rather than haphazardly distributed. Another
precipitation characteristic in eastern Africa documented in these series is
the marked alternation between rainy years and dry years—as opposed
to the grouping typical in the western Sahel. Overall, the dry and humid

periods on the eastern Sahel develop in close association with the monsoons over India and Southeast Asia, which, in turn, exhibit a remarkable
connection with variabilities in the tropical Pacific.

Once it was recognized that the droughts of the western Sahel occurred
in timely proximity to other fluctuations in the tropical belt, the search for
the climatic source of these variabilities began. Initially it was thought
that, since the Sahel rains occurred at the height of the northern summer
in connection with a northward advance of the Inter-Tropical Convergence Zone (ITCZ), the failure of that advance to take place was the root
of the problem. Soon after, however, it was established that precipitation
may not occur even in summers when the ITCZ moves inland. The first
reason offered was that the air drawn into inner western Africa by the
ITCZ was dry from its contact with cooler-than-usual waters along western Africa. This explanation had to be dismissed when measurements
showed sea-surface temperatures in the southern tropical Atlantic to be
warmer during ENSO years. But—and this is an important "but"—the
measurements did reveal colder-than-normal temperatures farther north
in the tropical North Atlantic in a belt stretching from the coast off Senegal
to the coast of the Guianas in South America. This observation is crucial
for understanding why there are fewer hurricanes in the tropical Atlantic,
the Antilles, and the Gulf of Mexico during ENSO years, an oddity dealt
with in chapter 7.

Thus the mechanisms that lead to the droughts in the western Sahel are
much more complex than previously advanced by some popularizers of
El Niño. Stefan Hastenrath, a meteorologist at the Universiy of Wisconsin,
proposed the most coherent explanation and elaborated on the reasons
for the longevity of these droughts. Studying the precipitation records of
western Sahelian stations from 1948 to 1983, and pairing them with sea-
surface temperatures of the tropical Atlantic as measured by passing
ships and at coastal stations in western Africa, he concluded that, over the
course of those forty years, there was a cooling of the Atlantic off western
Africa between latitudes 30° and 15°N, coupled with a warming south of
latitude 5°S. This caused a southward shift of the cloud bands typical of
the "equatorial convergence and near-equatorial wind confluence zone"
(as he describes the ITCZ over the tropical Atlantic). *Wind confluence zone*
is to be understood as the area where the northern hemispheric and
southern hemispheric trade winds converge. The southward shift of the
equatorial confluence zone originates with a long-term pressure rise over

the tropical North Atlantic that strengthens the northeast trades over western Africa and pushes the equatorial wind confluence zone southward. In the time series analyzed by Hastenrath, the rainfall zones of the western Sahel and the wind confluence zone moved southward in the order of 115 to 125 miles, a movement accentuated during the summer rain peak. If the mounting overgrazing and population increases in the Sahel are regarded against the backdrop of this climatic tendency toward less summer precipitation over the last forty years, the damage to this part of the world is easier to comprehend.

The rain variations in the eastern Sahel are more related—as already indicated—to influences from the Indian Ocean than from the Atlantic Ocean. Consequently, the analysts have focused on the behavior of the surface waters and the air flows from that ocean. Unseasonal warmings of the Indian Ocean are observed a year before an El Niño begins to show in the tropical Pacific; after the maturity phase of the event in the northern hemispheric spring, the warming becomes pronounced, which means that in the upcoming summer the Indian Ocean will be warmer than usual. Thus, instead of a regional high pressure center strong enough to send humid winds into India and eastern Africa, a convergence center for drying winds from the adjacent continents develops. It is this abnormal dry air flow that causes the droughts in the northern part of eastern Africa, the eastern portion of the Sahel, and the Indian subcontinent.

By now we are starting to realize how closely related to each other are the climatic variations of regions around the Indian Ocean. In the following section, we will turn to the catastrophic effects of ENSO-related droughts on populous India.

Famine and Weak Monsoons in India

Humans have always been dependent on nature's periodicities. Similar to the way in which, after Thanksgiving, media advertising reminds us of the imminence of Christmas, so were ancient civilizations alerted by natural signs that it was time to make certain preparations in their annual calendar of activities. To the ancient Egyptians, for example, the disappearance of Syrius from the western sky signaled that the annual flooding of the Nile was about to begin and that they should get ready for planting. Their agricultural calendar was ruled by the cycles of the river, whose

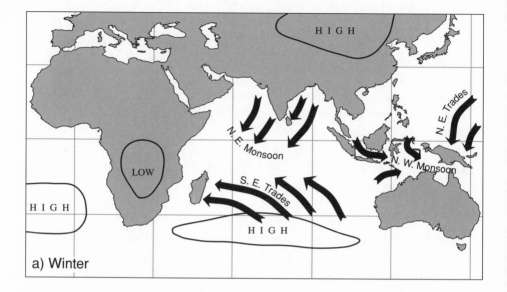

a) Winter

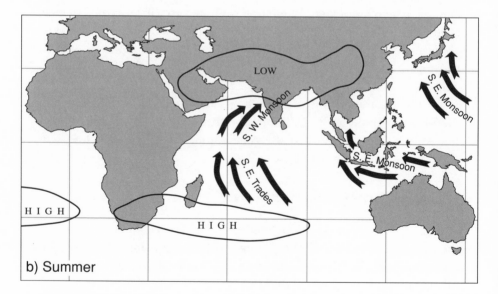

b) Summer

5.12. Monsoon paths in winter (a) and summer (b)

annual delivery of water and sediments was essential for the fertility of the soils. In the spring, agrarian communities and people all along the Nile Valley waited for these renewed signs of life.

In a similar manner, the early Indian civilizations were dependent on the rising and ebbing of the Indus, Ganges, and Brahmaputra Rivers. When the lowlands could no longer support the enlarging populations, people took to the uplands and drylands in search of new arable land. Water was not as readily available at these agricultural frontiers; the rains returning every year with the onset of the northern summer were the only source of the life-sustaining water. As population pressures kept rising and the Indians ventured into areas of irregular rainfall, rainfall uncertainty became more influential in their lives.

Monsoon, a derivative of the Arab *mausim* (season), actually refers to the seasonal changes of winds over the Indian Ocean realm and not to the rains. Many writers still use the word incorrectly, as a synonym for *rainy season* in that vast region, even though some monsoon winds do not bring rains. Furthermore, there are fundamental differences between the summer winds that blow from the southwest between western India and the African east coast, and the winter winds that blow from the southeast into the eastern segment of the Indian Ocean: the first are drying winds; the second are winds bringing rain.

The classic winter monsoons are air flows out of central Asia, where the cold continental temperatures give rise to dense, dry air masses. After crossing the Himalayas, these winds descend onto the Indian subcontinent, creating good weather and clear skies, and continue in a southeasterly direction across the northern Indian Ocean. Since those waters are cool during that season, there is not much humidity to be picked up, and the winds bring no winter rains to eastern Africa. In the eastern reaches of the Indian Ocean, the monsoons curve southward, attracted by the equatorial calms and by the Indonesian low, which is positioned over northern Australia at that time of the year. For this reason the drying monsoons over Indonesia and northern Australia blow from west to east and are called *northwest monsoons* by contemporary climatologists (Figure 5.12a).

After a pause in May—which, incidentally, is taken advantage of by climbers of Mount Everest, as detailed in Jon Krakauer's *Into Thin Air*, a gripping account of the ill-fated 1996 Everest climbing expedition—the direction of the winds over India and the Indian Ocean is reversed. When the Asian continent heats up in the course of the northern summer and the

Indian Ocean stays comparatively "cooler" than the surrounding land-masses, the airflow from ocean to land intensifies, reaching its maximum during the summer with torrential rains over India and Southeast Asia (Figure 5.12b). The city of Dehra Dun, at the foot of the Himalayas, receives 85 percent of its annual rainfall (eighty-nine inches) from June through September. While annual totals decline toward the south and west of India, the proportion of summer precipitation remains close to 80 percent. This means that a decrease in or the total absence of these seasonal rains has serious consequences for the rain-fed crops in regions that lack large rivers whose waters could be used for irrigation.

A fundamental distinction exists between summertime sea-to-land airflows that are *humid monsoons*, and monsoonlike flows that are dry. A good example of the latter are the southwest monsoons that blow over the western sector of the Indian Ocean and are supposed to bring precipitation to the arid northwest of India, Pakistan, and eastern Iran. As Hermann Flohn, M. Hantel, and E. Ruprecht (1970) explained, these monsoons are the prolongation of cross-equatorial southwest trades from the South Indian Ocean, which are so devoid of humidity that they form clouds over western India only for a few summer days, and if they ever do lead to rain, the drops evaporate in the extreme dry air before reaching the ground. Truly humidifying monsoon rains arrive with the easterly flows from the seas around Indonesia; they produce prolonged, heavy rainfall episodes over the eastern half of India, the plains of the Brahmaputra and Ganges, and Assam in the northeast. Indian climatologists, and Europeans like Flohn and his coauthors, attribute dry summers to delays and failures of the southeast monsoons. Over Indonesia, northern Australia, Indochina, the Philippines, and southern China, the humid summer monsoons blow from east to west as air from the equatorial Pacific is drawn into the low pressure cells that hover over the heated continents.

The electrified atmosphere and sense of anticipation while awaiting the arrival of the life-bringing rains set the mood of Louis Bromfield's novel *The Rains Came*, and numerous other literary pieces have also used this theme. Nevertheless, time and again the seasonal rhythm was broken when the summer rains were delayed or failed altogether, and the associated problems grew worse as the population of India increased and more marginal lands were brought under cultivation. With the advent of the Little Ice Age—the cooler, drier period that is documented worldwide from the 1500s to the late-1800s—the situation became critical, just as the colonial powers of Europe were struggling to establish their imperial hegemony over the splintered kingdoms of India. Although it can be assumed that climate-induced food crises were known on the subcontinent before the 1500s, the first reliable references to famines and droughts surface in colonial chronicles and popular lore about that time. In the nineteenth century, these occurrences were compiled in chronologies that appeared, for example, in the *Edinburgh Review* (1877), and in articles such as "The Famines in the World: Past and Present," published in the *Journal of the Statistical Society* by Charles Walford in 1878. In the twentieth century, the old chronologies that had been expanded and corrected by British and Indian scholars were incorporated by Australian researchers Peter H. Whetton and Ian Rutherfurd into the article "Historical ENSO Teleconnections in the Eastern Hemisphere" (1994), which offers useful insights into the role of El Niño in India's climatic history.

During the sixteenth century, famines occurred in India in 1500, 1509, 1520–21, 1540–43, 1554–56, 1576–77, 1592, and 1594–98, but only the famine of 1540–43 is attributed to generalized droughts. A comparison with the Quinn chronology shows that 1541, 1578, and 1591–92 were El Niño years in the South American Pacific. Not mentioned is 1588, the year when—according to Hubert H. Lamb—the city of Fatepur Sikri in India was abandoned due to monsoon failure, and also the year when the Spanish Armada was destroyed by a sequence of untimely North Atlantic storms in August.

During the seventeenth century, famines were reported in 1613–15, 1618, 1623, 1629–31, 1648, 1650, 1659–61, 1685, and 1687. Some of them were closely tied with El Niño episodes in 1614, 1618, 1624, 1660, and 1687.

Well-documented political developments permit the identification of droughts and famines during the 1700s. When England emerged in 1707 as the victor among the colonial powers competing for control of India, it also inherited that country's problems of food shortages and overpopulation. Members of the British colonial administration had to deal with the droughts, and their reports offer valuable insights into how they perceived the crises and tried to alleviate the famines of which the eighteenth century had its good share. Droughts in 1702–4, 1709, 1746–47, 1782–83, and 1791 occurred in concomitance with El Niño episodes, whereas those of 1718, 1733, 1737, 1739, 1744, 1752, and 1769–70 did not. Of special interest is a severe dry period that affected Andhra Pradesh and neighboring regions from 1789 to 1791—precisely in tune with the powerful ENSO episode of 1791—because it reveals how an extra-cold and dry winter in India prior to this episode developed into a pronounced drought when the summer monsoons failed to bring the expected rains (Grove 1998). It is interesting to observe the droughts' tendency toward longer duration and greater severity after 1770, the beginning of a drastic climatic change, which also resulted in higher hurricane frequency on the Caribbean Islands. This will be examined in the following chapter.

The nineteenth century began with droughts and famines in 1802–3, 1806, and 1812, all of which relate to El Niño events of different intensities in the tropical Pacific and significant global climatic anomalies, including extreme cold weather in 1816—dubbed "the year without summer"—due to a volcanic dust layer over most of the tropics (Chenoweth 1996). This period of severe climatic crises was followed by an interval during which the variations were less severe and the occurrences more spaced in time. Droughts in 1823–24, 1832–33, 1837–38, 1844, 1853, 1860, and 1864–66 occurred in phase with major or moderate ENSO episodes, providing further evidence of the link between monsoon failures over southern Asia and oceanic and atmospheric anomalies in the tropical Pacific. Only the drought of 1868 deviates from this pattern.

Matching the droughts of India with documented El Niño events becomes easier and more rewarding from the 1870s onward thanks to the existence of detailed surveys from British colonial administrators, which have been carefully scrutinized by contemporary scholars, such as B. Parthasarathy and associates (1987) and H. N. Bhalme, D. A. Mooley, and S. K. Jadhav (1983). Combining the information gathered from these sources with Whetton and Rutherfurd's list further illuminates the relations between monsoon failures and ENSO occurrences in the Pacific. Figure 5.13 offers a synthetic view of the monsoon rainfall variations in India and the warm phases of the Southern Oscillation between 1875 and 1992, illustrating how closely the pressure variations across the Pacific Ocean are associated with India's dry episodes.

The anomalous 1870s opened with a drought restricted mostly to the area around Marathwada (central India), in phase with the 1871 El Niño in the South American Pacific. Next came one of the most serious droughts/famines of the nineteenth century, that of 1877, which coincided with the powerful ENSO event of 1877–78. Fifty percent of the Indian subcontinent was affected, especially in the northwestern regions of

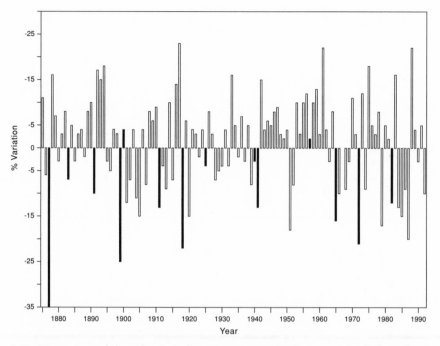

5.13. Monsoon and droughts in India, 1875–1992. El Niño years are darkened.

Rajasthan, Saurashtra and Kutch, Gujarat, and Haryana. After more than a decade of relative reprieve, the scourge returned in phase with the 1891 El Niño. This time, the northern Punjab and southern Rajalseema took the brunt of the water deficits. The century closed with one of the most devastating droughts in modern Indian history, in phase with the mighty El Niño of 1899–1900. Seventy-three percent of Indian territory was in the grip of that drought, which had its center in the central Indian states and spared only the northern regions at the foot of the Himalayas, the northwestern lowlands of the Ganges River, and Uttar Pradesh.

The first drought of the twentieth century, in 1904, coincided with a dip in SOI, but not with an oceanic El Niño disturbance. (This is excellent proof that not all depressions in the SOI need be accompanied by a warming of the tropical Pacific and that only the concurrence of both constitutes a true ENSO event.) The drought started in the northwestern regions of Gujarat, Saurashtra, and Kutch and expanded into Rajasthan and Uttar Pradesh the following year, so that by the end of this two-year period, 35 percent of India was affected. The same regions experienced another

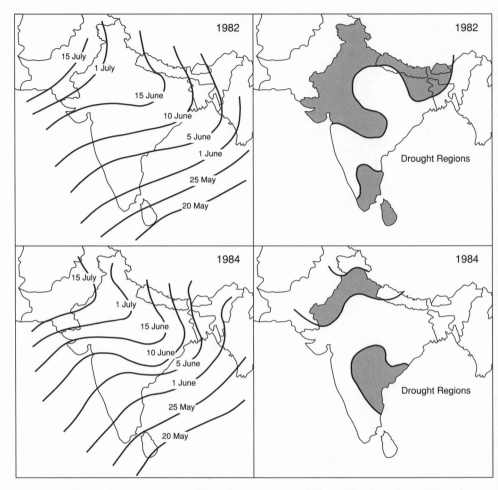

5.14. Time of monsoon arrival in India and regions affected by drought, 1982 and 1984

drought in 1911 and again in 1914, in phase with El Niños of medium strength. The worst drought of the first quarter of the century occurred in 1918 following a moderate depression of the SOI. An estimated 68 percent of India was affected, which makes this event second only to the catastrophe of 1899. Only the northern regions, Madhya Pradesh in the center, and the southern tip of the subcontinent were spared. Before those areas could recover, a new drought occurred in 1920—a year without disturbances in the tropical Pacific—involving 44 percent of the Indian territory, with critical areas in the north-central states. The following drought, in 1925, which is linked with a powerful El Niño off South America, included mostly the northwestern region of Rajasthan.

After a fourteen-year hiatus, droughts returned in 1939, 1940, and 1941, in concurrence with a prolonged and strong ENSO event during the same years. Yet these droughts affected barely 25 percent of the Indian territory, mostly in western Rajasthan, Saurasthra, and Kutch. An active policy of dam and reservoir contruction implemented after World War II served to reduce the impact of droughts, beginning with the one in 1948—which struck the Gujarat as well as Saurasthra and Kutch.

From 1950 on, it became even more patent that climatic variations in southeastern Asia and India had long-distance roots in the far Pacific: the droughts of 1951, 1965, and 1972–74 developed in concurrence with El Niño events in the tropical Pacific, and when the drought of 1982–83 developed in concomitance with one of the greatest ENSO events of the twentieth century, the mechanics of its origin and evolution could be studied in depth and used to explain the disastrous occurrences of previous centuries.

In this sense, the progression of the monsoons in 1982, 1983, and 1984 shows how rain deficits come about in India during extreme ENSO events. In 1982, the summer monsoon arrived on time in southern India at the end of May but then stalled prior to curving to the northwest in early June. Only by July did the monsoon reach the regions of the northwest—too late and too weakened. The ensuing rainfall deficits are presented in the accompanying precipitation maps of 1982 and 1984 (Figure 5.14). In 1983 (not shown) the monsoons were similarly delayed and, after a recurvature almost identical to that of the previous year, entered northeast India near Orissa, causing rain deficits in the northeastern states while normal precipitation fell in most of the south and west of the country. In 1984, the delay was repeated, but the recurvature occurred farther north over the Bay of Bengal, this time reducing summer precipitation in the east-central part of India as well as the arid northwest.

After remaining weak for another four years, the monsoon rains returned to normal strength in 1988, a year of strong cold water developments in the tropical Pacific. In 1991, however—with sinking Southern Oscillation Index values indicating that another ENSO episode was in the making—summer rainfall over India started to decline as expected. This time the recurvature in the arrival time of the monsoon took place deep in southern India, so that regions in the center and northeast of the country suffered from drought conditions, while the west and northwest received above-average precipitation for a change. In 1993, with SOI values still low but on the upsurge, deficit summer rains were recorded in the north-central states. Conversely, Bangladesh and portions of the northeast were inundated. In 1994, the SOI rose again, and the monsoon rains of that year returned to their accustomed levels.

The above-mentioned recurvature in the temporal and spatial arrival of the monsoon rains on the Indian subcontinent offer a clue to the mechanisms that control the onset of the summer rains and explain their delay and low amounts. According to Stefan Hastenrath (1990b, 1995), the intensity of a monsoon is determined by three main "predictors": the location of a high pressure ridge over India in the months preceding the onset of the rains, the intensity of the wind flow in the Indian Ocean across the equator, and the Southern Oscillation Index. These are the factors to look at to explain a successful or failed monsoon.

The establishment in spring of a high pressure ridge around 10,000 feet of elevation with its axis along the spine of India forces the jet stream over southern Asia to dip southward, and its persistence through the early summer can prevent the timely arrival of the monsoon and the onset of the summer rains. The southeast recurvature of the monsoon rains' starting dates depicted in Figure 5.14 suggests the location of this ridge that prevents the humid winds from reaching the subcontinent as it is progressively warming up.

The second factor, cross-equatorial airflows over the Indian Ocean, is related to the development of temperature differences between the ocean and the surrounding landmasses. Since water takes longer to warm up than land, at the onset of summer the Indian Ocean is comparatively cooler than the subcontinent, which makes for a steadier inland flow of humid winds and a more effective release of rains. However, when the thermal difference between land and water decreases due to warmer-than-usual temperatures in the Indian Ocean, the inland flow is considerably diminished.

At this point we may ask when and how is the Indian Ocean "warmer than usual"? Recent oceanographic research suggests that the Indian Ocean—although covering a smaller area than the Pacific Ocean and interrupted by the intrusion of the Indian landmass—has warming periods similar to El Niño in the Pacific. The areas of maximum warm sea are

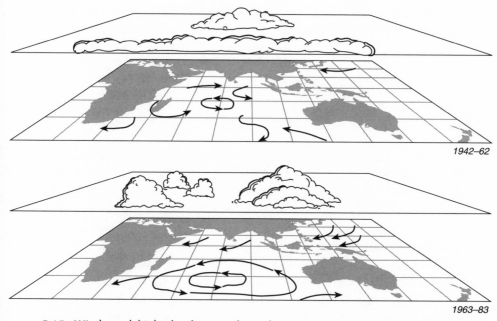

1942–62

1963–83

5.15. Winds and high clouds over the Indian Ocean, 1942–62 and 1963–83. Adapted from Reason et al. 1996.

located near the equator and off eastern Africa, from where the warming spreads *eastward*—that is, against the prevailing direction of the early summer monsoons. Temperature differences between ocean and continent are not pronounced under those circumstances, and even if there is strong convection over the warm waters, the humidity cannot make its way onto the Indian subcontinent due to the slackened winds.

The third factor controlling the monsoons, the Southern Oscillation, is less tangible than the other two, but its influence has been very consistent in recent times. The fact that there is a strong causal relationship between both the upper atmospheric circulation over India and the magnitude of the cross-equatorial flows in the Indian Ocean and the summer monsoons explains why not all droughts in India are reflections of ENSO events in the Pacific. The operating mechanisms were first suggested by Sir Gilbert Walker in 1923–24. As chief of the Indian Meteorological Service, he was trying to find concrete indicators for a link between the inter-annual variability of the monsoons over India and oscillations in the tropical circulation. He discovered the relationships between extremes in the monsoon intensity and the pressure seesaw between the Indonesian low and South

Pacific high that his successors called "Southern Oscillation." Today we know that during years when droughts in India concur with ENSO events in the South Pacific, the Walker circulation over the equatorial Pacific is displaced to the west, so that the branch of dry air descends over Southeast Asia and northern Australia. Thus, instead of humid air masses advancing westward, the airflow consists mainly of unsaturated dry masses that cause drought conditions in most of Southeast Asia, India, and the eastern half of Africa.

The extent to which these conditions are worsened by anomalies in the Indian Ocean was studied by C. J. C. Reason, R. J. Allan, and J. A. Lindesay (1996). They wanted to find out whether, over the course of the twentieth century, the interactions between water temperatures of the Indian Ocean and the airflow above had always followed the same patterns or whether variabilities could be detected. For the years 1963 to 1983—which include the Indian droughts of 1965–66, 1968, 1972–74, 1979, and 1982—they were able to develop a computer model that suggested the consolidation of a steady high pressure cell over the southern Indian Ocean; this cell forced humid air masses into Southeast Asia and East Africa, as depicted by the cloud development in the bottom half of Figure 5.15, and left the central part of the ocean exposed to the anticyclone's drying influences. During the years between 1942 and 1962—notable for the absence of devastating droughts—the said high pressure cell was weakened most of the time, the ocean on both sides of India was unusually warm, and an extended cloud cover hovered over the whole Indian Ocean, including eastern Africa, which during that period was spared severe droughts (Figure 5.15 top). The model developed by those three researchers illustrates how the oceanic and atmospheric conditions in that part of the world changed in consonance with what was happening in the Pacific basin.

In recent years, the scientific interest in past El Niño climatic variations has also led to the detection of nondocumented monsoon flows. Based on sedimentary deposits at the bottom of the western Indian Ocean, south of the Arabian Peninsula, deep-sea geologists S. C. Clemens, D. W. Murray, and W. L. Prell (1996) contend that the strength of past monsoons was greatly influenced by variations in the obliqueness of the earth's orbit around the sun and by changes in the precession of the equinoxes (the forward shift of the beginning of spring and autumn that has made it necessary to move the dates of the equinoxes from March 21 to March 22, and from September 21 to September 23). Microorganisms and traceable mineral deposits in sediment traps at the bottom of the Indian Ocean reveal that these seemingly insignificant changes led to the formation of ice masses during the Ice Age (Pleistocene) and have influenced the intensity and path of the monsoons for the past 2.6 million years.

Frank Sirocko, another geologist who infers climatic changes from deep-sea sediments, considers that the variabilities of prehistoric monsoons reflect distant geophysical variables, such as heat flux from the Indian Ocean, sea ice cover on the North Atlantic, changes in elevation of the Tibetan plateau, and snow cover over eastern Asia, plus distant effects of prehistoric El Niños, all of which are registered in fine stratigraphic deposits on the ocean floors (Sirocko 1996).

These "recording devices" indicate that the intensity and regularity of the Asian monsoons have caused sizable rain variations in the Indus Valley even before the dawn of civilization around 3,000 B.C., and that the documented monsoon failures since A.D. 1500 are but a moment on a timescale that goes far back into the geological past.

Fires of Australasia

At first glance, Australia may not strike us as one of the driest continents. Yet it possesses only 6 percent of the global surface freshwater and receives only 18 percent of the planetary precipitation, so that 83 percent of its territory is considered arid.

As in the case of other regions in the tropics, it was not until the occurrence of El Niño 1972–73 that international climatologists noticed the correlation between scant rainfall over Australia and the fluctuations of El Niño/Southern Oscillation. Around that time, Donald Heathcote published a very accurate survey of dryness in Australia, complemented by maps of the droughts that could be documented by instrumental series, but nowhere in his work is there any reference to ENSO episodes. This omission was remedied before long.

The Australian island-continent has a dry core centered in the uplands of Alice Springs in the interior. Only the northern, southeastern, and western fringes receive enough rain to support dense vegetation, and this is also where the population is concentrated. The rain mechanisms, however, are not the same in all these areas. The northern fringe and part of the eastern coast receive their maximum precipitation during the southern summer, when inland-blowing winds bring humidity from the sea. Also during the summer, the overheated waters of the Coral Sea and Arafura Sea spawn tropical cyclones that dump great amounts of precipitation over northeastern Australia, causing material damage and loss of life.

The same mechanism also prompts abundant rainfall over the Indonesian archipelago during the southern summer peak, which justifies dealing with the Indonesian droughts jointly with the Australian ones. This approach is also warranted when we remember that one of the poles of the Southern Oscillation is the Indonesian low pressure center (see chapter 1), as measured in Darwin on the north coast of Australia.

In southeastern Australia, particularly the densely populated state of Victoria, the rains are generated by a different mechanism: usually transient midlatitudinal depressions and the associated fronts reach maturity over the Australian Bight and the Tasman Sea and, continuing east, brew the storms whose consequences for marine traffic were analyzed in chapter 4.

The area around Adelaide and southwestern Australia is under the influence of westerly flows emanating from the zonal westerlies that prevail over the southern Indian Ocean, and experiences winter rains from transient depressions and fronts generated in the southern oceans. During the winter, the core of the continent remains bone-dry, and if that aridity is not relieved in the summer, this "patch of thatch" eats like a living organism into the greener borderlands.

To grasp the dynamics of the Australian droughts, we need to understand the blocking situations that tend to develop over southern and southwestern Australia during particular years. In the southern hemisphere—as opposed to the northern hemisphere—where landmasses are very reduced south of latitude 40 °S, there is a constant procession of anticyclones (high pressure cells) and depressions (low pressure cells) over the oceans. The high pressure cells, which are dominant during the winter, send cold air from the southern oceans into the interior of Australia, thereby blocking any warm and humid air that might be coming from the north. During summer, the traveling high pressure cells decrease in number and intensity, but if the anticyclonic dominance is not weakened in response to anomalies in the tropical circulation, most of Australia is blocked from receiving moisture from the surrounding seas, and generalized drought conditions set in; this happens most frequently during El Niño years.

The association between Australia's rainfall variability, temperature extremes, and tropical cyclone frequency and the ENSO-related circulation mechanism over the tropical Pacific was not formulated until the 1980s. Neville Nicholls (1992) contends, however, that already in 1877, when both Australia and India were affected by droughts, the Australian meteorologist Charles Todd suspected common mechanisms were the root cause, and in 1896, H. C. Russell of New South Wales addressed the coincidental drought occurrences in the two regions. H. Hildebrandsson is credited with being the first to suggest the existence of compensatory circulation mechanisms similar to those formulated by Sir Gilbert Walker in the 1920s. In view of these early insights, it seems odd that neither the aforementioned Heathcote, in his otherwise exhaustive treatment of Australia's droughts (Heathcote 1969), nor any other Australian scientists of his time suspected that a distant event, such as ENSO in the southern Pacific, was the modulator of the inter-annual fluctuations of their continent's climate. Today, there is no climatologist or environmentalist in Australia who does not accept that "El Niño/Southern Oscillation is a prominent feature of the ocean/atmosphere in the Pacific region and [it] has a marked effect on the climate of Australia" (Colls 1993).

Rainfall over Australia is abundant during the high phases of the Southern Oscillation (high pressures and cold waters across the eastern tropical Pacific), and cyclone generation is very active; during the low phases of the Southern Oscillation (low pressures and warm waters in the equatorial and eastern tropical Pacific), there is frequent blocking, regional or localized droughts, and lesser numbers of cyclones over northern Australia and Indonesia.

Because of the variable ways in which the climate controls mentioned above work in different regions, there are few generalized droughts that can be ascribed to a single cause, whereas regional droughts obeying one dominant control are more frequent. Instrumental records exist only from the 1840s on, which means that information about dry periods covers barely more than one and a half centuries. H. C. Russell collected anecdotal evidence about drought occurrences in Australia and drew up a list that appears in Nicholls's work (1992). Included are the years 1789–91, 1793, 1797, 1798–1800, 1802–4, 1808–15, 1818–21, 1824, 1827–29, 1833, and 1837–39, all of which, interestingly enough, are in phase with El Niños; only the droughts of 1798–1800, 1815, and 1818 emerge as isolated events. From 1840 onward, the available precipitation series convey an accurate picture of the critical fluctuations in many of Australia's arid regions and allow comparisons with similar environments in other parts of the world affected by major ENSO events.

D. Heathcote (1969), R. J. Allan (1985), and J. E. Hobbs (1988) produced illustrative surveys of Australian droughts since the 1880s that are useful for understanding the extent of these disasters and their associations with ENSOs. For the whole continent, the first three decades after the 1840s were marked by erratic inter-annual variations punctuated by low rainfall in 1854, 1859, and 1869—all of them moderate El Niño years off Peru. During the 1870s and 1880s, these variations were made worse in the central and southern regions by the occurrence of global anomalies. A record annual low in 1876 was followed by a rainy 1877 that happened to be one of the major ENSO episodes of the nineteenth century, while a more generalized dryness that affected almost half of the continent in 1886 occurred in conjunction with monsoon failure in Indonesia and eastern Africa and unrelated to any ENSO event. A drought in 1888, which can be paralleled with the moderate 1887–89 El Niño off Peru, affected eastern Australia as well as a fringe along the west coast, sparing the northwest and center. During the serious El Niño of 1891, the effects of abnormal dryness were more pronounced in the western part, but the following year brought drought conditions all along northern Australia, which is to be expected when the Indonesian low is strengthened and the number of tropical cyclones reduced. Another drought in 1894, restricted to Australia's western side, had no relation with atmospheric and oceanic anomalies in the Pacific basin, which means it was caused by variations in the water and air circulation of the southern Indian Ocean between Africa and Australia. In 1897, the country experienced a drought in the south-central part and extreme northeast, but not on the southeastern and western fringes. The possible connection between this particular drought and a moderate El Niño episode that was reported in northern Peru that year needs to be further investigated, since the rather strange distribution pattern of this drought suggests a blocking situation.

The spread of the drought of 1900–1902 followed a pattern that was repeated during the major ENSO episodes of the twentieth century: the whole north and northeastern regions of Australia, especially York Peninsula, were strongly affected, suggesting the influence of the strengthened Indonesian low, which is an indicator of warming across the equatorial Pacific. The drought of 1905 was as serious as the drought of 1877; it involved 95 percent of Australia and spared only the temperate southwest.

The anomaly coincided with extended dry spells in the eastern hemisphere of the Southern Oscillation, but it had no major El Niño correlates in the eastern tropical Pacific.

After almost a decade of good rainy years, dry conditions returned and bottomed out in 1914 with a drought affecting chiefly the central part of the continent, the pattern seeming to indicate a connection with the medium-intensity El Niño episode of that year. Close to three decades followed during which conditions in the western Pacific were not conducive to generating widespread dryness, but the droughts in 1912–13 and 1918–19 occurred too close to ENSO episodes in the central and eastern Pacific to reject an association. Dry episodes in 1924 and 1925, and a severe drought in 1940, were in phase with the major 1940–42 El Niño and affected much of southeastern and western Australia (where they even caused land abandonment). It was only with the reoccurrence of the droughts during the "new El Niño era" beginning with the 1957–58 episode that a closer association with ENSO events in the Pacific Ocean became evident (Figure 5.16). Thus the dryness that affected northern and

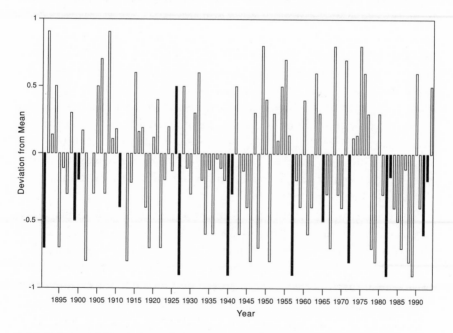

5.16. Rain variability in Australia, 1885–1994. El Niño years are indicated by dark bars.

southwestern Australia in 1958 and 1959 must definitely be considered the sequel of upset conditions in the tropical Pacific, and droughts in the center of the country in 1961 and 1963 can be linked to minor ENSO episodes during those years. The drought of 1965, which involved most of the eastern half of Australia, confirmed patterns that were becoming obvious and left no doubt that Australia was among the main areas affected by ENSO occurrences.

During the severe worldwide climatic anomaly that occurred in phase with the ENSO episode of 1972–73, precipitation over northern and eastern Australia was insufficient during the first year, but there was a powerful rebound to high rainfall during the second. This rebound is interesting because brisk jumps in annual precipitation, air pressures, and sea-surface temperatures are common during the transitions from El Niño to its opposite, La Niña. A reduction in summer precipitation in 1976 and 1977 was an apparent response to the somewhat restricted El Niño of 1976. These cases make it clear that almost every ENSO event of the post-1950s presided over precipitation deficits in much of eastern and northern Australia—a good reflection of the inter- annual climatic variations at the western pole of the Southern Oscillation.

Better documented and with discernable signs of that control were the onset and development of the El Niño in 1982–83, which started to be felt in northern Australia in 1981. The blocking situation developing in those years was determined by the displacement of the summer convection area to the central and eastern equatorial Pacific, which brought Australia under the influence of persistent anticyclonic conditions, with resulting severe precipitation deficits. The whole eastern half of the country, from Darwin to Adelaide, suffered from rainfall shortages, whereas the winter rains in the western half—albeit scant even under normal conditions—did not decline by much.

The ecological consequences of this drought were felt not only in nature but also in many sectors of the economy. Lack of water caused a sharp drop in the 1982 production of wheat, barley, oats, and sugarcane, but yields were back to normal the following year—a clear case of the brisk transition from the dryness caused by El Niño to the extreme wetness and higher cyclone frequency associated with the subsequent La Niña (Figure 5.17). At the end of the 1982–83 ENSO episode, the agricultural sector had lost an estimated AU $500 million. The fact that the shrimp harvest in the Gulf of Carpentaria dropped to the lowest level of the century illustrates that the changes in the ocean's salinity, on which these crustaceans depend, occur in tune with the fluctuations of the Southern Oscillation. Cattle numbers decreased from 26.2 million in 1980 to 22.2 million in 1984, and the sheep population declined from 136 million in 1983 to 133 million in 1984. Bushfires destroyed natural vegetation, artificial pastures, and cropland, and in the infamous "Ash Wednesday conflagration," fires raging from Adelaide to Melbourne claimed forty-nine lives, the highest toll since 1944. The overall damage wrought by ENSO 1982–83 was among the most extensive of the composite natural hazards suffered by Australia in the course of the twentieth century, and convincing confirmation of the vulnerability of this island-continent to the variabilities of the tropical atmospheric-oceanic circulation.

The prolonged but weaker ENSO episode of 1992–94 announced itself in 1991 with a drop in SOI values and an incipient warming of the central Pacific. In the course of the summer, drought spread from Queensland to New South Wales, exerting unrelenting stress on the natural forests and

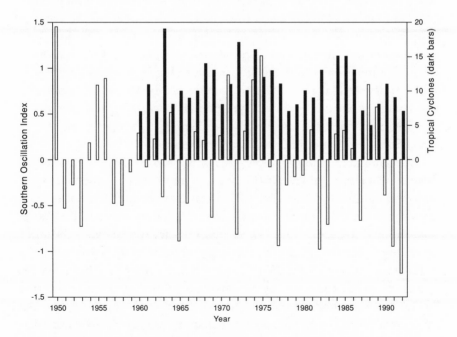

5.17. Southern Oscillation indices and number of cyclones in northern Australia, 1950–92. SOI values are to be read on the left vertical axis; number of cyclones on the right axis.

their fauna. The Darling River decreased to a thirtieth of its average flow, which, in combination with the cloudless skies and high temperatures created by the blocking situation, led to an explosion of toxic blue-green algae in the rivers of Queensland, New South Wales, and even Victoria. Koalas starved in the dry forests, and platypuses suffocated in dried-out waterways. Cattle and sheep perished along dwindling watering sources and algae bloom rendered undrinkable the water of languishing streams. Conditions escalated with the arrival of fall and winter, particularly in regions where these are the driest seasons of the year; in other areas, the overall dryness was aggravated by below-average seasonal rainfall. In the summers of 1992 and 1993, a slight rebound in summer precipitation brought some relief, but it was not until the Southern Oscillation recovered its strength and the tropical Pacific Ocean returned to cooler conditions at the end of 1994 that sufficient rains finally returned to Australia.

As noted earlier, the inter-annual rainfall patterns of neighboring Indonesia also reflect ENSO variabilities. This is because in years with El Niño conditions in the tropical Pacific, the Indonesian low pressure cell is not as deep as in normal years and the area of ocean warming, convection, and raininess moves farther east into the central equatorial Pacific. Consequently, summers all across the Indonesian archipelago become drier than usual. When such dry summers are sandwiched between two usual rainless winters, Indonesia goes through a period of nearly eighteen months of precipitation deficit, the result of the weakening of the eastern monsoons which bring ocean humidity and rains to the islands.

Inter-annual rainfall variations are not of great concern to subsistence farmers in a region that receives copious rains every year due to its location near the equator, but a shortfall in seasonal precipitation has serious implications for the natural vegetation. The Indonesian archipelago is covered by tropical rain forests and monsoon-dry woodlands—the latter becoming dangerously fire prone during prolonged periods of dryness. To make things worse, lately, the islands' once lush vegetation has been aggressively reduced not only by national and international companies that sell lumber and wood chips to Japan, Singapore, and Hong Kong, but also on several islands by immigrant farmers from overpopulated Indonesian regions. The dictum that once the original vegetation cover is removed from a humid tropical environment, the exposed soil and the secondary vegetation become extremely vulnerable to progressive desiccation can be verified in Indonesia; there, this drama is being played out just as the frequency and severity of El Niño occurrences have soared.

A pathbreaker on many fronts in El Niño research, the late William Quinn is also credited with being the first to recognize the connection between droughts in Indonesia and warm and humid phases of ENSO in the eastern tropical Pacific when he examined, in 1978, several ecological disruptions in the Pacific rim lands in relation to El Niño occurrences. Using information about salt production on Madura Island collected by previous researchers and reports on reduced crops in the rest of Indonesia, Quinn and his colleagues established that 77 percent of the droughts reported in these sources coincided with El Niño events in the eastern tropical Pacific. In their list, dry years correspond to El Niño events of 1844, 1877–78, 1891, 1911, 1925–26, 1932, 1940–41, 1953, 1965, and 1972–73, and even the slight 1976 warming of the equatorial Pacific was reflected in a widespread summer rainfall deficit in Indonesia.

However, the deleterious effects of these dry episodes did not become obvious until the occurrence of the 1982–83 ENSO. As in the case of northern Australia, a pronounced decline in seasonal precipitation began toward the second half of 1981 and continued through the summers of 1982 and 1983; precipitation returned to normal levels only with the resumption of the eastern monsoon at the end of the northern summer of 1984. At the peak of the event, fires started to clear land raged out of control, claiming numerous lives and displacing more than 80,000 rural inhabitants. The rice fields did not yield the expected harvests, and the specter of famine hovered once again over the impoverished rural masses and the colonists who had imprudently moved into lands previously occupied by tropical forests.

The return of the rains in 1984 could not halt the progressive deterioration of the natural habitats. The agricultural colonization of previously undisturbed forest areas, added to the expansion of oil palm and rubber tree plantations, plus the swallowing of natural forests by logging companies that accompanied Indonesia's growth frenzy in the 1980s worked together to reduce the islands' natural resources to their most vulnerable on the eve of the major ENSO episodes of 1991–94 and 1997–98.

Summer rains were scarce in the northern summers of 1992, 1993, and 1994, prompting a flare-up in the fires that individuals and companies—taking advantage of the arid conditions—had lit to clear new land. By fall 1994, when the humid eastern monsoon had been weak for four years in a row, smoke from northern Sumatra polluted the air in Singapore, Kuala Lumpur, and other cities along the Klang Valley of Malaysia. Wildfires destroyed 3.5 million hectares on Kalimantan (Borneo), as compared to 8 million hectares in the much larger Amazon basin over the same time period. After a short respite brought about by copious summer rains in 1995 and 1996, the looming ENSO event of 1997–98 destroyed all hope of a return to normalcy and a halt in the destructive practices of land clearing. The precursors of El Niño 1997 began to be felt in May—spring in the northern hemisphere—when the persistence of the dry western monsoon prevented the eastern monsoon from moving in during summer and fall. Fires laid in preparation for the planting season by slash-and-burn cultivators proceeded to rage throughout the summer when no rains came. Forest fires on Kalimantan and East Sumatra spread to peat bogs, where they were especially difficult to extinguish. Smoke development was so heavy that it caused an airplane to crash in the Kalimantan airport, killing 132 people. The fires spread to seventeen natural parks and protected areas, exterminating terrestrial animals and birds to such an extent that ecologists detected radical changes in the composition of avian communities as fruit eaters and omnivores were replaced by insect-eating species. By the end of 1997, 8,000 square miles had been devastated, and Indonesian health authorities became alarmed by the increase in respiratory and cardiovascular diseases in the cities.

During 1998, the situation grew worse as the fires continued to burn out of control and new ones were being ignited by irresponsible cultivators and reckless plantation owners. The Indonesian government proved all but powerless in the face of this emergency. At a meeting of the Association of South East Asian Nations (ASEAN) held in September of 1998, the usually polite delegates—especially those from neighboring Singapore and Malaysia—did not mince words when talking to their Indonesian counterparts. The embarrassed officials admitted that their government was to blame for not taking action sooner; now that the effects of El Niño–induced droughts had been added to those of environmental degradation (to which the authorities had turned a blind eye), the losses to the national economy amounted to $4.4 billion in just two years. Seeing the pressing need for action, ASEAN created a body to monitor the ENSO climatic variations and to develop brigades for preventing or at least minimizing the effects of large-area fires.

El Niño and its damaging sequels were the catalyst for the adoption of preventive measures in Australia, too. Nine Economically Sustainable Development Working Groups were formed in the early 1990s to study and reduce the impact of natural hazards and climatic variabilities on agriculture, forestry, fisheries, mining, tourism, and transportation. Even prior to this action, the government encouraged research on the relationship between climatic fluctuations and global climatic variations, and particularly on the increase of carbon dioxide in the southern hemisphere and its influence on global warming. An article by Australian scientists P. H. Whetton, A. M. Fowler, M. R. Haylock, and A. B. Pittock (1993), based on a global circulation model, places the recent increase in flood and drought incidents on their continent in the context of contemporary climatic changes induced by the worldwide increase of carbon dioxide.

These examples demonstrate how a natural phenomenon, such as El Niño, can lead to national and even international policies. In a world that is becoming increasingly more vulnerable to natural disasters, practical applications of scientific knowledge of this kind are badly needed.

When Crops Were Scarce in Mexico

Upon the arrival of the Spanish conquerors, the highlands of central Mexico were among the most densely populated regions in the New World. Moreover, in the basins and on the high plateaus flourished one of the most advanced cultures—the Aztecs—comparable only to the Inca in Peru and the already declining Mayan cultures of Guatemala and Yucatan. Crucial for the survival of large organized groups is an adequate supply of food, and this was guaranteed in Mexico by a large labor pool, plenty of water, and soils of high fertility. The humidity was delivered by seasonal rains coming either from the Caribbean Sea or from the Pacific Ocean. Lofty mountain peaks—many of them volcanoes—along the Sierra Madre Oriental to the east and the Sierra Madre Occidental to the west trapped part of this humidity in their ice and snow caps and released it slowly in the form of meltwater throughout the dry season. The plateaus were dotted with lakes and ponds of different sizes—remnants of the last glaciation some 14,000 years ago—that stored part of the overland flow and provided water for the agrarian communities.

Whether the Aztecs and other groups who lived in the highlands of Mexico before the emergence of advanced civilizations experienced food crises, and if so, whether these crises were due to climatic variations, is not known, for no written sources exist. Nevertheless, archeological findings suggest that drought-induced famines unleashed massive population movements and repeatedly precipitated the fall of regional powers in pre-Spanish times.

A total transformation of the pre-European modes of agrarian production began when the Spaniards arrived: while maize continued to be the main staple, wheat farms, cattle ranches, and horse-breeding farms were added to accommodate the Spanish palate and provide much-needed transportation. Expansion into previously uncultivated areas was a risky venture because it necessitated incorporation of semiarid lands of large inter-annual variability located in the rain shadow of the two sierras. It was not long before the effects of these transgressions were felt. During the early times of the conquest, the Mexican highlands had plenty of water and the rural landscapes presented themselves in lush greens—a result of the worldwide increase in humidity during the sixteenth century. But, shortly after, they began to experience droughts and freezes that reduced agricultural production as the global climate turned cooler and drier. The Spanish administration kept records of these crises, from which a sequence of abnormal years in Mexico can be extracted and compared with environmental crises elsewhere. A cursory review of these records reveals the numerous imprints left by ENSO events in the economic and social history of the country.

However, one should resist the temptation to hold ENSO developments in the tropical Pacific responsible for all of Mexico's environmental crises. The climate of this vast country is a composite of tropical and subtropical controls, of Pacific and Caribbean wind flows, and—to complicate things further—of strong continental influences from North America, during the winter months. This complexity can lead to erroneous interpretations of global circulation patterns, especially if the weather influences from the northern hemisphere are disregarded.

As mentioned above, there is no written proof attesting to climatic extremes during pre-Hispanic times, and environmental crises whose manifestations were not uniform across the geographic regions of Mexico did not figure prominently in chronicles even in colonial times. Thus substitute sources of information have to be searched out. Most valuable in this context is Enrique Florescano's *Precios del maíz y crisis agrícolas en México, 1708–1810,* the work of an economist-historian that investigates the reasons for the volatility of the price of maize during the eighteenth century.

Florescano found that the fluctuations were due primarily to climatic crises such as droughts, freezes, and floods, which—since he finished the book in 1969—he did not relate to ENSO variabilities. In a later work, he concentrates mostly on droughts and refers more frequently to anomalies in the tropical Pacific (Florescano 1980). The series provided by Florescano can be expanded backward using indirect evidence, collected by the British geographer Sarah Metcalfe, on climate change in Mexico.

According to these sources, the first indications of cultural change–inducing climatic variations emerge with clarity between A.D. 600 and 900, when humid conditions in the Mexican high plateaus encouraged expansion of agricultural communities. A relatively long period of prosperity was followed by prolonged droughts during the twelfth and thirteenth centuries, which caused a contraction of the agrarian frontiers and triggered the collapse of the Toltec empire in A.D. 1168. Intensification of recurring droughts during the thirteenth century forced tribes in northern Mexico to migrate southward in search of greener lands; one of these tribes was the Aztec, who erupted later into the fertile basin of Mexico and founded a city on the island of Tenochtitlan in Lake Texcoco in A.D. 1345. This lake, along with others and with swampy areas in the high plateaus of central Mexico, testifies to extreme wetness during the first half of the fifteenth century, but this period of sufficient water was followed in 1450–54 by a severe drought. At the time of the Spanish arrival—and lasting into the early 1600s—the climate in the central Mexican highlands was again very humid. These were, however, the last wet episodes of colonial times. The seventeenth century became increasingly dry, and we know of serious droughts in 1624, 1661, and 1692. A comparison with records of El Niño events affecting northern Peru reveals that the Mexican droughts of 1624, 1661, and 1692–94 occurred in phase with ENSO events of moderate intensity in the tropical Pacific (Quinn 1992).

During the 1700s, the frequency of droughts increased, and their repercussions in food shortages and social unrest became more apparent, as documented by Florescano. Figure 5.18 shows the year of occurrence and degree of severity for each of these droughts. Degree 1 means that the droughts were restricted to particular regions and did not cause national crises, while degree 2 means that they spread over several regions, causing generalized famines and institutional breakdowns. A dry period between 1708 and 1711 can be linked to the strong 1707–8 El Niño that had negative sequels in other regions of the tropics. Other droughts in 1720,

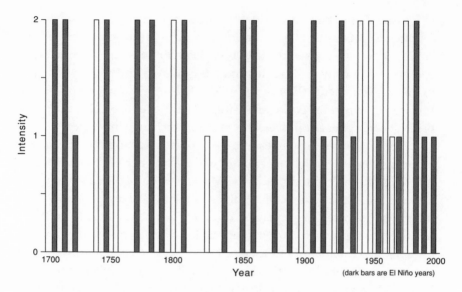

5.18. Droughts in Mexico in historical times, 1700–2000

1728, and 1785–86 also coincided with El Niño events, and still others followed ENSO events in the tropical Pacific in 1749, 1771–72, and 1792. As causes of poor or lost harvests in years such as 1711, 1749–50, 1780, and 1785, Florescano cites "scarce rains" and "frosts in autumn." The latter points to the possible association of the dry spells with cold wind invasions from the North American continent that are inherently dry and kill crops. Harvests were also poor due to drought conditions in 1724–26, 1741–42, 1755, and 1768–70, but there is no connection with ENSO events, so other explanations need to be explored. The same goes for the excessive rains and flooding between 1761 and 1763. Overall, the eighteenth century was marked by drastic climatic variations in central Mexico, as it was in most of the Western world and the Pacific basin.

The nineteenth century began with widespread droughts in 1800–1801 that do not relate with ENSO events, but the droughts of 1808–10 and 1822–23 might have mirrored moderate El Niño episodes mentioned by Quinn (1992). The picture becomes confused after the latter episode, for the country plunged into a period of war during which hunger and deprivation were not caused by natural disasters alone. Harvest failures due to lack of rains affected Yucatan in 1822–23 and in 1834–35, in both cases a year before an El Niño outburst, whereas the widespread drought of

1850–52 coincides with the moderate El Niño of 1850. Climate-related disaster surfaced anew in conjunction with the major global El Niños of 1877 and 1891, when vast grain-producing areas in the central part of the country lost most of their annual production. Granaries in Durango were looted by hungry mobs in 1877, and in Mexico City and Oaxaca food had to be rationed and storehouses placed under the custody of militia in 1891 and 1892. Dryness caused by deficient summer rains in central and northern Mexico in 1884, 1894, 1903, 1925, 1932, 1942, 1957, and 1965 (Jáuregui 1979) coincide well with major ENSO events. Absent from this enumeration are the El Niños of 1911 and 1972–73, which were of dire consequences for the Latin American countries open to the Pacific but went almost unnoticed in Mexico. Droughts between 1944 and 1947, on the other hand, happened during a period of unsignificant ENSO developments in the Pacific.

When the recent major El Niños started with the episode of 1972–73, meteorologists began to take a closer look at rainfall deficits in Central America and Mexico, and they later discovered the influence of the tropical Pacific in droughts during the 1982–83 and 1997–98 events. Meteorologists Teresa Cavazos and Stefan Hastenrath took up the task of reviewing the relationship between precipitation variations all over Mexico and recent El Niño occurrences and found that the low correlation between the two in some regions has to do with the climate controls in that extended country, for there are distinct influences from the Pacific Ocean and from the Caribbean Sea. Along the Pacific side of Mexico, cool winds traveling atop the California Current determine dryness during the winter months. During the summer, the drying winds are replaced by humid oceanic flows that deposit rains along the Pacific coast, the western Sierra Madre, and the basins of northwestern Mexico. With the progression of summer, there is also a northward advance of the bands of clouds and precipitation associated with the shift of the Inter-Tropical Convergence Zone in the eastern Pacific. During strong El Niño events, the ITCZ does not accomplish its northward progression and remains near the equatorial zone of the eastern Pacific, which reduces precipitation along the Pacific slope of Central America, from Panama to Mexico. When El Niño brews in the tropical Pacific, the climate in western Mexico usually returns to normal at the end of summer, but not before passing through an autumn of active cyclogenesis in the adjacent Pacific off Mexico that manifests itself in an elevated number of hurricanes. This behavior explains the frequent references in the historical records of Mexico to flooding in years following heightened ENSO events in the tropical Pacific.

The climate in eastern regions of the country is dominated by airflows from the warm Caribbean Sea that vary with the strength of the North Atlantic trade winds. The amounts of precipitation that fall on Mexico's Gulf coast, the eastern Sierra Madre, and the eastern expanses of the central plateau are determined by the intensity of these flows. In non–El Niño years, which are characterized by a high incidence of tropical hurricanes and increased humid flows from the Atlantic, eastern Mexico receives abnormally high volumes of precipitation during spring and summer, and these are years of abundance for that part of the country. During El Niño years, however, westerly winds prevail in the upper troposphere, the ITCZ is located far south over the Pacific, and the dry north-hemispheric trade winds are strong—all factors that contribute to rainfall deficits in the summer.

Along the northern Mexican border, the climatic peculiarities are similar to those in the Southwest of the United States. Just as ENSO winters are very rainy in California—due to the increased generation of fronts and depressions over a warmer-than-usual Pacific—the states of northwestern Mexico (Baja California, Chihuahua, Sonora) tend to receive more rainfall. During fall and winter they experience the same cold waves (*nortes*) as the continental United States, waves which have been responsible for crop losses and famines in the historical past. These cold outbreaks are not related to ENSO episodes, and this constitutes further evidence that not all the climatic variabilities that affect Mexico are linked to oceanic and atmospheric pulses in the tropical Pacific.

It is undeniable that water supply was crucial for the progression of the agricultural frontiers in northern Mexico and that this progress was repeatedly upset by droughts that took their toll on populations in pre-Hispanic as well as colonial and early-republican times. Wars and revolutions aggravated the country's food problems, and it was not until the establishment of authoritarian rule by the PRI (Institutional Revolutionary Party) that water management projects were implemented in north-central Mexico, and reservoirs and canals were finally built. Today harvests are so plentiful that large surpluses can be exported to the United States. Water management has had a long tradition in Mexico. One need only look at the dykes, drainage canals, raised fields, and irrigation ditches that have been unearthed or are still in use all over the areas once occupied by the high cultures of Mexico. They ensured in the past that appropriate amounts of storable crops, such as corn, could be raised.

The study of Mexican droughts has revealed the extent to which variabilities in the South Pacific affect their genesis, but it has also pointed to other factors contributing to precipitation irregularities, such as cold spells from North America and the role played by tropical hurricanes. It is precisely the conditions under which those hurricanes evolve that require us to look more closely at La Niña, the startling counterpart of the El Niño phenomenon.

6

~

Altered States: From El Niño to La Niña

In the Americas the years when rains fail and temperatures plunge are as dreaded as the wet and stormy years of El Niño. Scarce runoff in rivers and low levels in reservoirs depress agricultural production, shepherds see their flocks dwindle as pastures dry up, and urban populations endure electric shortages.

During their search for the reasons behind rainfall variability in the circum-Pacific area, scientists turned their attention toward the oceans when they realized that these dry episodes coincided with cold water expansions in the eastern Pacific. Peruvian and Chilean oceanographers were the first to recognize the sequels of these *Anti-Niños* during the late 1960s and to match them with the wet El Niño episodes. In the late 1970s, George S. Philander, a geophysicist without experience in South America, disliked the term *Anti-Niño* because of its similarity with *Antichrist* and promoted *La Niña* instead. Today *La Niña* is used to refer to cold water conditions in the Pacific Ocean and atmospheric anomalies over the Atlantic Ocean.

La Niña: The Disruptive Sister

La Niña comprises generalized cold waters in the tropical Pacific, a strong Peru Current off the coast of western South America, a shallow thermocline in the equatorial Pacific, and a large pooling of warm waters in the western Pacific. There is little evaporation from the rather cool surface waters and little transfer of caloric energy from ocean to atmosphere, conditions that promote droughts in areas near the Pacific Ocean that experience raininess during El Niño episodes. Lack of stimuli from the Pacific leads to severely cold winters in continental North America and frequent midwinter and early-spring snowstorms, as the polar jet stream is enhanced by the cold input from the Pacific Ocean.

The signs of La Niña are different in the "eastern hemisphere" of the Southern Oscillation. High sea-surface temperatures are registered in the tropical Atlantic and Indian Ocean, and increased evaporation and caloric energy are released into the atmosphere from these water masses. It rains copiously in Australia, the monsoons bring abundant precipitation to India and East Africa, and South Africa enjoys good harvests thanks to the bountiful water supply.

How do all these phenomena fit into the general picture of interactions between the surface waters of the Pacific Ocean and the Southern Oscillation? During La Niña years, the Southern Oscillation Index is relatively high, which means a very strong South Pacific high pressure cell and steady southeast trades in the tropical Pacific. Over Indonesia, on the other hand, the low pressure deepens and becomes a center of convergence for the warm and humid air masses from the western Pacific. The robust southeast trades activate the upwelling (upsurge of deep cold waters) along the west coast of South America and along the equatorial belt, so that the air over the comparatively cold waters stabilizes; the sky is clear, sun radiation strong, and precipitation scarce. The wind shear of the strong trades causes a "piling up" of warm water in the western Pacific, where increased evaporation and convection produce copious rains, so that a La Niña event is manifested in a sharp increase in rain in Australia, New Guinea, the Philippines, and Indonesia (Figure 6.1).

One of the best ways to identify a La Niña episode in its place of origin—the southeastern Pacific—is to scrutinize the records of sea-surface temperatures. The station of Chicama, which is typical for northern Peru, recorded conspicuous dips in temperature during 1938, 1950, 1954, 1964,

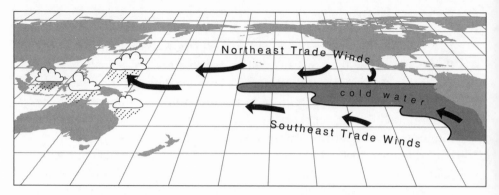

6.1. Cooling of the eastern Pacific and warming of the western Pacific during La Niña. Modified from Philander 1989.

1968, 1970, 1978, 1985, 1988, and 1999. The relationship between these sea-temperature drops and the high phases of the Southern Oscillation is shown in Figure 6.2; the corresponding SOI values appear below. The match is close to perfect for the mentioned years. With this convincing proof of an association between La Niña and the high phases of the Southern Oscillation, the question that arises is, how are these features reflected in the climatology of adjacent regions?

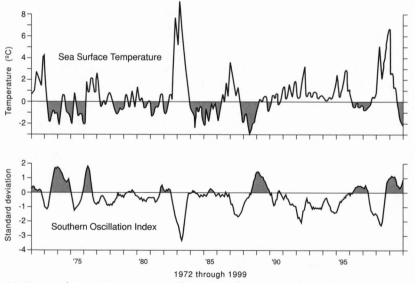

6.2. Sea-surface temperatures at Chicama and corresponding values for Southern Oscillation Indices.

In the chronically dry coastal desert of Peru, lack of rain caused by these conditions makes no difference since most of the river oases receive their water from the Andean snow caps, which, in turn, are fed by humidity from the tropical lowlands east of the Andes. Cold water in the eastern Pacific is optimal for Peru's fisheries, and the country enjoys veritable fishing booms during these La Niña years. At the same time, the sierra and the altiplano experience abundant rains that ensure good harvests and the proliferation of llama and sheep herds.

Not so positive are the effects of La Niña in the semiarid belt of central Chile, known as *Norte Chico*. Agricultural and pastoral activities in this coastal region depend on the rather modest winter rains that usually energize rivers and regenerate the few snow caps that exist in this part of the Andes. The Chilean geographer Hans Schneider synthesized the precarious conditions of life in the semiarid Norte Chico (Figure 6.3). Droughts have been frequent there since around 1770—a time that fits well the global climate deterioration detected in other parts of the world—and have been worsened by agricultural and pasturing practices that increased

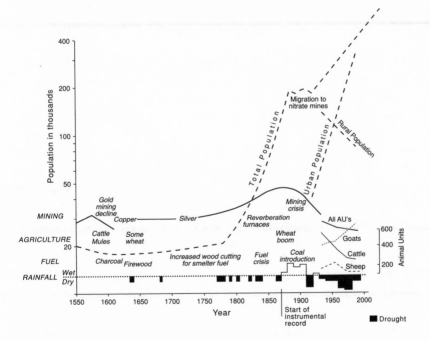

6.3. Human and environmental implications of droughts in Chile's Norte Chico. Adapted from Schneider 1982.

desertification and land degradation. Originally, that region was well suited for raising cattle and mules (the latter were widely used in gold, silver, and copper mining). In addition, the smelting of silver and copper required large volumes of hardwood, which took its toll on the native vegetation. As the population increased, so did activities harmful to the environment, such as sheep and goat herding and the demand for charcoal, both contributing to deterioration of brush and natural pastures and to enhanced regional desertification. The decline of mining at the turn of the twentieth century was not accompanied by a demographic contraction, although a large number of males left for the bigger copper mines and nitrate fields of northern Chile; instead, the pressures on agricultural land increased, and droughts became even more of a crisis. The cold waters in the southeastern Pacific and the strong South Pacific anticyclone's blocking of the rain-bringing winter fronts made the droughts in the Norte Chico more frequent and prolonged, particularly those associated with La Niña.

On the positive side, however, the greater frequency of El Niño episodes after 1957 brought more winter rains to this region that replenished the water reserves—now stored in huge and efficiently managed water reservoirs—and permitted it to become a modern center of export-oriented grape production. As a consequence, the dominant rural population of past centuries has now become predominantly urban.

In consonance with the seesaw interactions between the tropical Pacific and the tropical Atlantic, which are especially active during the warm and low phases of ENSO, La Niña episodes in the tropical Atlantic are characterized by ocean warming. This condition is favorable for the generation of cyclonic depressions, which are likely to develop into major hurricanes when they move into the western tropical Atlantic. This realization has led climatologists to expect increased hurricane activity in the Caribbean region, along the west coast of Central America, and in the Gulf region of North America during La Niña years.

Not much was known about the peculiarities of La Niña until Peruvian and Chilean oceanographers detected the existence of this unpleasant counterpart of El Niño. Originally, the cold episodes in the Pacific Ocean were thought to occur midway between two El Niño events, but a different picture emerged as they started to occur with greater frequency in the 1970s. Table 6.1 lists conspicuous La Niña years since 1870, compiled from reliable air and ocean measurements. The data show that the cold

Table 6.1
Association of hurricanes in the Caribbean basin with El Niño–Southern Oscillation events or Anti-Niños in the tropical Pacific Ocean

High hurricane years	Anti-Niños	Low hurricane years	ENSO events
1999	1999		
		1998	1997–98
		1997	1997–98
1995	1995		
		1992	1992–94
1988	1988	-	-
		1983	1982–83
1979	1979	-	-
-	-	1976	1976 *
-	-	1972	1972
1969	1968–69	-	-
-	-	1965	1965 *
1961	-	-	-
1958	-	-	1958 *
-	-	1957	1957
1955	1955	-	-
1950	1950	-	-
-	-	1941	1940–41
1939	1939	-	-
1936	-	-	-
1933	1933	-	-
1932	-	-	1932
1926	-	-	1926
-	-	1922	-
-	1917	1917	-
1916	-	-	-
-	-	1914	1914 *
-	-	1913	-
-	-	1911	1911
1906	1906	-	-
1901	-	-	-
1898	1898	-	-
-	-	1897	1897 *
1893	1893	-	-
1891	-	-	1891
1887	1887	-	-
-	-	1884	1884
1878	-	-	1878
-	1875	1875	-
-	-	1868	1868 *
1865	1865	-	-
-	-	1862–63	-
-	-	1858	1857–58 *
1850	-	-	-
-	-	1847	-
1842	-	-	-
1838	1838	-	-
1837	-	-	1837 *
-	-	1836	-
1831	1830–31	-	-

(continued)

Table 6.1—*Continued*

High hurricane years	Anti-Niños	Low hurricane years	ENSO events
-	-	1828	1828
1827	-	-	-
-	-	1823	-
1818	-	-	-
-	-	1814	1814
1813	1813	-	-
-	-	1808	-
-	-	1801–2	1802–3
-	-	1798	-
-	-	1797	-
1791	-	-	1791
1787	-	-	-
-	-	-	1785–86
-	-	1783	-
-	-	1777	1777–78 **
1772	1772	-	-
-	-	1770–71	1771 **
1766	-	-	-
-	-	1761	1761
1756	-	-	-
1747	-	-	1747
1733	-	-	-
1728	-	-	1728
1714	-	-	1714–15
-	-	1707	1707–8
-	-	1701	1701
-	-	1696	1696
-	-	1687–88	1687–88
1681	-	-	1681
-	-	1671	1671
-	-	1660	1660
1656	-	-	-
-	-	1652	1652
1642	-	-	-
1634	-	-	1634
-	-	1624	1624
-	-	1618–19	1618–19
1614	-	-	1614
-	-	1607	1607
1605	1605	-	-
-	-	1591	1591
1579	-	-	1578
1568	-	-	1568
1565	-	-	-
1554	1554	-	-
1551	-	-	1552
-	-	1541	1541
1530	-	-	-
1528	-	-	-
1508	-	-	-

* A moderate El Niño according to Quinn, Neal, and Antúnez de Mayolo 1987.
** Not a documented El Niño, but with copious winter rains in Chile.

episodes tend to follow major ocean warmings in the Pacific, but sometimes they precede these events, as they did in 1964, 1956, 1938, 1924, and 1910 (Caviedes 1973). Obviously, El Niño and La Niña are more closely connected than previously assumed, and they represent two opposite faces of the Southern Oscillation. If this is so, what mechanisms explain the brisk shifts from one anomalous condition to the other?

Sudden Change in Ocean and Atmospheric Systems

The previous section emphasized repeatedly the briskness with which El Niño events emerge and the abrupt transitions into a La Niña state, or vice versa. The realization that this occurs when a warm ENSO phase flips over into a cold one invites a search for the hidden mechanisms that place the two events in such close proximity and precipitate sudden changes in sea and atmospheric systems.

We are so accustomed to progressive change in nature that it may surprise us that sudden changes also have their place and are not expressions of disorder or chaos. In 1981, I used *catastrophe theory* to illustrate the rapid transition from cooler oceanic-atmospheric conditions in the Pacific Ocean to El Niño, and vice versa. The intriguing question was, why does the process continue all the way through in certain years, whereas in others—when sea and air indicators seem to announce the imminence of such an event—it does not?

Catastrophe theory is based on a mathematical model advanced by the European mathematicians René Thomm and Christopher Zeeman. It holds that changes in natural states are controlled by factors tied to one another along certain planes or topological surfaces. On a horizontal plane where there is no energy application, changes in states are not likely to occur: if we let a drop of water or a marble fall on a flat surface, it will stay where it was placed. If, however, we tilt that surface, that is, apply energy to lift one side, the drop of water or the marble will move along the slope. If we apply energy to a pliable surface from two directions at the same time, a pleat or fold will appear. Assuming that such a pleat is created on the surface of an impermeable material, the water drop will "jump" from the lip of that pleat onto the lower part of the surface in what is referred to as *cusp catastrophe jump*. In nature, this corresponds to the transition from one state to another, but not in a linear or progressive manner. Good examples of such brisk transitions are the passage of car-

bon hydroxide or solid ice from a frozen/solid state directly into gas—
skipping the liquid state—or of snowflakes turning into water vapor in
the dry coldness of the North American prairies.

Cusp catastrophe theory can also illustrate the transition from cold
oceanic conditions and weak southern trade winds to the warm oceanic
conditions of an El Niño through a sudden jump. Looking at Figure 6.4, let
us start with situation A, which corresponds to normal air and oceanic
conditions in the tropical Pacific: the high pressure is strong, and the
southern trades are steady, leading to intense upwelling along the west
coast of South America and across the equatorial Pacific. When climatological conditions along the line connecting A to B weaken, the high pressure and the dependent trade winds decay, yet no oceanic alterations—to
be gauged along the vertical dimension of the cusp—will be evident. Situation B represents slack winds and still-cool waters before the brisk onset
of an El Niño, which at a certain moment in its maturation process will
transit from point B to C, jumping through the cusp. In the case of El Niño,
this "sudden" transition actually lasts for two to three decisive months,
during which the preparatory phase either can resolve into generalized
warm water conditions across the whole tropical Pacific, or it can dissolve. The latter happened in 1976, when, after all indicators pointed toward an imminent El Niño occurrence, it did not materialize; this El Niño
had been "aborted." In *cusp catastrophe theory,* this would correspond to
the transition from point B to D, that is, a slow, progressive transition
above the pleat, but not a sudden jump through the cusp. Also of note is
that a return from position or state of nature B to the initial position A is
logically possible, and that upset climatic parameters need not always
lead to an El Niño, but that returns to "normality" without energy expen-
diture are common. Grasping these principles, namely the possibility of
returns from B to A and of gradual passages from B to D, helps us understand why even with sophisticated forecasting techniques and the help of
computers, it is still difficult to predict an El Niño occurrence beyond six
months in advance.

A return from the ocean-atmosphere conditions at position C to those
dominating at position B is impossible. Reversals of this sort can happen
in some chemical processes and also when water vapor transits into solid
ice (snow crystals) without first passing through the liquid state. In the
Pacific Ocean, however, conditions can return to "normal" (position A)
only through C and D—all of these being progressive rather than sudden

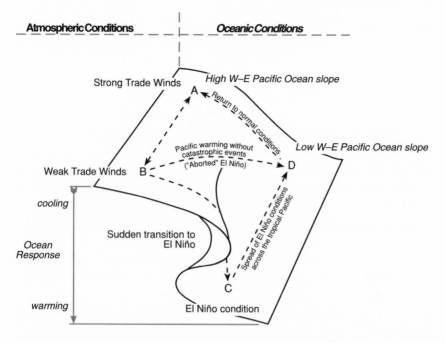

6.4. Application of cusp catastrophe theory to atmospheric and oceanic conditions leading to El Niño in the tropical Pacific

changes of nature. Thus cusp catastrophe theory illustrates the states of nature prevailing in the tropical Pacific both on their way into and out of altered conditions.

There is another "disorderly" process in ENSO events awaiting explanation: the rapid passage in the tropical Pacific from El Niño conditions to the opposite state of La Niña. Cusp catastrophe theory does not accommodate a transit from C to A. However, the mathematical solution known as *chaos theory* does precisely that. The theory holds that normality persists in natural systems for as long as there are no perturbing influences. If a pendulum is set between two magnets ("attractors"), it will swing between these two extremes, but if a third magnet is placed within the magnetic radius of the other two, this third and perturbing action will send the pendulum into an erratic motion that to us would look like a "chaotic" response. However, in the natural world, such "chaotic" responses have their place, as in the case of the heart valves opening and closing.

Oceanographer Geoffrey Vallis explains the sudden transitions from normal sea-atmosphere conditions to perturbed El Niño and La Niña conditions through the *bifurcation effect* in chaotic systems. The departing point—as in catastrophe theory—is that during normal air circulation, the eastern tropical Pacific is cool, the thermocline is close to the surface in the eastern tropical Pacific and deep in the western Pacific, and the winds from the east (trade winds) are strong. If the latter slacken due to a temporary weakening of the South Pacific anticyclone, the other two factors will be subsequently affected by the presence of three attractors instead of two (Vallis 1986) so that the system will bifurcate or split along the 0 axis as shown in Figure 6.5.

Ocean warmings and coolings reflect seasonal changes in sun radiation and wind direction, but since the oceans' reaction to these inter-annual variations is slow, a low-grade instability may persist for several years before resolving into a full-fledged El Niño. During an unstable period of cold waters, a slight increase in the relative power of one of the attractors suffices to send the system into an El Niño condition, which is also an unstable condition. Figure 6.5 illustrates the transition process by means of a topological butterfly: after remaining in unstable cool-water

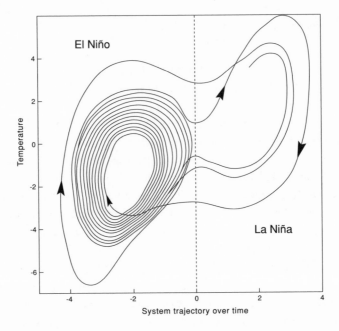

6.5. Chaos theory explaining sudden transitions from El Niño to La Niña. From Vallis 1986.

conditions for several annual cycles—left wing of the butterfly—the state of nature transits to the right wing through a "chaos" passage. In this case, the warm ocean conditions dominating in the right wing are those of an El Niño. After remaining there for a few cycles, the ocean system will pass to a cold condition, or La Niña, which is more or less pronounced depending on the magnitude of the reversal. It is due to these brisk passages that the two extreme states occur so close together in the ENSO time series.

The fact that northern hemispheric winters in the wake of an El Niño episode are so severely cold and abundant in precipitation is due to the combined effects of the large amounts of humidity that were stored in the atmosphere during the warm months and the precipitous cooling in-duced by La Niña. Those special cases when an El Niño event is preceded by La Niña can also be explained with the help of chaos theory: when southeast trades that have grown extra strong, due to a strengthening of the South Pacific anticyclone, experience a precipitous collapse (which heralds the coming of an El Niño), this represents a brisk transition to the opposite state, that is, from cold conditions to generalized warming in the tropical Pacific.

The climatic consequences of these abrupt changes and the effects of La Niña, particularly in the tropical Atlantic, will be explored in the next section.

Tropical Waves and Cape Verde Islands Cyclones

It took some time to accept that weather developments off the western coast of Africa lie at the root of the hurricanes that batter the Caribbean Islands and wreak havoc in the Gulf states and along the mid-Atlantic coast. Excellent coverage by governmental agencies and the active use of satellite imagery to illustrate hurricane developments in the tropical At-lantic allow the general public to follow the genesis of tropical depres-sions and know what to expect from those that make it all the way across the Atlantic.

Today the Cape Verde Islands, a group of small islands situated at lati-tude 15°N off the coast of Senegal, are known among hurricane buffs. These former volcanic peaks are bathed by the cold Canary Current and fanned by the constantly blowing winds from the Azores-Bermuda high pressure center located in the North Atlantic. In protected locations, plan-tations of subtropical crops, such as sugarcane and bananas, have been doing well since the islands were discovered by Portuguese navigators in the fifteenth century. Slaves were brought in from the African coast, some 500 miles away, and the population today is composed of about 400,000 Creoles and Africans. What makes the islands interesting—apart from the attractive blend of Portuguese and West African racial elements and cultural traditions—is their proximity to the breeding ground of the tropical depressions that file across the tropical North Atlantic from summer to autumn.

The Cape Verde Islands lie at an important hub of climate interactions. During winter the air above them is stabilized by the surrounding body of cold water, and arid conditions are imposed by the harmattan winds from northern Africa. After the solstice in June, however, the seasonal northward shift of the North Atlantic high, the abating of the northeast trade winds, and the rise of temperatures in the eastern tropical Atlantic allow the Inter-Tropical Convergence Zone to advance northward and summer rains to reach the islands. Along with these developments over the tropical Atlantic, major upper-air alterations occur over the northern half of continental Africa. The *Tropical Easterly Jet* (TEJ), which originates south of the Himalaya and Tibet plateau and flows at an altitude of about twelve kilometers (7.5 miles) during the northern summer, makes a slight bend over the western tip of Africa (Liberia and Sierra Leone) and then proceeds in a northwesterly direction over the Atlantic. This results in "easterly flows" at the surface level, which are activated as the waters heat up in the course of the summer, oscillating between a maximum of sixty-nine waves in a year of warmer waters in the Atlantic (La Niña years) and forty-nine in a year of colder waters in the tropical Atlantic (El Niño years). Localized low pressure cells (tropical depressions) develop periodically over abnormally heated seas and are propelled westward by the easterly flows during summers without El Niño in the tropical Pacific.

These tropical depressions increase their speed as they move into higher latitudes, where a geodynamic component called Coriolis force kicks in, so that within a few days they reach the eastern side of the Caribbean Islands. At that point, some gain enough energy and rotation speed to be classed as hurricanes, while others weaken during their advance into the latitudes of the northern Bahamas, Florida, Georgia, or the Carolinas. On this course, tropical depressions and hurricanes are doomed since they come in contact with cooler waters and northern air masses that dissolve them.

We have examined how small-scale depressions can be generated over an abnormally warm tropical Atlantic off western Africa and then be propelled westward by easterly flows to end up as hurricanes—the televised progress of these depressions provides an excellent illustration. But the same dynamic forces hold more surprises: Ever since Europeans set foot on the Antilles, they have been puzzled by sporadic locust invasions erupting from the vast expanses of the Atlantic Ocean. For a long time, these events were seen as bad omens or freaks of nature because the possibility of transoceanic insect migration challenged the imagination before the airflows over the tropical Atlantic were better understood. Prior to exploring how the locusts could have accomplished a 2,000-mile voyage over open sea, let us look at their multiplication dynamics in northern Africa.

The sub-Saharan countries are the prime habitat for desert locusts. During dry years—which correspond, as we saw in chapter 5, to ENSO events—these insects live as isolated individuals near where they hatched. Short rainy episodes affect both their social habits and their physiology: coloration and body proportions change, metabolic and oxygen-intake rates increase, and they become more active and "nervous" (Walsh 1986). Those hatching after rainy spells rapidly exhaust the greens available, and subsequent generations, whose multiplication is activated by new rains, find less and less food; this emergency triggers their swarming behavior. Since the air flows from east to west during rainy years, it is very common for locusts bred in the early summer in eastern Africa (Ethiopia and Sudan) to start on a westward migration—interrupted by periods of egg laying and regeneration—that takes them to the western Sahel. From there, after a last stop at the Cape Verde Islands, a major and final jump across the Atlantic is possible when air-flow circumstances are favorable.

Locust and grasshopper swarms were sighted in 1948–49, the mid-1960s, 1974, and 1978–79, all years when the tropical Atlantic experienced warm water conditions, but the best-documented and most convincingly explained episode occurred in the fall of the 1988 La Niña event. That summer, the rainy season was very active, fostering the growth of leafy vegetation in the savanna grasslands of Mali and Mauritania and of bumper crops in northern Senegal. The extreme wetness also prompted high activity among the desert locusts, which, having devoured the leafy vegetation, invaded the cultivated fields. As their food sources dwindled, the swarms' mobility and nervous behavior increased. In early October, when the rains began to recede and their food supply was all but gone, swarms moved south into Senegal, Gambia, and Guinea-Bissau, helped by the seasonal winds (Figure 6.6). Simultaneously, a second locust wave erupted, this time in the western Sahelian states, and traveled toward the coast. Mature swarms descended on the Cape Verde Islands around October 3, followed by immature swarms near the end of the month.

How did these migrations fit with the air circulation then prevailing? A wide band of equatorial calms stretched along the West African coast up to 25°N latitude and from there into the tropical Atlantic until merging with the ITCZ in midocean. When the calms subsided in early October, they were replaced by offshore winds induced by the TEJ that took locust swarms from the coast of Mauritania and Senegal to the Cape Verde Islands in one day. Howard C. Richardson and David J. Nemeth, who describe this episode in detail (Richardson and Nemeth 1991), assert that with wind speeds of thirteen to eighteen miles per hour, the locusts could have covered the distance within twenty-four hours. After a short rest, the swarms took to the air again on October 9 and started arriving on the

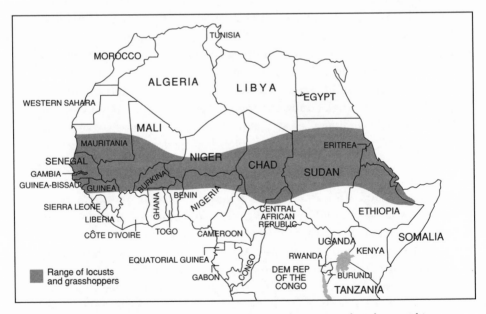

6.6. Regions affected by the outburts of locust plagues in sub-Saharan Africa

Windward Islands in the Lesser Antilles on October 13. Subsequent swarms left the Cape Verde Islands on October 10 and landed on the Leeward Islands and the Greater Antilles on October 14. By then, another visitor from the east, tropical storm Joan, had also made landfall on the Antilles.

The 2,600-mile journey of the locusts within as little as five days was made possible by very special meteorological conditions. North of the migration path, the elongated Azores-Bermuda high pressure center, whose peripheral winds blow from east to west, contributed to maintain the equatorial easterlies that facilitated the swarms' first leg from the African coast to the Cape Verde Islands. The same conditions had also propelled the developing tropical storm Joan, which, upon entering the Caribbean area, was upgraded to Hurricane Joan on October 18.

For such a journey to be successful, the flow of easterly winds must remain steady for several days, which is what happened in early October 1988. Flying in swarms also allows mature and immature locusts to cover long distances that could not even be attempted in individual endeavors and permits them to take a well-established path downwind. The ITCZ-associated easterlies are a further migratory advantage because they not only facilitate takeoff but provide the thermal lift that allows the swarms to glide up and down between 600 to 1,000 feet without having to beat their wings, thereby conserving energy and avoiding fatigue. Still, the locusts that arrived on the Antilles after the five-day journey of October 1988 were utterly exhausted. The fact that there were twenty females for every male indicated that young and gravid females possessed greater endurance than males. The arrival of tropical storm Joan a few days later helped to disperse the swarms and thus impaired their ability to survive in the new environment. The plague was finally stamped out through pest control, predators and domestic fowl, and the unaccustomed hardships encountered under the islands' tropical canopies.

This fascinating case of the desert locusts' flight across the north tropical Atlantic in the fall of one of those years when the airflow is from east to west illustrates the path often taken by tropical depressions. Nineteen eighty-eight exemplifies conditions predominating in the central Atlantic in opposition to ENSO occurrences in the tropical Pacific. During this La Niña year, the Pacific off South America was particularly cold, and the continent itself experienced one of the coolest winters of the past fifty years, due to cold waves moving up from the southern tip into the high-

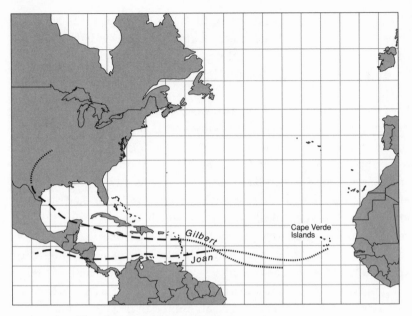

6.7. Tracks of hurricanes Gilbert and Joan in 1988

lands of central Brazil and even Amazonia. Opposite conditions prevailed
in the tropical Atlantic, where the waters between Africa and the Caribbean were unusually warm and evaporation was strong. Detailed studies
of hurricane development during this particular year by Avila and Clark
(1989) and Lawrence and Gross (1989) reveal that 1988 was the most active tropical-storm season since 1969, another year with cold water conditions in the Pacific and a high Southern Oscillation Index. Sixty-two "African waves" were spawned between the end of May and mid-November,
twelve of them reaching tropical-storm strength, and five hurricane
strength. Among the five hurricanes were two unforgettable ones: Gilbert
and Joan (Figure 6.7).

On September 3, Gilbert was "born" off the African coast as a tropical
wave; on the ninth, it reached tropical-storm status north of the Guianas,
and the next day was upgraded to a hurricane south of Puerto Rico. West
of the Cayman Islands, its pressure plummeted to 888 millibar—the lowest ever measured during the twentieth century. As a category 5 hurricane, Gilbert made first landfall on Yucatan, September 14, and a second
at Taumalipas state, Mexico, three days later. On September 18–19, it
curved to the northeast and, after a third landfall in central Texas, finally

ran out of steam over Oklahoma. Gilbert caused severe flooding on Jamaica, Grand Cayman, the coast of Taumalipas state, and Padre Island in Texas; it claimed 318 lives, 202 of them in Mexico. Damages were estimated at $5 billion, including $2 billion each for Jamaica and Mexico.

Joan, introduced earlier in connection with the amazing transoceanic flight of locusts, started out as a tropical wave on October 5 and attained storm status in the mid-Atlantic by the tenth. After passing the Windward Islands, the storm followed an unusual southern track along northern Venezuela and Colombia to finally make landfall at Bluefields, Nicaragua. Cutting straight across Central America, it reached the eastern Pacific Ocean on October 26 and was renamed Miriam. By the end of this lengthy journey, Joan had caused 216 deaths. Nicaragua was hardest hit, with 148 dead and $1 billion in material losses—half of the overall damages inflicted. There were also reports of locusts landing on Trinidad in connection with the hurricane.

To recapitulate: The life of a hurricane begins with the development of tropical waves off the coast of Africa between 7° and 20°N latitude. The waves move rapidly westward, and near 35°W longitude, some of them reach "tropical depression" or "tropical storm" strength as they gain energy and humidity from the warm sea. Near 60°W longitude—not far from the Antilles—additional energy inputs prompt the rise to hurricane status in certain cases. Some 50 percent of the storms curve northward between 65° and 75°W longitude, which takes them over the Lesser Antilles and the Bahamas—while sparing Florida and the Gulf states—to dissipate over the open ocean between 35° and 45°N latitude. Of the other 50 percent, more than a third penetrate the Caribbean Sea and curve into the Gulf of Mexico, where they gain strength and make a landfall on the coast of Gulf states. Depending on the intensity of the recurving, they may even return to the Atlantic Ocean via the northern Florida peninsula. This group is probably the most powerful and devastating of all tropical storms and hurricanes. The rest are those that move parallel to the northern coast of South America and, staying on this westerly course, cross Central America to be incorporated into north tropical Pacific systems or simply dissipate over these somewhat cooler waters.

Because tropical storms and hurricanes absorb energy from the surface of the tropical Atlantic, large numbers form when the ocean is warmer than usual and the high pressure cell over the subtropical Atlantic is weakened and more distant than normal from South and North America.

In such years, the hurricane season starts early—around June—and lasts into November, with the most devastating tropical storms and hurricanes occurring during late September and October, and their action reaching farther north along the outer Caribbean Islands and the U.S. East Coast than in other years.

During La Niña years, such as 1979, 1981, and 1988, the number of tropical waves, depressions, and hurricanes is decidedly higher than during major and moderate El Niño years (1972, 1977, 1982, 1983, and 1986). This observation supports the thesis that the frequency of storms and hurricanes in the Atlantic is related to anomalous oceanic and atmospheric circulations during ENSO events. Such a connection can be convincingly demonstrated by looking at the number of hurricane days per year from 1900 to 1990; years with recorded El Niño occurrences in the tropical Pacific definitely have fewer hurricane days than those with their counterpart, La Niña (Figure 6.8). What are the atmospheric circulation conditions that lead to decreased numbers of tropical depressions and hurricanes during ENSO in the tropical Pacific? They are as follows: the sea-surface temperatures in the north equatorial Atlantic are usually cooler than normal, and the winds generated by the South Atlantic high pressure center cause a northward displacement of the dry air and cooler waters on the east side of North and South America.

Inversely, during La Niña events, the Pacific Ocean undergoes a surface cooling that is mirrored in the Atlantic by a warming tendency, which leads to a higher frequency of tropical waves, tropical depressions, and hurricanes heading toward the Caribbean Islands, Central America, and the U.S. Southeast. The question now arises whether these tendencies, detected in recent records, also hold true for earlier times. If one could prove that there were fewer tropical storms and hurricanes during proven El Niños of earlier years, this would provide indirect evidence that years with higher frequencies represent undocumented La Niña events, and in this manner the short La Niña series could be extended farther back in time. The next section explores the possibilities of using historical sources on hurricane occurrences to detect hidden La Niñas in the past.

Mighty Hurricanes of the Past and Present

On his second voyage to the West Indies in 1494, Christopher Columbus left a small detachment on the northwest coast of Isabella Island, now the

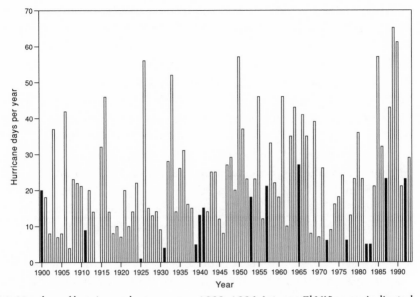

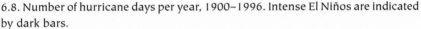

6.8. Number of hurricane days per year, 1900–1996. Intense El Niños are indicated by dark bars.

Dominican Republic. Toward the end of June, a fierce storm took the Spaniards, who so far had been enjoying beautiful summer weather, by surprise. As the storm pounded the island, even the natives ran for cover, lifting their arms in supplication and calling out to the god of storms, Orkan. This is considered the first encounter of Europeans with tropical storms in the New World. Columbus himself was to experience another one when he returned to Isabella in October of 1495.

Hurricanes continued to visit during the conquest and settlement of the Caribbean Islands, and the reports increased along with the population and maritime traffic in the region. Accounts from Spanish, French, English, and Dutch settlers or military garrisons contain a wealth of information on tropical storms and hurricanes, the basis on which nineteenth-century researchers, such as André Poey and Marcos Melero, compiled catalogs of past storms that served as data banks for later researchers. The motivations of these pioneers were merely historical: to pinpoint the places that had been devastated and to account for the losses in lives and ships. Nobody ever wondered about the origin of the storms, much less about a relationship with climatic variabilities elsewhere.

While conducting bibliographic searches at the Library of Congress in the mid-1970s, I came across two works on the history of hurricanes in the Caribbean: Luis A. Salivia's *Historia de los temporales de Puerto Rico y las Antillas, 1492 a 1970* (1972) and José C. Millás's *Hurricanes of the Caribbean and Adjacent Regions, 1492–1800* (1968). The first lists the hurricanes that hit Puerto Rico and the Antilles; the second is a thorough collection of historical hurricane occurrences from the time of Columbus up to 1800. As with the list of shipwrecks along the coast of Chile compiled by Vidal-Gormaz (see chapter 4), these series offered great potential for detecting climate variabilities. Recent hurricane data from C. H. Neumann, B. R. Jarvinen, and A. C. Pike's *Tropical Cyclones of the North Atlantic Ocean, 1871–1986* (1988) were a useful complement. This detailed and exhaustive compilation differentiates between "tropical depressions," "tropical storms," and "hurricanes"—which is of great value for assessing the developmental stages of tropical disturbances—and contains helpful cartographic presentations of cyclone tracks. To lay the grounds for a more detailed study of hurricanes' frequency and occurrence in historical times, I published in 1991 a five-century survey of hurricane landfalls, month of occurrence, and their association with the low phases (El Niño) and the high phases (La Niña) of the Southern Oscillation (Caviedes 1991). An article by Alison J. Reading (1990) deals with hurricanes in the Caribbean based on English sources, but its coverage is incomplete since she does not include information from Spanish historical documents. The synthesis of historical sources that follows is presented to illustrate the relationship between hurricane frequency and the two phases of ENSO in the tropical Pacific.

When one consults historical series of this kind, certain differences in their reliability must be taken into account. For example, due to smaller island populations and comparatively lower numbers of ships circulating in the waters of the Caribbean and tropical Atlantic, reports on cyclone activity in early colonial times are sparse. There are areal restrictions in a work such as *Tropical Cyclones of the North Atlantic Ocean,* which deals only with hurricanes that entered the Caribbean basin, that is, the area included between the arc of the Antilles/Bahamas to the east, the coast of Central America to the west, the coast of Venezuela and Colombia to the south, and the Gulf coast of Mexico and Florida to the north. Taking into account that the probability of being hit by a hurricane increases with landmass size, the analysis of observed occurrences focused on the larger and more populated islands of the Greater Antilles, as well as on key islands of the Windwards, where cyclone recurvatures are frequent.

During the last 100 years, major hurricanes have occurred at an average of three per year. Active years are considered those with more than six hurricanes. These numbers are only good for reference because during periods of generalized climatic tranquility, three may constitute a large number. For this reason, a moving scale of events per year is recommended to ensure greater accuracy. The difference between hurricane frequency and hurricane intensity should also be noted. For example, 1992 (an El Niño year) was a low-frequency but high-intensity year: Andrew was the only one of that season's three hurricanes that hit the mainland, but the devastation it wrought in southern Florida was the gravest of the last decades. Also, the terms *hurricanes* and *tropical storms* are not interchangeable. While both are stimulated by transient tropical waves that circulate in the tropical Atlantic, the latter often make their way toward the Caribbean without reaching hurricane strength. The average number of tropical storms per year is twelve, but there are fewer during El Niño years and more during La Niña years. It is also very possible that in historical records tropical storms may have been mistaken for hurricanes, which would influence the accuracy of that count.

The 1500–1990 series displays a marked increase in the number of recorded hurricanes after the 1770s (Figure 6.9). This may be due to increases in the island populations and maritime traffic. It can also be argued that the higher hurricane frequency toward the third quarter of the eighteenth century was in response to a major climatic variability corresponding to the declining Little Ice Age, the implications of which will be discussed in the next chapter. A closer review of the series before and after 1770 offers some interesting insights into hurricanes in the Caribbean and climatic history elsewhere (Table 6.1). Three minor surges in hurricane frequency around 1530, 1550, and 1570 could be interpreted as distant echoes in the aftermath of El Niños in the Pacific. From the end of the 1500s to the early 1640s, there were far fewer reported hurricanes, followed by three more minor surges in 1656, 1680, and 1694–95. It is interesting to note that a study on the prices of sugar produced on the Canary Islands—roughly 1,000 miles north of the Cape Verde Islands—has revealed periods of dryness and high prices in 1609–11, 1650–53, and 1662, as well as periods of excessive rains that correspond to wetness in the eastern tropical Atlantic during 1638, 1642, 1654, and 1665 (Gimeno at al.

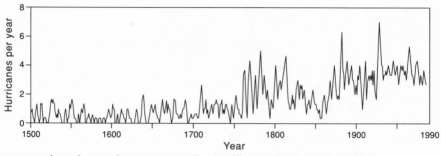

6.9. Number of major hurricanes on the Caribbean Islands, 1500–1990

1998). The high-frequency hurricane year of 1642 coincides with the 1642 surge in precipitation, while the hurricane years of 1656 and 1657 and the heavy rains of 1654 on the Canary Islands occurred soon *after* the 1652 El Niño episode that caused copious rains in Peru and a severe drought in northeastern Brazil. It must be stressed at this point, however, that, notwithstanding these suggestive coincidences, other major El Niño occurrences during that century—in 1607, 1624, and 1687–88—were not followed by high hurricane incidences in the Caribbean.

During much of the eighteenth century, hurricane activity was quite subdued; only a major peak in 1714 can be matched with a period of climatic restlessness punctuated by El Niños in 1713 and 1715, a drought in China in 1714, and by low levels of the Nile River in 1715 and 1716. Toward the end of that century, the notorious hurricane seasons of 1786 and 1790–92 occurred in close temporal vicinity with the moderate El Niño episode of 1785–86—which caused summer rains in northern Peru and was in phase with a drought in northeastern Brazil—and with the intense El Niño of 1791. Other El Niño episodes in 1701, 1720, 1728, and 1775 were not followed by an increase in hurricane frequencies in the Caribbean. From 1766 to the end of the century, there was a noticeable rise in the number of hurricanes. According to Luis Salivia (1972), eight hurricanes affected the Caribbean Islands—Trinidad and the Bahamas excepted—as well as the coasts of the Gulf of Mexico between July and November of 1772. Further, 1780—referred to in historical sources as "The Great Hurricane Year"—and 1787 experienced five and seven hurricanes, respectively. This surge, which is also shown in Alison Reading's compilation, lends more substance to the contention that around the 1770s, a rather serious climatic oscillation was experienced worldwide.

After a period of relative remission during the early 1800s, a rising trend peaked in the late 1830s, indicating the reactivation of hurricane-producing mechanisms during the first third of the nineteenth century, as illustrated by a high frequency of hurricanes in 1813, 1818, and 1837–38. The rise was followed by a distinct plunge in hurricane occurrences between 1850 and 1860, a decade characterized by relative climate tranquility in other parts of the world as well. The 1870s show a conspicuous increase in the number of hurricanes reported, which is not only the result of improvements in observation techniques and record keeping but the reflection of a new climatic revolution of global proportions. Surges in hurricane activity occurred in 1878, 1887, 1893, and 1898—the last two being years with La Niña conditions in the tropical Pacific. During the last decade of the nineteenth century, the interesting feature of cold and warm events in the Atlantic appearing the year before or after a major ENSO episode in the tropical Pacific began to take on clearer contours. The coincidence between the high number of hurricanes in 1878 following the strong 1877–78 El Niño in the tropical Pacific and western South America is a remarkable comprobation of this trend.

During the twentieth century, further improvements in information quality opened the way to even more accurate comparisons between the tropical Atlantic and tropical Pacific. In the wake of powerful El Niño events in the tropical Pacific, hurricane activity surged at the turn of the century to peak during the 1920s and 1930s, two decades that did not experience many ENSO episodes. The number of days with major hurricane conditions is an appropriate measure of the severity of a given hurricane season and very useful for identifying the influence of ENSO in the Pacific Ocean upon hurricane development in the Atlantic during the twentieth century, when El Niños and La Niñas became clearly discernible. As displayed in Figure 6.8, El Niños correspond to years with a low number of hurricane days up to 1928. Whereas the high-frequency hurricane seasons of 1899 and 1906 preceded El Niño events in 1900 and 1907, the active tropical cyclone and hurricane year of 1916 followed the moderate 1915 El Niño, indicating once again that hurricane frequency rises in close conjunction with warm ocean episodes in the Pacific.

Even though 1925–26 was a strong El Niño year, the frequency of tropical storms in the 1920s was one of the lowest for any period in the twentieth century. The 1930s started with the moderate El Niño of 1932, in phase with a severe drought in northeastern Brazil. This event coincides perfectly with the triad of 1931, 1932, and 1933, which not only had a very large number of tropical depressions and hurricanes in the tropical Atlantic and Caribbean Sea but marked the beginning of the infamous "dust bowl" years in the North American Midwest.

The 1940s started out with the strong 1940–42 El Niño, during which hurricane frequency was reduced, but the increase in cyclone activity from 1942 to 1945 might be considered the Atlantic's delayed response to the Pacific warming. The rest of the decade was not very active as far as ENSO developments in the Pacific or hurricanes in the tropical Atlantic are concerned, pointing to relative tranquility in global climatic conditions.

La Niña occurrences in 1950, 1955, and 1969 confirmed that the generation of tropical storms and hurricanes in the tropical Atlantic is enhanced during years with cold waters in the Pacific and warm waters in the Atlantic. Active storm seasons occurred in 1958, at the outset of that year's El Niño episode, and in 1966, one year after El Niño 1965.

The increasing recurrence of ENSO variabilities that started with El Niño 1972–73 and the corresponding transitions to La Niña signaled the beginning of a period of active climatic fluctuations exemplified by the increase in Atlantic hurricanes during 1979, 1981, 1988, 1994, and 1999. A remarkable characteristic of these recent La Niña episodes is that they tend to occur in close proximity to their "brother" (El Niño), which may reflect—as explained in the previous section—the briskness with which prolonged ocean and atmospheric warming episodes in the Pacific Ocean come to an end and conditions return to relative normality.

The probability of a connection between the climatic systems operating in the tropical Pacific and those operating in the Atlantic was first proposed by Edward B. Bennett (1966). He suggested that El Niño events in the Pacific are preceded by strong anticyclonic (high pressure) conditions over the southern Caribbean Sea that favor the northeast trade winds' crossing the isthmus of Panama into the tropical Pacific following the pull of the lows that develop over the warm Pacific waters. During the early 1980s, William Gray of Colorado State University proposed the existence of a connection between the variations of the Pacific *Quasi Biennial Oscillation* and the occurrence (or absence) of hurricanes in the tropical Atlantic. (The QBO is a twenty- to twenty-two-month pulse clicking over the tropical Pacific that makes the tropospheric winds flow from west to east and then from east to west at two-year intervals.) Gray noticed a marked decrease in the number of tropical depressions and hurricanes when the flow is from west to east (El Niño years) as compared with the years when the flow is from east to west (non–El Niño years). Notice the coincidence with the paths followed by tropical depressions and by the locust swarms in October of 1988 from the coast of Africa to the Antilles and the shift of the high-elevation winds over the tropical Atlantic during those extreme La Niña years. How long has this pulse been beating? A recent study of marine sediments from coastal Venezuela dating back to A.D. 1200 suggests that variations of ENSO character have been frequent in the tropical Atlantic since A.D. 1300, precisely the period when the North Atlantic exited the Medieval Warm Period and entered the cooling trend towards the Little Ice Age (Black et al. 1999). If so, the alternation between years with abundant hurricanes and years with few must have become established about 700 years ago.

This extended review of seasons with a high frequency of hurricanes in the Caribbean has revealed that these seasons coincide mostly with La Niña years or that they occur in close proximity to strong ENSO events. The claim that the return from abnormal warmer and humid periods to colder and drier periods does not happen gradually but in sudden jumps—as explained through "cusp catastrophe theory and "chaos theory"—is thus substantiated. Ascribing the recent increase in tropical depressions and hurricanes to more frequent and persistent ENSO fluctuations—possibly in response to global warming—is certainly not unwarranted.

7
~

Imprints of El Niño in World History

Dramatic turns of events have occurred under the imperatives of climate, but very few of them have been associated with El Niño crises, perhaps because historians are not familiar with the teleconnections that sew a perplexing array of environmental, economic, political, and human circumstances into the El Niño "quilt." This book has offered numerous examples of how El Niño occurrences have modified human communities. In several instances, the destiny of entire civilizations was radically altered by its impact.

In retrospect, and knowing that these events were caused by global climatic variabilities, we can see that—as in classic Greek tragedy—the protagonists played into the designs of destiny by knowingly or unknowingly violating the dictates of climate. How could the characters involved have known that the climatic circumstances under which their plans were put into action would be exceptional?

Our review of historical events in which the climatic influence was obvious will begin with the recent past. This approach offers a better understanding of the physical circumstances surrounding these events because climate has not changed much since they occurred. The first three examples—the failed German siege of Stalingrad, the disastrous campaign of Napoleon in Russia, and the Ethiopian drought that precipitated the fall of Emperor Haile Selassie—are fascinating developments that were presided over by severe climatic conditions. Although these conditions were not outright responsible for the outcome, they surely aggravated critical situations that the protagonists themselves had created. Analysts of political, military, and social history often ignore the contribution of environmental concomitants, but—considering the impact of variabilities such as ENSO on human affairs, economic development, and environmental stability—the climatic-historical perspectives that this chapter introduces may enrich the interpretation of history in light of natural crises.

Hitler's Change of Fortune at Stalingrad

During World War II, the bloodiest standoffs in the European theater of operations took place around the Russian city of Stalingrad. Originally called Tsaritsyn, the settlement had been founded in the Middle Ages at a strategic point on the sluggishly flowing Volga to support trade with nomads from central Asia and to ward off Mongol, Turk, and Cossack invaders who periodically raided the thinly populated eastern flank of the Russian kingdom. During the Bolshevik revolution, 1917–20, the region was fiercely contested by the royalist White Army and the revolutionary militias under the leadership of Joseph Stalin, who, against all odds, drove out the last of the czarist resistance forces. In recognition of this "liberation," the city of Tsaritsyn had its name changed to Stalingrad, following the tradition of other cities along the Volga that had been renamed to glorify father figures of international communism and consolidating the personality cult that characterized the rule of Stalin over the nascent Soviet Union.

Stalingrad, now Volgograd, lies at the western edge of the central Asian steppes, wide-open to continental heat during the summer and the influx of frigid air during winter. Despite its location at a lower latitude than more hospitable European cities, such as London, Brussels, Paris, Frankfurt, and Prague, the brutal summer-winter contrast and the swift transitions from one season to the other make for a climate that is very hard to live in.

What brought the armies of Adolf Hitler to such a forbidding place? After dealing swiftly with his contenders in western Europe, Hitler went on to attack the Soviet Union in April of 1941. Supported by allies like Ukraine, Romania, and Hungary—which had suffered the brunt of Soviet expansionism—the German war machine moved swiftly into the heart of European Russia in the summer of 1941. It was not long, however, before the invaders found themselves slowed down by countless skirmishes against the evasive Soviet troops that only occasionally engaged in frontal combat. By summer's end, the Germans had reached the outskirts of Moscow but were not able to enter the city. Meanwhile, Hitler made a decision against the advice of his generals that would lead to his ultimate downfall at the eastern front: he ordered part of the troops involved in closing the circle around the retreating Soviets to divert to the southeast in order to build a front aimed at conquering the coal mines of the Donetz and cutting off the oil supply lines from the southern Caucasus. Initially the move was successful. The southern Ukraine fell, and motorized divisions rushed into the Caucasus. But with winter approaching, a massive Russian counterattack forced the Germans to withdraw to a defensive line west of Moscow and weather the winter there. By the spring of 1942, 800,000 casualties heralded the turn of Hitler's fortune.

On the southern front, the advance toward Crimea and the Caucasus Mountains began in May of 1942. At first quick and successful, it came to an ominous standstill as the summer progressed, and most of the German objectives, including the taking of Stalingrad, were not achieved. General Friedrich Paulus, chief of the Sixth Army, was to seize the city—a manufacturing center of engines for tractors, tanks, artillery guns, and chemical products—with troops taken from the German thrust into the Caucasus. Paulus had distinguished himself on the western front in France and on the beaches of the British Channel, where his troops had repelled the Allies' counteroffensive in 1940. When sent to the southern Russian front in the summer of 1942, he advanced quickly eastward along the Don River (Figure 7.1) and reached the vicinity of the Volga at the end of August; but the battle for the city of Stalingrad that was to ensue would turn into a gruesome nightmare for experienced and fresh troops alike.

At Kremlin headquarters in Moscow, Joseph Stalin had stipulated that the city that bore his name should not surrender until the last armed man and woman had fallen; not even strategic withdrawals were allowed, and execution awaited any who made the attempt. Reinforcements for his

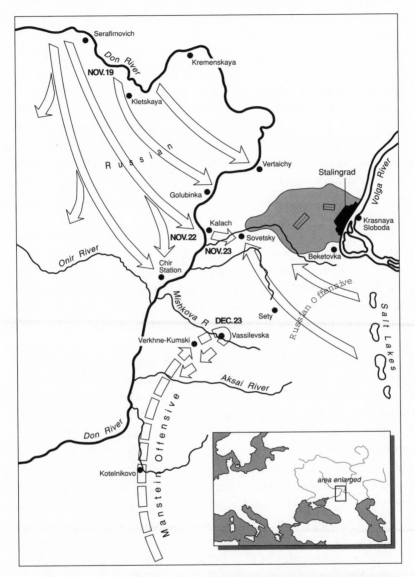

7.1. The German/Russian front at the Don River and the Stalingrad "Cauldron" in 1942. White arrows are thrusts of the Red Army on November 22 and 23. The broken arrow shows the German offensive of General Manstein, foiled on December 23.

troops were ferried from Krasnaya Sloboda, on the east bank of the Volga, across the two-mile-wide river in suicidal trips that tainted the waters red with blood. Throughout September and October, the streets of Stalingrad shook with machine-gun fire and grenade explosions as the fighting for the control of individual streets and buildings degenerated into hideous carnages. Despite the huge Soviet losses, the Germans were unable to take the city. Instead, unaccustomed to that kind of warfare, they saw their energies dwindle and their spirits sink. Realizing that Stalingrad had become a senseless drain of men and materials, Paulus and several other generals at the southern Russian front tried to persuade Hitler to allow a strategic withdrawal from the partially occupied city before the arrival of winter. Hitler was incensed; such a shameful move was simply beneath the superior German forces!

Most military analysts agree that Stalingrad was not as significant in the strategic game as perceived by the two reckless leaders, for whom human lives were expendable. Hitler became as obsessed with the desire to see the city under German control, even if in rubbles, as Stalin was about not surrendering the city of his name.

The long and costly siege of Stalingrad was a strategic blunder, in that it forced the Germans to maintain a more than 600-mile-long front along the Don River from south of Moscow to the lower Volga, deep in enemy territory. That task was entrusted mainly to Hungarian, Italian, and Romanian troops, whose military capabilities were significantly inferior to those of the well-equipped Germans. East of the front, a Soviet army that had suffered heavy losses but was far from annihilated, readied its human and material resources for the winter, Russia's legendary "ally." Meanwhile, the German generals pondered the daunting prospect of having to survive five months of severe winter in a ghost city, far from supplies and reinforcements. At the end of October, the Volga began to ice over as a winter arrived that was to be even colder than the preceding one.

The weather developments from November 1942 through January 1943—the crucial months of the Stalingrad siege and German capitulation—can be followed by reviewing meteorological records from the German Weather Service, which since the early 1930s had been compiling daily weather situations of central Europe according to a consistent classification of particular weather types (*Grosswetterlagen*). Even though the characterization of these weather situations is specific to central Europe, its application to Stalingrad at the eastern edge of Europe is pertinent because it permits us to link local weather to air masses that usually progress from western to eastern Europe.

The German thrust on the Caucasian oil fields and the lateral move on Stalingrad were initiated in August of 1942, when the steppes were basking in the dry summer heat. Weather conditions were generally good in September and October, and clear skies facilitated German operations in the air and over land. The first cold waves arrived out of central Asia toward the end of October, and the rains that resulted from their collision with humid airflows from the west or southwest transformed the ground into a mudfield. By early November it was obvious that a particularly severe winter lay ahead: the rapidly changing atmospheric conditions pointed to an instability that is common during years with anomalous climatic patterns. Today we know that in continental Europe, the decaying phase of ENSO in the tropical Pacific is marked by severe winters with excessive snowfall and repeated outbreaks of cold. This was precisely the case in the winter of 1941–42, when the sustained 1940–41 El Niño in the eastern Pacific was caused by low temperatures and heavy snows over most of continental Europe. The severity of that winter had been one of the reasons for the Germans' failure at Moscow and for the loss of lives and materials that forced their ultimate retreat. The winter of 1942–43 could be expected to be even worse because it was coming in the wake of a warm ENSO, when conditions usually flip to the other extreme, La Niña.

During most of November, the weather alternated between opposites (Table 7.1). On some days, southwesterly winds brought balmy weather but also cloudiness that hindered air operations; on others, air masses from the northwest released their moisture as frozen rain and snow flurries. With Germany's Sixth Army bogged down in Stalingrad and the thinly spread Italian, Romanian, and Hungarian troops immobilized along the Don River line, the Russians attacked on November 19, a day of gusty winds and snow drifts, and quickly annihilated the Romanian troops and Paulus's northern brigades. On November 20, under similar weather conditions, the Russians launched a new offensive from the southeast that could not be stopped by Romanian and German defenders, and by November 23, a quarter million of Paulus's troops were caught in the grip of two formidable Russian pincers. The Germans were now confined to a "cauldron" forty miles long and twenty miles wide; their lifelines were two airstrips over which this quarter of a million men were to be supplied by airlift (Figure 7.1). However, as the weather continued to

Table 7.1

Weather conditions in eastern Europe and military operations around Stalingrad, November 1, 1942–January 31, 1943

Date	Weather conditions	Operations and field conditions
November 1–3	Cyclonic southwest flow: precipitation	Bloody street fights for dominance of Stalingrad's city center
November 6–8	Humid and cold	First ice floes on the Volga announce arrival of freezing season
November 9–15	High pressure: cold but clear skies	Russians push into the Don boundary in preparation for counter-offensive against Germans in Stalingrad
November 16–23	Cyclonic depression: cold, snow flurries, gusty winds	Russian attack against German-Romanian lines begins on November 19; Russians attack from the south on November 20; 250,000 Germans are trapped in the "cauldron"
November 24–28	High pressure: clear skies, dry, cold	German air supply begins into two airfields inside the cauldron on November 27; General Manstein's tanks advance from the south to rescue the encircled German troops; frozen snowfields
November 28–30	Trough over Europe: sleet and snowfall	Suspension of airlift; Russian tanks overrun Romanian lines
December 1–3	Trough: bad weather, sleet, snow flurries	Russians cross the frozen Volga and recapture sectors of Stalingrad
December 4–5	High pressure: dry and cold	Manstein's tanks are stalled by Russian assaults and lack of fuel
December 6–9	Changing highs and lows: snow flurries	Suspension of airlift; renewed Russian tank attacks

Date	Weather	Events
December 10–14	Cyclonic southwest weather: snowfall	Russians begin second thrust from the north aimed at retaking German stronghold at Rostov, on the Sea of Azov
December 15–18	Cyclonic south weather: mild but humid	Italian forces collapse at the Don River line
December 19–22	Cyclonic southwest weather: snowfall	Short-lived German counterattack on enclosing Russian forces
December 23–24	High pressure: dry and very cold	Manstein turns back south at Vassileyska, 20 miles short of the cauldron; the troops of General Paulus are doomed
December 25–28	High pressure bridge: drifting snow	Impaired visibility; no airlift from airfields
December 29–31	Trough: rain, sleet, blizzards	German troops and tanks begin withdrawal from the Caucasus
January 1, 1943	Cyclonic west flow: abundant snowfall	Preparation of final Russian assault to reclaim Stalingrad
January 2–5	Trough: rain, sleet, snow	No airlift; Germans lack food and ammunition supplies
January 6–8	Northern high: cold, windy, clear skies	Russians' terms of surrender to General Paulus are rejected
January 9–10	Central high: cold, drifting snow	Subzero temperatures; Germans are dying of exposure and malnutrition
January 11–18	Southern flow: mild, partly cloudy	Airfield of Pitomnik falls to Russian attackers
January 19–21	Cyclonic southwest flow: snowfall, mild	Gumrak airfield is taken by the Russians; German isolation is total
January 22–24	Northeast high: continental cold wave	Sporadic fighting; Germans are corralled in city pockets
January 25–31	Cyclonic southwest weather: abundant snow	General Paulus capitulates in downtown Stalingrad on January 31

deteriorate and the Russians began to take command of the skies around Stalingrad, this proved extremely difficult.

Hitler finally realized the seriousness of the situation and ordered General Erich Manstein from the Caucasian front to rush his panzer divisions to the rescue. Manstein, who at the beginning of the war had cleverly outmaneuvered the French defense at the Maginot Line, was expected to open a corridor into the cauldron, while Paulus was to break through the Russian circle and meet up with Manstein's tanks. The rescue attempt that started on November 27 was soon slowed down by sleet and snow flurries generated by a trough over central Europe, while Paulus's troops, starving and pitifully short of ammunition and oil, were too weak to accomplish anything from within the circle. In the skies, the Luftwaffe was barely able to keep the besieged forces supplied in this bad weather. In early December, atmospheric conditions fluctuated rapidly between heavy snowfalls associated with the passing of cyclonic depressions from the west or southwest and cold outbreaks from the interior of Asia, which prevented Manstein's advance and further debilitated the troops in the cauldron.

Meanwhile, the Russians used the opportunity to move fresh troops across the frozen Volga and reinforce their armies. The bad weather that continued throughout the month worked to the advantage of the Red Army: a big counteroffensive was launched on December 17 with the objective of trapping Manstein's forces and blocking the Black Sea route that could be used by the Germans in the Caucasus as an escape.

Threatened by the prospect of losing all his forces in southern Russia, Hitler authorized the retreat of Manstein's troops to the west to spare them the fate of the doomed Sixth Army. On December 23—only thirty miles from their encircled comrades—Manstein turned back south and hastily organized the westward escape of the remaining German troops. Hitler and his General Staff had chosen to sacrifice the troops at Stalingrad so that they would keep the Russians occupied and prevent them from intercepting the German armies on their retreat from the Caucasus and the Black Sea. For five more weeks, Stalingrad continued to be the scene of bloody skirmishes between the weakening Germans and the Russians, who continued gaining strength. One by one, the airfields fell to the Red Army, and on January 31, 1943, Friedrich Paulus saw no sense in prolonging the butchering of his men and capitulated. This most pathetic German defeat of World War II, which had started with the failure to capture Moscow during the previous winter, marked the beginning of the end of Hitler's rule.

Although maniacal decisions, strategic mistakes, planning errors, and logistic miscalculations all figure in the defeat of an army considered almost invincible, these human shortcomings were exacerbated by a natural cause: weather. A cursory comparison between weather conditions during the winter of 1942–43 and those of previous winters reveals that the latter had been marked by severe extremes and high variability of weather: steady flows from the west that alternated with weather systems from the east and north accounted for more fluctuations and greater longevity of generalized weather conditions (synoptic situations). The winter of 1942–43, on the other hand, was characterized by what is referred to in German meteorology as *mixed circulations*, that is, successive invasions of air masses from different directions that produce permanently covered skies, snowfall, frozen rain or sleet, blizzards, and gusty winds from changing directions. During the intermittent anticyclonic conditions—which in central European winters are equated with clear skies and glacial temperatures—previously fallen snow and rain freeze solid, and roads and structures are buried under thick snowdrifts mobilized by blinding blizzards. These changing conditions indicate that the climatic controls over Eurasia were tremendously erratic during the extinction phase of the 1940–42 El Niño episode. The return to positive values of the Southern Oscillation Index in October of 1942—after a period of more than two and a half years of low SOI values, or warm ENSO conditions—is a sure indicator that, in the fall of 1942, the global climate was passing through one of those abrupt El Niño/La Niña transitions described in chapter 6.

In table 7.1, the sequential episodes of the siege of Stalingrad as presented in historical narratives by William Craig (1973) and Antony Beevor (1998) have been related to the *Grosswetterlagen* that occurred between November 1942 and January 1943. The relevance of these *Grosswetterlagen* for the outcome of the siege has been validated by meteorological research conducted in the recent past by Klaus Fraedrich. This meteorologist from the Free University of Berlin has studied the repercussions of the extreme phases of ENSO in the climatic anomalies of Europe, and his findings—backed by 107 years of observations–coincide amazingly well with the weather conditions reported for Stalingrad during the winter of 1942–43 (Fraedrich 1994, Fraedrich and Müller 1992). His meteorological analysis and subsequent statistical testing demonstrate that, in Europe, warm

ENSO episodes (El Niño) cause cooler and wetter winter conditions resulting from higher cyclonic activity, while cool ENSOs (La Niña) cause milder and drier winters because of anticyclonic dominance. The reason for the enhanced cyclonic activity (low pressures and stormy weather) during El Niño is that the tail end of the cyclonic track over the North Atlantic shifts farther south than usual over the British Isles and Scandinavia, and over the east-central Mediterranean. That route cuts across the Balkans and northern Turkey into the Ukraine and the Caspian Sea, propelling a continuous succession of humidity-laden depressions into that part of Russia (Figure 7.2); these weather systems brought freezing rains and heavy snowfalls during the siege of Stalingrad. Also validated by Fraedrich's findings are other weather situations mentioned in historical accounts, such as the very cold airflows from the east during those winters and more frequent than normal directional changes of the air masses. During La Niña years, cyclonic depressions pass farther north over Scandinavia and northern Russia, while the center of the continent remains under the influence of a high pressure cell (resulting in clear, cold weather).

The weather conditions during the months after General Paulus's capitulation also deserve some remarks. When El Niño 1940–42 flipped over into La Niña, the greater weather stability in Europe made it possible for the German troops—about to be encircled again by the Red Army—to effect an orderly withdrawal from the Caucasus and the northern Black Sea and to contain the Russian offensive during most of 1943 and 1944, when the winters—though cold—were not as changeable as the winter of 1942–43 had been. When the German forces finally collapsed, it did not take long before the Russians were in the Ukraine, Romania, Hungary, and Poland, and in April of 1945 the Red Army was the first to enter Berlin.

A recurrent theme brought up by World War II commentators is the fear the Germans had of Russian winters and of doing battle in the vastness of that land. They had had experience with this fateful combination more than a century earlier while being part of and sharing the fate of Napoleon's Grande Armée in the steppes of Russia. In the following section we will examine the circumstances under which czarist troops, the Russian winter, and El Niño joined forces to shatter the dreams of global domination of another European despot by the name of Napoleon Bonaparte.

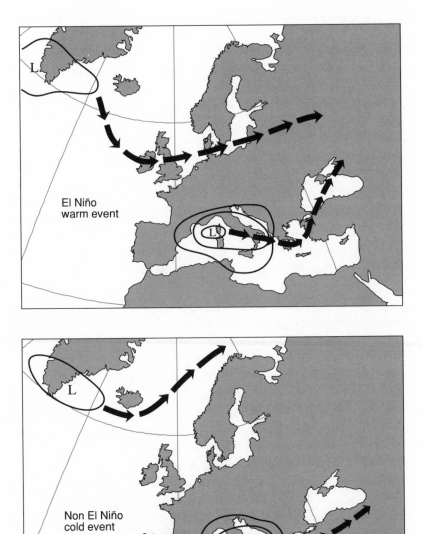

7.2. Cyclone routes across Europe during El Niño and non–El Niño years. Adapted from Fraedrich and Müller 1992.

Who Defeated Napoleon in Moscow?

Within a few years, Napoleon Bonaparte, a short artillery officer from Corsica, ascended into the upper ranks of the French revolutionary army due to his opportunism, extraordinary intelligence, and political shrewdness. Having distinguished himself among the postrevolutionary elite in the 1792 campaign against the northern Italian allies of Austria, Napoleon rose to one of the three director positions in the Republic of France and, after deposing the other two, emerged as the country's supreme director in 1798.

This meteoric rise to absolute power was based on his subjugating many of the small states and kingdoms that existed in continental Europe at the end of the eighteenth century, a policy that set France on a collision course with the great powers of Austria, Prussia, Russia, and England. Napoleon's armies, modernized according to the newest canons of warfare, defeated those powers individually or in alliances, shaking to their foundations empires such as Austria, Spain, Russia, and Turkey. By 1810, France dominated, either directly or through puppet governments, every country from the Iberian peninsula to Sweden, and from the English Channel to Egypt. Only England, separated from continental Europe by the sea, was able to resist and challenge the French domination.

In April of 1812, Alexander I of Russia had no choice but to declare war on France in an effort to break the continental blockade and ease the animosities of independent states, such as Poland and Lithuania, which he coveted. Russia found an eager ally in France's traditional enemy, England, which already supported the Portuguese and Spanish resistance in the European southwest, and backed the Turks who harassed the French in the Balkans and the eastern Mediterranean. When Sweden promised to join Russia and England under the condition that it would receive Norway at the end of the war, Napoleon decided it was time to take care of Russia, the instigator of these machinations.

As usual, Napoleon's initial advance was swift and effective, his forces swelled by international contingents from Italy, Poland, Lithuania, Holland, Belgium, Switzerland, Croatia, and Austria, plus a conglomerate of troops from the non-unified Germany, which included Westphalians, Saxonians, Hessians, Bavarians, Wurtenbergians, and Prussians. Even France's former enemies, Austria and Prussia, were coerced into joining the Grande Armée so they might safeguard their own possessions in eastern European territories and keep England out of the continent. Especially for the Prussians, this was a very divisive issue since, in previous wars against the French, many of their nobility had offered their services to the czar, thus bringing to the Russian troops the discipline and strategic savvy for which the Prussians were renowned since the wars of Frederick the Great.

The theater of operation for the push into the heart of Russia in 1812 was White Russia (today Byelorussia or Belarus), an expanse of swamps and dense forests between eastern Poland and the Central Russian Uplands west of Moscow. To reach Moscow, the invaders had to cross river after river, squeeze through narrow gorges in the Central Russian Uplands, and make it through the Pripet Marshes, south of Minsk (Figure 7.3). All of this—while taking considerable effort—was accomplished

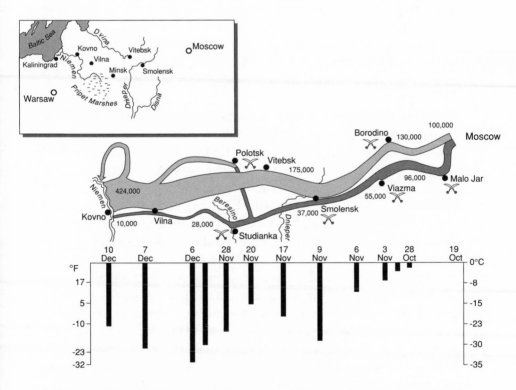

7.3. Route of Napoleon's campaign in Russia in 1812. Redesigned from an original of Charles J. Minard published in 1861.

without their ever having to confront the bulk of the Russian army, which had opted for a strategic withdrawal for the time being in order to minimize losses. The French advance into the heart of Russia was effected on three fronts: the first, along an axis running through Lithuania, was assigned to French and Prussian troops; the second, heading directly toward Moscow from northern Poland through Vitebsk and Smolensk, was under the command of Napoleon himself; and the third, starting off in the Austrian territory of Galacia and bypassing the Pripet Marshes, was allocated to the temporary Austrian allies.

Encouraged by the relatively speedy advance, particularly of the central front, Napoleon thought that the taking of Moscow and ultimate surrender of the Russians would be a matter of weeks—the same mistake in thinking that Hitler would make in 1941–42. But the military advisors to the czar had other plans. Against the suggestion of most Prussian generals at the service of the czar to launch a counteroffensive before Napoleon would reach Moscow, it was decided to prolong the strategic withdrawal into winter. This proved a clever move because the invading forces had spread themselves thin and with each passing day moved farther away from friendly Poland and Lithuania, and from their supplies in the rearguard. Enemy territory was most unwelcoming: as the fall rains started, roads turned into veritable mud-traps and there was no cooperation to be coaxed from the locals.

On September 14, 1812, Napoleon's 128,000 troops entered an almost deserted Moscow. Over the next two days, fires broke out in different sectors, which they were forced to extinguish in order to save the few provisions left behind. Discouraged, Napoleon decided to leave the ghost city as soon as possible, and on October 19, he took his troops (down to 96,000 after only one month of occupation) along a southern route toward Smolensk, where he intended to establish winter quarters.

By early November and with the weather deteriorating, they had taken great pains to retreat to Vyazma in the Central Russian Uplands, 100 miles short of Smolensk. Having endured repeated snowstorms and weakened by constant attacks from a now growing body of Russian troops under the leadership of Prince Mikhail Kutusov, a mere 60,000 men remained in fighting condition, while some 30,000 stragglers kept slowing down their withdrawal. While at Vyazma, Napoleon received notice that back in Paris General Claude Malet, not expecting him to return from Russia, had attempted a coup d'état. Deeply troubled by these signs of dwindling support and loss of confidence in his leadership, Napoleon considered returning to France.

The withdrawal resumed in a somber spirit of impending doom: the rivers were frozen, the horses were dying for lack of forage or being fed to the able-bodied men—the stragglers being left at the mercy of marauding Cossacks. On November 9, a mere 41,500 soldiers reached Smolensk, where many more died from starvation and exposure, as hardly any food, fodder, or firewood was left in the ravaged city. In the meantime, the Russians had seized Vitebsk, closing the road to Vilna in Lithuania, so that 37,000 French and allied troops were forced to retreat via Orscha, a route unknown to them. After crossing the Dnieper on November 20, the exhausted men reached Studianka, a crucial crossing on the Berezina River northeast of Minsk, only to be subjected to an all-out attack from the Russians. A ferocious battle raged from November 26 through 28, after which the battered survivors managed to cross the Berezina; left behind were 5,000 dead and countless starving and wounded men. Only 7,000 of the French troops remained in fighting condition, and 21,000 demoralized allied forces were in disarray. In view of the hopelessness of the situation, Napoleon left the field on November 29 and rushed back to Paris to salvage his personal future there.

One of his most able commanders, General Joachim Murat, took the remains of the troops to Vilna, but the place was so unsafe that on December 10, just one day after their arrival, they continued the retreat in the direction of the Niemen River, which was secured by Prussian allies under the command of General Yorck von Wartenburg. Wartenburg, however, realizing that all that was left of Napoleon's Grande Armée was the name, signed a declaration at Tauroggen, near Kovno, stating that Prussia was withdrawing her troops. With this defection, the fate of the Grande Armée was sealed and Napoleon's Russian campaign had come to a tragic end.

A short return of Napoleon to Saxony and Prussia, where fresh French troops achieved an odd victory over a new alliance of Russians, Prussians, and Swedes, was but his swan song. In August of 1813, Napoleon was forced to sign an armistice, and a year later he capitulated in Fontainebleau before the combined armies of British count Wellington, Prussian general Wittgenstein in the service of the czar, and his former allies, Prussian general Gebhard Blücher and Austrian general Karl Philipp Schwarzenberg.

Napoleon's Russian campaign has been, perhaps, the most analyzed military expedition of modern times. In 1861 the French engineer Charles J. Minard produced one of the best graphic illustrations of the attrition and losses of the Grande Armée (Figure 7.3). The shrinking width of the bands representing the number of soldiers eloquently depicts the magnitude of the military disaster (some 424,000 men departed from Kovno in the summer of 1812, but barely 10,000 returned to Vilna at the end of the year). At the bottom of the graph, the temperature scale shows the frigid temperatures that prevailed during the retreat from Moscow to Kovno during that bitter winter which added to the loss of soldiers on the battlefields, also shown.

An authoritative study of the catastrophic campaign was conducted by one of the protagonists, the Prussian general Karl von Clausewitz, who became a famed war strategist during the nineteenth century. Among other decisions made by Napoleon, the general especially criticized the imprudence—repeated 120 years later by the Germans at Stalingrad—of spreading thin the invading troops without adequately securing supplies in the rearguard. The virtues of strategic withdrawal when faced with a far superior enemy were extolled by Clausewitz, who gave credit to the Russians for letting the vastness of their country and the severity of the continental winter break the invaders' backbone before attacking. Since the writings of Clausewitz were required reading for successive generations of Prussian and German officers, the lessons learned from Napoleon's campaign should have sent shivers down the spines of Hitler's generals when they saw their obsessed leader repeat the same mistakes.

Still, a key consideration in these analyses is that winter has repeatedly been Russia's best ally, and the question is, was it the severity of the winter of 1812 or the tactical and strategic blunders that doomed Napoleon's Grande Armée? Giving too much importance to the climate belittles the ingenuity of man, but disregarding weather when making strategic decisions is not prudent either. In Russia, the winters of 1812 and 1942 are cases where the climatic element favored the victors and magnified the losers' mistakes.

From a global climatic viewpoint, the early 1800s had been rather uneventful. The oscillations of the eighteenth century were subsiding—probably due to the decline of the Little Ice Age—and the lingering effects of El Niño 1803–4 remained confined to the eastern Pacific Ocean. At the beginning of the 1810s, a tendency toward cooler global temperatures was enhanced by dust veils in the atmosphere from volcanic eruptions on Saint Vincent Island (Antilles) and on Celebes (Indonesia). In the context of the ensuing cooling and subsequent alterations in the atmospheric circulation, a moderate El Niño in the tropical Pacific caused a severe drought in India in 1812, and as the tropical pendulum swung rapidly to the other extreme, the number of Caribbean hurricanes rose suddenly in 1813.

Unlike the German campaign into southern Russia, Napoleon's advance into central Russia cannot be supplemented with systematic weather observations, and the only indications that inclement weather dominated during his withdrawal from Moscow, between October and December of 1812, are lateral references to the sufferings endured by the men in the field: freezing temperatures, sleet, snow flurries, glacial winds, and intermittent blizzards that aggravated the lack of food and adequate shelter, plus the abysmal wasting away of the horses that were essential for the transport of equipment and provisions (Nafziger 1998). The parallels between the German demise at Stalingrad and Napoleon's withdrawal from Moscow are striking. In both campaigns, it was difficult to move equipment and provisions at the hasty pace demanded: as the continental winter set in, General Paulus rapidly ran out of food, fuel, and ammunition, and Napoleon lacked sufficient provisions for his men and forage for the beasts of burden. Also in both cases, autumn turned into an early and especially brutal winter within a few weeks, one of the global sequences—as we know now—of the swift transition from El Niño to La Niña. In fact, Fraedrich and Müller (1992) report that during La Niña episodes in Europe, the depressions responsible for miserable weather take a more northerly route, which increases the number of rain and snowfall events over north-central Europe. These adverse weather situations, in alternation with short periods of continental cold waves and strong winds that led to blizzard conditions, sapped the energy of the west European troops, who were not accustomed to such a rigorous climate.

In light of these arguments, the defeat of Napoleon and his subsequent fall from power seem to have been caused not only by human acts or the will of God—as the Germans put it, *Mit Mann und Ross und Wagen hat sie die Herr geschlagen* (With man, horse, and cart the Lord struck them down)—but by the convergence of an untimely El Niño and ill-planned human actions.

The Sahel Droughts and the Fall of Haile Selassie

For centuries and with wanton regularity, droughts and famines have descended on the so-called Horn of Africa, particularly the highlands of Ethiopia. Emperor Haile Selassie, the country's ruler since 1941, was rudely awakened from his complacency in 1972–74, when, using the turmoil caused by a devastating drought in the eastern Sahel, a group of Marxist army officers seized the opportunity to remove him from power. Inner political intrigues, Soviet strategic ambitions, Western miscalculations, and, not least, a natural disaster converged to throw Ethiopia and neighboring countries into a state of instability from which they have yet to recover.

Located at a crossroad in eastern Africa where the effects of the seasonal monsoons interplay with the dry harmattan winds from the Arabian Peninsula, Ethiopia is frequently plagued by water shortages. Agriculture and livestock husbandry in the highlands depend on the rains of the *belg* (February to May) and *kirmet* or *meher* (June to September) seasons, for little usable water can be drawn from rivers, lakes, or underground reserves. Whenever *belg* and *kirmet* rains fail and the summer monsoons are feeble—as happens during El Niño years—coffee trees wither, seasonal staples wilt, and herds are decimated. In certain drought years, locust plagues (as detailed in chapter 6) will add to the misery.

Not only a hub of climatic influences, Ethiopia is also a country where the mixing of ethnic groups and nationalities has not been greatly successful and the political equilibrium is rather unstable. The largest ethnic group are the Oromo in the central part of Ethiopia, followed by the Tigreans and Amhara in the north, the Shankella in the west, the Sidamo in the south close to Kenya, the Somalis in the southeast, and the Afars in the north-central region—all differing in ethnicity, religion, customs, and mode of livelihood. In the central highlands, most are cultivators and Ethiopian Christians; those in the north, east, and southeast are predominantly herders and Muslims; and in the areas near the Sudan and Kenya, pastoral animists are dominant (Figure 7.4).

Written Christian Orthodox traditions and Arabic historical records permit the identification of famines and pestilences in Ethiopia, many of which are related to climatic crises in the rest of the world and registered in the western hemisphere since medieval times. These sources—scrutinized by Richard Pankhurst (1990)—yield early references to climate-induced famines during 831–49, 1252, 1271–73, 1344–72, 1435–36, and 1454–

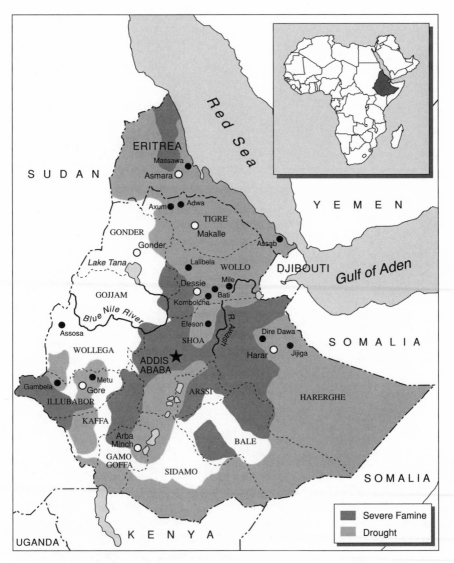

7.4. Drought and famine in Ethiopia

68, but their anecdotal and legendary character obscures the exact circumstances under which the disasters occurred. Still, these data are valuable
for identifying their coincidence with periods of global climatic crises.

Information became more trustworthy during the 1500s, when Western missionaries began to arrive in the country and the possibilities for
cross-referencing increased. According to these sources, Ethiopia experienced a drought in 1540 that claimed a large percentage of the cattle in the
north and was accompanied by a locust outbreak in most of the central
highlands. This episode correlates with the first El Niño documented in
northern Peru and with a drought in central India, making it part of a
global anomaly. Another drought and concomitant food crisis occurred in
1567–68 in conjunction with the El Niño of those years (Wolde-Mariam
1986).

During the seventeenth century, famines associated with ENSO events
occurred in 1618, 1625–27, 1633–35, and 1653, while the famines in 1611,
1650, and 1678 seem unconnected to Pacific anomalies. During the eighteenth century, the droughts of 1700 and of 1702 were probably repercussions of the global 1701 El Niño, while of the other five infamous
droughts, only that of 1747 coincided with a global anomaly. A strong El
Niño that affected the Pacific rimlands in 1791 does not appear to have
had consequences in Ethiopia.

With the arrival of the nineteenth century, the country experienced an
increase in the number of droughts occurring in phase with anomalies of
worldwide extent: the drought of 1812 brings to mind the failed Russia
campaign of Napoleon; that of 1828–29 caused heavy cattle losses and
was aggravated by a cholera epidemic; and that of 1850 provoked generalized dry conditions but spared human lives.

The most intense and best-documented drought/famine of Ethiopia
between 1888 and 1892 resulted from the convergence of several aggra-
vating circumstances. First there was an outbreak of rinderpest (cattle
plague) when Italian invaders arrived in Eritrea and northern Ethiopia
with infected horses from India. The plague decimated cattle and the oxen
needed in the country's subsistence-level agriculture. Then in 1890, the
summer rains declined and became even scarcer as the major 1891 El Niño
spread across the tropical belt. In addition, locust swarms in 1889 and
1892, along with a proliferation of caterpillars, wiped out the few crops
still left after three consecutive years of dryness (Pankhurst 1990). Cholera, typhus, dysentery, and smallpox epidemics broke out, while hyenas,

lions, and leopards fed on abandoned corpses and, in time, even grew so bold as to attack the weakened survivors at their villages. Depopulation ensued especially in the rural areas of Gojjam, Shoa, and Harerghe, and about a third of the country's entire population perished from the combined effects of these disasters. Political implications were far-reaching: Menelik, the emperor at that time, made use of the emergency situation to annex Somalian and Kenyan territories that had been abandoned by the inhabitants, while the Italians, who in 1885 had occupied the northern port of Massawa, found little resistance as they penetrated deeper into the country. These confrontations with nature, with Somalians and Kenyans, and with the invading Italian troops strengthened Ethiopia's ability to deal with foreign enemies but lessened its ability to handle environmental crises and demographic emergencies.

Among the droughts of the twentieth century, those between 1916 and 1920 may be distant echoes of El Niño events in 1917 and 1918, and the one of 1927–28, which ravaged northern Wollo, followed in the wake of the major 1925–26 El Niño. But the droughts of 1934–35 and those of 1947–50, which affected the coastal lowlands and most of Wollo, do not coincide with any ENSO event, although the latter anticipates India's severe 1951 drought. A drought related with the major 1957–58 El Niño affected particularly the northern regions of Tigre, Wollo, and Eritrea, where water had become scarce two years earlier, was now coupled with the now-familiar outbreaks of epidemics and locust plagues. Governmental inefficiency showed up again as the seriousness of the crisis was played down and international aid was squandered. The drought catastrophes of the late 1950s claimed some 397,000 lives (Wolde-Mariam 1986).

During the second half of the twentieth century, Ethiopian droughts faithfully mirrored atmospheric disturbances of global extent, starting with the 1965–66 occurrence which perfectly corresponds with the moderate 1965 El Niño. That drought affected particularly the north-central highlands of Wollo, which did not receive much relief from a government that had learned nothing from previous emergencies and was mired in incompetence and corruption. Things went from bad to worse when the 1971–74 drought unfolded in the Sahel in consonance with El Niño 1972–73. One of the peculiarities of this event is that the first news about insufficient *meher* rains came from the northern districts of Wollo in September of 1972, three months before the El Niño would manifest itself in the eastern Pacific. As usual, the warning signs were not heeded in Addis Ababa, and by the end of that year, western Wollo was in the grip of dryness. In the course of early 1973, when the spring rains also failed, most of the eastern and southern regions were in the grip of drought. In an effort to escape starvation, peasants and herders began to flee from the drought-stricken north to the coffee regions in central Ethiopia and to the wetter southwest. Only after personally visiting the Wollo region in November did Emperor Haile Selassie order measures to alleviate the hunger and halt the mounting outmigration. Apparently, though, the seriousness of the situation was not fully recognized; relief arrived late, and much of it ended up in the wrong hands.

For years now, the inefficient administration of the aging Selassie and his growing seclusion had alienated the people who once idolized him and fostered resentment among progressive sectors of the Ethiopian society. Discontent fueled by Soviet advisers was spreading fast even in the armed forces, the supporters of his authoritarian rule. The ideological infiltration had begun during the 1960s, when Haile Selassie—in view of the Soviet Union's growing involvement in the Near East after the Suez Canal crisis and the Yom Kippur War—started to flirt with that superpower. Soon, advisers from Russia made their influence felt in Ethiopia's intellectual circles and in the armed forces. Their messages of liberation not only from the capitalistic West but also from the rule of the old emperor were readily received by the country's idealistic emancipationists. Among the latter, the Dergue—a military group whose Amharic name (which means "committee") revealed Soviet inspiration—was waiting for an opportunity to seize power. The occasion presented itself when the drought-stricken country in addition had to deal with the decaying morale and growing unruliness in the armed forces and when insurgencies from various ethnic groups could not be contained due to the fading authority in Addis Ababa.

In September 1974, after nearly a year of influential participation in the government, the Dergue leaders rather unceremoniously dethroned the aged emperor and took the reins into their own hands. The change of power did not translate, however, into any appreciable relief from the desperate situation in the country, since the new power was more concerned with consolidating its hold on the country than with alleviating the rampaging famine. The scarce food available as well as external aid went to the army, which was busy quelling insurrections and preventing secessionist movements in twelve of the country's fourteen major regions.

The bloodbaths characteristic of communist takeovers did not spare Ethiopia. Challenges to the authority of General Mengistu Haile Mariam, the Dergue's supreme commander, were suppressed with utmost sever- ity, such as execution without trial even for dissidents in his own military ranks. Disillusioned by the regime's failure to deal with the food crisis that had ravaged the country for four consecutive years, former backers of the coup began to resist the military, and Muslim groups who had re- belled against Haile Selassie's rule now rose against Mengistu in protest of his collusion with the atheistic Soviet Union.

The deterioration of the populations struck by the natural disaster con- tinued for several years after the coup. At the same time, political devel- opments exacerbated by the military takeover became more dangerous to the country's stability and territorial integrity. In the late 1970s, at least eight groups were fighting for independence, among them the Eritreans, Somalians, Tigreans, Oromo, and the Gojjams on the Sudanese border. The Dergue dictatorship had to deal with all these insurrections and with growing unrest among the starving peasants, who, in the best communist tradition, had been forced into relocation programs away from their homelands.

And then the scourge returned. The first repercussions of the powerful El Niño of 1982–83 were felt in 1984, when a drought devastated the dis- trict of Korem, in Wollo, and claimed 60,000 lives. In other highland re- gions, the *belg* rains failed, prompting an outflow of famine refugees into the western regions of Gojjam, Wollega, and Illubabor (Figure 7.4). But it was only a matter of time before the latter regions were also affected. In the spring of 1985, the drought spread westward, forcing new waves of refugees from Wollega and also from Tigre into Sudan. With Ethiopian refugees joining the Sudanese in their flight toward the banks of the Blue Nile, the disaster acquired international proportions. In Addis Ababa, the military regime of Mengistu did little to stop the outflow of people con- sidered "enemies of the system." After a brief rainy interlude in 1985, drought conditions returned in 1987–88, echoing the moderate 1987 El Niño that had started in late 1986. The flow of famine refugees into Sudan increased, and peasants from the central highlands, who had been herded into makeshift villages in the north of Sidamo and Bale, fled into neigh- boring Somalia.

By now, all support for the repressive rule had vanished, and in May of 1991—deserted by his Marxist friends and military epigones alike—General Mengistu Haile Mariam was deposed by his own Ethiopian People's Revolutionary Democratic Front. Without support from the collapsing Soviet Union and with the Cuban advisers gone, the country finally extricated itself from the communist shackles. The cost had been enormous, however: nearly 1 million people had starved to death or been killed in armed conflicts; over 2 million had been displaced into neighboring countries (only to find even worse conditions there); and Eritrea—now an independent country—was definitely lost.

A drought had toppled Emperor Haile Selassie in 1974, and seventeen years later, another triggered the demise of the military man who had usurped his power. El Niño had been the instigator in both dramas.

High Waters of the Nile

The droughts of sub-Saharan Africa and the events that precipitated the fall of Emperor Haile Selassie as well as the demise of his successor, General Mengistu, have an undeniable relationship with ENSO events in the tropical Pacific. Similar relationships can be traced back for other places far removed from the Pacific as long as reliable documentation and credible references exist. Speculations about anomalous floods of the Nile River cannot be used to support the contention that past El Niños influenced major cultural revolutions in Egypt. Only those references which are backed by credible archival information can be interpreted against the backdrop of ENSO climatic variations.

With this basic consideration in mind, William H. Quinn (1992) studied the records, kept in Cairo, of the Nile's flood levels between 622 and 1900 to compare their fluctuations with known phases of the Southern Oscillation. Then, to construct a series of years amenable to comparisons, he used British records from before the opening of the first Aswan dam in 1902, and hygrometric observations on the Blue Nile and Atbara River for subsequent years. These two rivers collect the waters from tributaries flowing out of western Eritrea and the Ethiopian regions of Gonder, Gojjam, Wollega, and Shoa, thus reflecting the rainfall variabilities in those areas. The periods of dryness mentioned in the previous section are faithfully reproduced in the flood-level fluctuations of the Nile downstream. In the Ethiopian highlands, whose rivers feed the Blue Nile, there is an initial period of rains during the early northern spring that does not affect the water levels of the Nile in Egypt. As continental warming increases in spring and peaks in midsummer, the *meher* or *belg* rains swell the rivers and creeks that descend from the western mountain slopes onto the plains, where they are anxiously awaited by the pastoral communities of western Ethiopia and Sudan. During June and July, these waters flood the riverine lands of the lower Nile, leaving a carpet of sediments whose extraordinary fertility sustains the population of Egypt. The contributions of the White Nile to river levels and sediment loads in northern Sudan and upper Egypt are difficult to trace due to the dispersion of these waters into the vast swamps of El Sudd in southern Sudan.

After the winter low, the rising of the Nile in late spring was always welcome because it meant renewal of the fertile sediment layers and replenishment of the numerous wells, cisterns, and man-made ponds that allowed cultivation throughout the summer. In years when rains in the eastern Sahel and the Ethiopian highlands were scarce, the Nile would not carry the expected sediment load nor the water needed to satisfy the agricultural requirements. Since we now know that episodes of dryness in eastern Africa and the Sahel are linked to failures of the summer monsoons over the western Indian Ocean, and that droughts in the eastern half of sub-Saharan Africa relate to altered summer circulation over southeastern Asia (Indonesia included), it is legitimate to look for teleconnections between this part of Africa and the Southern Oscillation in the Pacific. Thus, when sea warming and humidity increase in the eastern tropical Pacific (that is, when the El Niño phenomenon occurs), East Africa experiences droughts due to monsoon failures, and the rimlands of the Indian Ocean also suffer from rain shortages and pervasive droughts. Abnormally low levels of the Nile that surface in historical records have a plausible causal relationship with warm/low phases of the Southern Oscillation, while the high Nile levels correspond to cold/high SO phases.

The water stands of the lower Nile were already measured during Hellenistic times when Egypt was ruled by the dynasty of Ptolemy, one of Alexander's generals. During Roman times, the measurements were continued in the Nile delta and also in Thebes in middle Egypt by a special caste of Christian Copts, who performed that task thereafter. The most accurate measurement devices were the *nilometers*—wells into which waters from the Nile were diverted and their levels measured on an apposite column. The Arabs who succeeded the Hellenistic masters were well aware of the importance of the Nile water levels for the cultivation of crops in lower Egypt and made sure that nilometers in the proximity of

Cairo were periodically read and records duly kept. The logs of Arab geographers and travelers contain numerous references to the water stands
measured by these nilometers and to memorable low water periods since
622, the beginning of the Muslim era.

These accurate records of the years, or rather clusters of years, during
which the Nile levels were deficient permit us to draw parallels with the
droughts and famines of Ethiopia detailed in the previous section. According to the findings of Quinn, the lowest levels occurred around 650,
689, 694, 842, 903, 967, 1096, 1144, 1200, 1230, and 1450. We know of corresponding famines in Ethiopia during 831–49, 1145, and 1454–68, but the
other episodes are isolated occurrences. Quinn was able to pinpoint a
large number of low-level episodes between 800 and 1250, during a period of global warming known among paleoclimatologists as the Medieval Warm Period (A.D. 1000–1250). This is consistent with the current
knowledge that an activation in the frequency and intensity of El Niño–
like events takes place during warm periods.

During the sixteenth century, when the Western nations became more
diligent and accurate in their recordings of climatic variabilities in other
parts of the world, Nile flood-level records deteriorated under the rule of
the Ottoman Turks. Still, anecdotal information allows the recognition of
low levels in 1553, 1641, 1650, and 1694, all of which correlate with distinct
ENSO events in the Pacific. As to the relative small number of these occurrences, Quinn reminds us that this was during the Little Ice Age, when the
northern hemisphere underwent a cooling that suppressed the energy
outbursts typical of ENSO events.

From 1700 on, the correlations between the Nile's flood levels and
anomalies in the tropical belt are closer, and their reporting is more pre-
cise. Three of the strongest eighteenth-century El Niños—in 1720, 1728,
and 1791—had repercussions in extremely low flood levels and in significant droughts in India, as we saw in chapter 5. The low flood of 1769–70
does not correspond with any of the El Niños on the Quinn list, but these
years are mentioned by authors such as Hamilton and García (1986) as an
El Niño episode responsible for a drought in India. There is also a note in
Captain James Cook's logs indicating that he encountered warm water
conditions in the central Pacific in 1769. The possibility of warm ENSO
conditions developing in the central Pacific around 1770 without spreading to the eastern Pacific is interesting because in my research I also noticed an abrupt change in the conditions necessary for the genesis of hur-

ricanes in the tropical Atlantic around that year (Caviedes 1991). Such short-lived abnormal episodes in the tropics might also be considered indications that the Little Ice Age was entering its decaying phase. ENSO episodes of minor proportions during 1737, 1743–44, and 1782–83 are also reflected in low flood levels of the Nile according to a list of events contained in the article by Whetton and Rutherfurd (1994).

For the nineteenth century, both the Quinn and the Whetton and Rutherfurd series on the Nile coincide in relating El Niño 1824–25 with low-level floods in phase with a drought in India and Australia, thus revealing anomalous precipitation conditions over most of the eastern hemisphere of the Southern Oscillation. Another period of moderately low flood levels toward the end of the 1820s seems to correlate with the major El Niño of 1827–28, and the steep drop in the Nile flood levels in 1837 with the ENSO of that year. A reduction in the severity of ENSO episodes from the 1840s to the 1860s is associated by some authors with the extinction phase of the Little Ice Age. Nevertheless, extreme lows were recorded during 1844–46, 1854, and 1864–68, when the Nile flood level reached its lowest point since 1700 (Whetton and Rutherfurd 1994). The interconnectedness between the two events became apparent again when the powerful El Niño of 1877 was reflected in extremely low Nile flood levels, as well as during the 1888, 1891, and 1899–1900 episodes—all of this supporting the contention that after the 1870s, the repercussions of ENSO events were being felt worldwide with greater intensity.

During the twentieth century, this trend became more pronounced despite the flow-regulating role of the Aswan dam (Figure 7.5). It is interesting to note that low levels in 1913, 1925, 1940–41, 1957, 1966, and 1972 coincide precisely with El Niño occurrences, while the Nile surges correspond invariably to what is now recognized as La Niña years, that is, years with cold temperatures in the tropical Pacific, such as 1916, 1929, 1938, 1954, and 1964. Although the Quinn series does not include recent La Niña occurrences (it ended in the early 1970s), the evidence suffices to show that the rhythms of the Nile are more closely related to the interannual pressure and humidity variations in the tropical Pacific than was previously assumed.

Thus the fluctuations in the Nile flood levels extracted from the available records reveal a plausible connection with the monsoons and the Southern Oscillation and reflect climatic variations, such as the Little Ice Age and the Medieval Warm Period, which affected the magnitude and

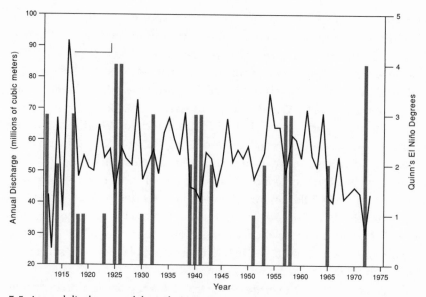

7.5. Annual discharges of the Nile River at Dongola and severity degrees of El Niños (gray bars). According to Quinn 1992.

frequency of the Southern Oscillation extremes. This makes it necessary to turn to the historical implications of one of these two long-term climatic variabilities, the Little Ice Ages.

Storms and Doldrums of the Little Ice Age

In his memoirs, the French philosopher Blaise Pascal complains about the miserable conditions under which he did most of his writing: an omnipresent cold numbed his fingers and forced him to pace continuously in the room in order to stay warm. The 1600s were not pleasant for Europe: interminable wars bled the nations, and during the short interludes of peace, plagues and famines further decimated the debilitated populations. All of this happened against the backdrop of bitterly cold winters and rainy or suffocatingly dry summers that ruined crops or created conditions favorable for fires, such as the infamous "great fire of London." Fierce storms raging across the seas eroded coastal lands and caused countless shipwrecks.

Historians and geologists call this period the Little Ice Age, analogous to the Ice Age whose adversities were endured by our prehistoric ancestors. The conceptualization of this particular harsh period by contemporary earth scientists stems mostly from historical references to storms, cold temperatures, harvest failures, famines, and abandonments of settlements or from indirect evidence, such as traces of glacial advances in high mountains and variations in pollen spectra or sedimentation. Absolute determinations of the temperatures then prevailing have been possible only recently, using radioactive methods and tree-ring temperature indicators. Interestingly, when first proposed by the Quaternary specialist F. E. Matthes, the term *Little Ice Age* (*LIA*) was based largely on historical references rather than empirical evidence, a circumstance that lends credibility to the use of historical sources to re-create past environments as explained in chapter 2. The Little Ice Age of the second millennium A.D. was not the first cold recurrence in recent earth history; there were other cold periods in northern Europe, such as the Dryas (10,300 B.P.) and the Pre-Boreal (4000 B.P.). The difference is that this latest cold period was experienced by inquisitive populations, who observed its manifestations and left records that contribute to a better understanding of such an abnormal climatic period.

In its purest expression, LIA was a truly northern hemispheric occurrence, enhanced by the predominance of continental masses that cool down faster than water masses and react quickly to the cooling influences of air from polar latitudes. These processes were less pronounced in the southern hemisphere because of the reduced continental masses in the higher latitudes and the buffering effect of the "Southern Ocean"—the conjunction of the southern Pacific, Atlantic, and Indian Oceans that encircles the Antarctic.

As to the time interval involved, the historical testimonies of climatic deterioration seem to point to about 300 years, between A.D. 1550 and 1850. Today, absolute chronology indicators such as oxygen isotopes trapped in ice core samples, coral growth rings, and tree-ring widths enable us to reconstruct the thermal conditions of the northern hemisphere during the last 1,000 years. In the resulting temperature curve (Figure 7.6), departures from the 1,000-year average depict the climatic oscillations that have occurred from A.D. 1000 to the present. Although there is a plunge in the early 1300s, a distinct temperature drop after 1450 signals the true beginning of LIA. Subsequent temporary warmings occurred at the beginning of the 1500s, around 1510–20, near 1560, 1610, around 1780–90, interspersed with cold recrudescences between 1580 and 1590, 1680 and 1720, and 1810 and 1840. The Little Ice Age dragged on into the early 1900s, since it was only after 1910 that temperatures in the northern hemisphere started an upward trend.

In the following pages an attempt will be made to establish concrete linkages between the climatic anomalies that occurred during LIA in the northern hemisphere, particularly in Europe, and the responses in the tropical oceanic-atmospheric circulation to this prolonged cooling episode.

The manifestations of LIA in continental Europe and the contiguous Atlantic Ocean exemplify the upset global conditions during that period. Considering Europe as representative of these changes is a matter of geographic pertinence. No other continent in the middle latitudes receives so many different influences: maritime flows from the Atlantic Ocean, moderating effects from the Gulf Stream, upper-latitudinal westerlies, cold air masses from the Eurasian plains, and subpolar airflows from Greenland and Scandinavia.

Among the numerous indicators of the LIA climatic deterioration in western Europe, a few are of primary importance to explain subsequent responses. It has been estimated that the North Atlantic between Iceland and northern Scotland was 5 °C colder than at present, and that this cooling was coupled with the Gulf Stream curving away from the North American continent farther south than it does today; namely, near the

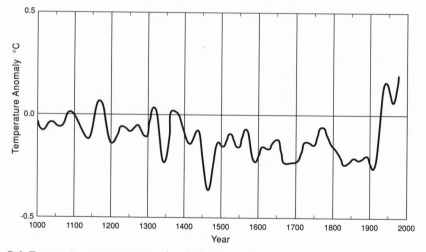

7.6. Temperature variations in the northern hemisphere over a 1,000-year average (A.D. 1000–1998). From Mann et al. 1999.

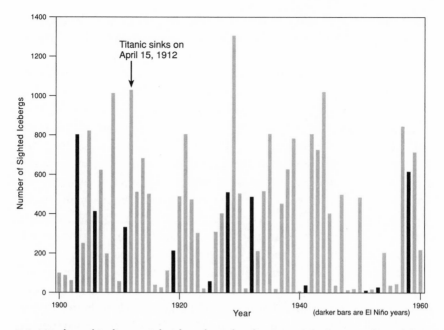

7.7. Number of icebergs sighted at the Labrador Sea, 1900–1960. Adapted from Birch and Marko 1986.

latitude of Nantucket Island. These two circumstances prompted a southward shift of the North Atlantic oceanic front (the zone of encounter between subpolar and midlatitudinal waters) and of the atmospheric polar front. This increased the frequency of collisions between polar and temperate air masses over the North Atlantic, so that fronts and cyclonic storms were much more active than they are today. Consequently, the likelihood of icebergs breaking off from the icepack frontage on the Labrador Sea became much higher.

In an enlightening contribution about the effects of contemporary El Niños on winter weather in the Canadian Atlantic and on the number of icebergs drifting southward, J. R. Birch and J. R. Marko (1986) report that during such years the intensified Icelandic low causes a strengthening of the Baffin and Labrador currents, which mobilizes a larger number of icebergs and permits more of them to drift farther south to the Grand Banks of Newfoundland. The authors' contention that these effects tend to continue into the spring of the year after particularly strong El Niño episodes is substantiated by 1912, which had the highest iceberg count between 1900 and 1929 (Figure 7.7). Thus one might speculate that the

Titanic would not have met her tragic end on April 15, 1912, had it not been for an El Niño occurrence in 1911 that sent icebergs drifting farther south during the subsequent northern spring. This major tragedy in recent history also appears to be tied to the vagaries of El Niño, reflecting the relation of air and sea conditions in the North Atlantic with those of the distant tropical Pacific (Newell 1996).

Another feature of the LIA circulation was the frequent generation of blocking situations from the strengthening of anticyclones over the North Atlantic, which happens when the meandering within the westerlies intensifies, that is, when the zonal westerly flow curves either over the central North Atlantic or over an axis that runs from Scandinavia to the central Mediterranean basin. In both instances, instead of a straight *zonal* flow of the westerlies from west to east that inhibits air mixing, there is a *meridional* flow from higher to middle latitudes, or vice versa, which is conducive to the mixing of temperate and polar air, to frontal or cyclonic development, and to the formation of spells of bad weather. Based on historical sources, Hubert H. Lamb (1988) showed that during LIA there was a reduction in the southwesterly winds that bring balmy weather to the British Isles and an increase in winds from the northwest and northeast, which prompted the worst storms in the North Sea and North Atlantic in centuries.

Understandably, all these alterations in the wind and circulation conditions during LIA had a strong impact on nature and on humans. Pollen analyses from the Canadian northlands suggest that the boreal forests retreated south and were replaced by tundra vegetation from the north during that time; in Iceland, the timberland became depleted because of excessive cutting and the trees' declining power of regeneration; in Scandinavia, the northern boundary of grain cultivation, which had run near latitude 63°N during the Medieval Warm Period, retreated southward; in the highlands of Scotland, crop failures and famines left villages and hamlets desolate; in southern England, vineyards that had flourished during the late Middle Ages ceased to produce; and in continental Europe, repeated clusters of years with summer temperatures so low that crops would not reach maturation caused hunger and starvation. Specifically remembered for their glacial temperatures were the years 1613–14, 1683–85, and 1784–85, the latter two occurring in phase with El Niño phenomena.

On the North American continent, the failed attempts to establish colonies in northern North Carolina on Roanoke Island and in southeastern Virginia at Jamestown between 1587 and 1612 can be blamed on the harsh climate during these centuries. Using tree-ring data, David W. Stahle and his colleagues (1998) established that the fledgling colony on Roanoke Island off Cape Hatteras succumbed to a pervasive drought that spanned the summers from 1587 to 1589, and that the high mortality rate among the British colonists of Jamestown in 1607 was linked to a seven-year drought that struck as soon as they set foot on the coastal wetlands of Virginia. These episodes underline the abruptness of the climatic fluctuations in the northern hemisphere during one of several cold recrudescences of LIA.

The seas of western Europe were very stormy between 1530 and 1799. Hubert Lamb pinpointed the worst years as 1588, 1694, 1703, 1717, 1756, 1791, 1792, and 1795. Of particular historical interest are the storms of August 1588, which destroyed the fleet of the Spanish Armada and were associated with the passage of transient depressions generated by the meandering course of the westerlies so typical of LIA. Apart from causing large numbers of maritime accidents (see chapter 4), the storm-driven waves altered shorelines and eroded or inundated coastal lands, especially in northern Germany and the Netherlands.

The manifestations of perturbed atmospheric circulations over the northern half of the Atlantic Ocean, such as the extreme meanderings of the westerly flow, frequent development of blocking situations, and greater exchanges of heat and cold as arctic waters moved south, resulted in increased storminess during the winters and lower temperatures during the summers. Periods of anticyclonic dominance prompted dry interludes, such as the previously mentioned droughts that wiped out the colony at Roanoke Island ("The Lost Colony") and endangered the continuity of Jamestown, and those that unleashed the Great Plague of 1665 in Europe and the fire of London in 1666. The north-and south-hemispheric advances of subpolar circulations toward the equator must have caused a contraction of the tropical belt. As a consequence, the exchanges of air and water masses in the Pacific and Indian Ocean realm must have occurred in the direction of the parallels with less possibilities of mixing, whereas those in the Atlantic Ocean—due to its elongated shape—must have followed in a meridional direction, prompting a more turbulent mixing of heat and cold. This easily explains the higher frequency of front and storm developments in the North Atlantic during LIA.

The aggressive advance of subpolar air and water masses in the high latitudes of both hemispheres also explains the higher storm activity in the southern seas, which prompted the all-too-frequent shipwrecks in the waters of Chile and New Zealand, outlined in chapter 4. A description of the predominant climatic characteristics of LIA in the high latitudes of Pacific South America is offered by Antonio Lara and Ricardo Villalba (1993) in an interesting article on temperature reconstruction for southern Chile derived from tree rings of the southern coniferous giant alerce (*Fitzroya cupressoides*). Some of these longest-lived trees of the southern hemisphere are over 3,600 years old. The authors found traits in the tree rings suggesting that in the maritime southern hemisphere the lowering of temperatures during the cold episodes of LIA was less severe than in the northern hemisphere and that cooling or warming periods did not always coincide with those of the northern latitudes. Nevertheless, a prolonged cooling period between A.D. 1490 and 1700 seems to have been an echo of the northern hemispheric LIA, and a cooling from A.D. 1750 to 1800, the reflection of the first signs of the LIA's collapse. Interestingly, the studies of Lara and Villalba offer no evidence of a South American correlate to the northern Medieval Warm Period between A.D. 1080 and 1250 (Figure 7.8).

Worldwide, the LIA cooling epoch meant a reduction of El Niño episodes for lack of caloric surpluses and the generation of more La Niña–like episodes, which caused droughts not only in middle latitudes—as demonstrated by the examples from Europe and North America—but also in tropical regions such as India, Ethiopia, and northeastern Brazil. Also, the LIA climatic "extremes" resulted in a higher frequency of brisk transitions between clusters of cold years with increased frontal activity and storms and clusters during which anticyclonic dryness dominated. The numerous freezes and droughts mentioned in historical sources from colonial Mexico, as well as in China and Japan, confirm that these were typical features of the global LIA.

The Little Ice Age came to an end in a convulsive way. Although the commonly agreed date is 1850, the beginning of the decline was announced toward the end of the eighteenth century by several spasmodic climatic interludes, such as a rise in hurricane frequency in the Caribbean during the 1770s and the explosive ENSO of 1791 which corresponded

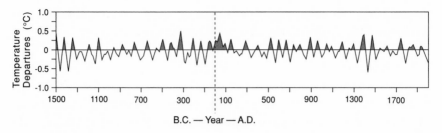

7.8. Temperature departures in the southern hemisphere, 500 B.C. to A.D. 1000–1990. Adapted from Lara and Villalba 1993.

with droughts in India, Ethiopia, and Brazil. The actual end was marked by unsettled climatic conditions worldwide during the 1870s. From a strictly geochronological viewpoint, the beginning of the contemporary warming around 1910 may be considered as the definite exit from that long period of inclement weather.

El Niño Echoes from the Far Orient

At the time when El Niño 1972–73 occurred, the People's Republic of China was just opening up to the West after decades behind the "bamboo curtain." A window that allowed a glimpse behind the curtain was Hong Kong, and it is from students from this southern tip of China that I first heard about the droughts and torrential rains affecting their country during the ENSO event of those years. This made me realize that the effects of El Niño do not stop at the Pacific shores of Asia. In subsequent years, as China opened up even more, Chinese meteorologists revealed the advances they had made while cut off from the international scientific mainstream. Among the subjects they had explored was the relationship between ENSO and climatic variations in eastern Asia. Intrigued by the contemporary manifestations of these phenomena, they had also searched Chinese anecdotal and historical sources for clues of past El Niño occurrences.

Japanese scientists, by contrast, had maintained close contacts with their European and North American peers after World War II. The renowned Japanese climatologist Masatoshi Yoshino, for example, studied with Hermann Flohn in Bonn, Germany, and after his return interested many students in the intricacies of the monsoon flows over the Far East and the implications of El Niño for Japanese climatic history.

In this section, several advances on this theme made by Chinese and Japanese scholars since the 1980s will be reviewed with the purpose of unveiling traces of past El Niños in some of the long historic series of their respective countries.

To understand the climatic variations that have affected China now and in the past in association with the warm and cold ENSO phases, we must first familiarize ourselves with the climate mechanisms operating in that vast country and the ways in which they relate to circulations over Asia and the western Pacific. Northwest China is dominated by continental controls; therefore temperatures and rainfall are not influenced by ENSO. The rest of the country is under the regimen of the monsoons and receives maritime flows from the western Pacific that depend on the variabilities of the Southern Oscillation and El Niño developments. The effects of these two modulators, however, are far from homogeneous throughout Chinese territory.

Rainfall in the monsoon-dominated regions occurs mainly during the summer months, when the polar front recedes north and makes room for the air masses of the southwest monsoons that originate in the warm, humid reaches of the Indian Ocean and the Sea of Indochina. An initial period of precipitation in June and early July called *Mei-Yu,* or "Plum Rains," results from the combined action of southward thrusts of the withdrawing winter front and the initial incursions of monsoon flows; this is also a feature of Japan's precipitation regime known as *Bai'u* rains. After midsummer, humid air from the southwest mixes with maritime air from the Pacific, whose humidity content largely determines the year-to-year rain variability in China. If the western Pacific subtropical high expands during that time, droughts occur along China's east coast, and precipitation and floods increase in central China. As the high pressure moves northward, so do the rains and floods, while droughts now affect the lands south of the Yangtze River. In years when the eastern Pacific is cold and the western Pacific is warm, rains are copious in central China, and snows unusually heavy on the Tibet Plateau. These are responses to oceanic and atmospheric conditions associated with El Niño and La Niña, respectively (Zhang and Crowley 1989).

Due to these interactions connected with the intensity of the monsoons and the type of the sea and air conditions in the tropical Pacific, the rains, or lack thereof, show up over China in very peculiar ways. During El Niño years, southern China is affected by floods and northern

China by cold and dryness; also, more cyclones than usual develop in the western Pacific south of China and Japan, raising the level of humidity in the coastal regions of these countries. Under La Niña conditions, southern China experiences droughts, and the north floods. During the transitional periods between El Niño and La Niña, floods occur in central China around the Yangtze River, and dryness affects all other regions.

The instrumental series of China have been extended into the past via several of the proxy methods discussed in chapter 2. So, for instance, the flowering dates of plum and cherry trees allowed the scholar Zhu Kezhen to identify cold and warm periods in Chinese climatic history for the last 5,000 years. Other scholars, like Xu and Wen, threw light on climatic variations since the beginning of the Christian era by analyzing local chronicles from central China. But the sources most applicable to tracing past El Niños are those of S. W. Wang and Z. C. Zhao (1981) and C. Wang and S. Wang (1987), because they deal with short-term temperature and precipitation tendencies that make it easier to pinpoint ENSO episodes than long-term fluctuations that tend to mask El Niño occurrences.

Some peculiar variations in a precipitation series assembled by S. Hameed, W. M. Yeh, M. T. Li, R. Cess, and W. C. Wang (1983) for Beijing

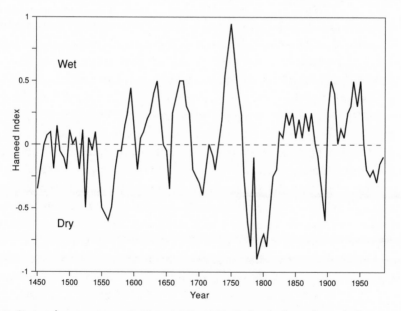

7.9. Dry and wet years at Beijing, 1450–1975. Redrawn from data of Zhang and Crowley 1989.0

from 1450 to 1974 are reminiscent of major ENSO occurrences, such as the rainfall anomalies of 1578–79, 1624, 1671, 1747, 1844, 1877, 1891, 1905, and 1941. Of special interest are the droughts of 1785, which correspond to an El Niño of that year from the Quinn list (1992); and the very cold winter of 1892, which occurred in the wake of the strong 1891 ENSO episode (Figure 7.9).

Regarding longer periods, the century around A.D. 1000 was warmer than usual but was interrupted by several clusters of cold years. Then China experienced a colder period from 1450 to 1890, when droughts became more frequent than before, suggesting something similar to the Little Ice Age that was affecting the other continents of the northern hemisphere (Zhang and Crowley 1989). Intensifications of the cold trend during the 1600s and late 1800s occurred both in China and Europe. But there were also humid interludes in the drawn-out Chinese LIA, which caused catastrophic flooding on the Yellow River in 1482, 1662, and 1843, and on the Yangtze River in 1368 and 1870, all dates within one year before or after El Niño events. Precipitation deficits in northern and western China due to monsoon failures during the seventeenth century at the LIA peak suggest that, at that time, the monsoons were more restricted to the southern part of the country. This was a response to distant happenings, such as prolonged snow seasons in Eurasia, which tend to weaken the monsoons in the subsequent summer, and westward shifts of the North Pacific high pressure center, which is one of the symptoms of warm and humid ENSO events in the tropical Pacific. Under extremely weak monsoon conditions, China suffered prolonged and extensive droughts that resulted in severe hardships, such as the infamous famines of 1805, 1877, and 1891, which coincided with similar calamities in India and eastern Africa.

Although China is one of the regions receiving distant echoes of ENSO, not all of its catastrophic dry and humid episodes during the last 1,000 years have been exactly synchronous with worldwide variabilities. For instance, a warming period during the eleventh century occurred before the Medieval Warm Period in Europe, and the Chinese LIA reached its peak in the middle of the seventeenth century rather than at the end, as did the European LIA. This indicates a disjunction between the cooling trends in Europe and East Asia, probably because the extreme Orient is more exposed to the tempering influences of the Pacific Ocean, whereas Europe lies open to the fluctuations of the cooler North Atlantic. With the onset of global warming during the twentieth century and the increase in oscillations of El Niño signature, China also began to record more ENSO-related anomalies, and during recent decades, the effects of El Niño have been showing up with greater clarity and more intensity in the country's precipitation anomalies.

Japan differs from China in the way it receives and reacts to ENSO impulses because, little perturbed by continental influences, it is wide-open to the maritime stimuli from the Pacific Ocean and the warm Kuroshio Current. Also, the Japanese islands are located farther north than the tropics and subtropics of Asia and thus receive the brunt of ENSOs without continental interferences. El Niño developments in the eastern tropical Pacific mean that the usual pooling of warm waters in the western Pacific moves farther into the central Pacific than during normal years, so that the Kuroshio Current weakens. Accordingly, during such abnormal winters, an increase in cold air onslaughts from the Siberian high pressure brings freezing temperatures and dry air to most of Japan. During El Niño summers, the southeasterly monsoons that carry summer humidity to southern Japan and central China lose intensity, and cold, dry winters are followed by summers with lower than normal temperatures and a persistence of the *Bai'u* frontal precipitation.

Inversely, in years of normal air and ocean circulation across the tropical Pacific, the Kuroshio Current is adequately fed by the pooled warm waters in the western Pacific. This keeps winter temperatures up and provides enough humidity for abundant rains and snowfall, whereas during summer the Japanese islands receive sufficient precipitation from the strengthened monsoons. These normal conditions are more pronounced during La Niña years because of the greater contrast between the warm waters and humid air in the western Pacific and the cold waters in the eastern Pacific. According to Yoshino and Yasunari (1986), the *Bai'u* rainy spell disappears earlier during La Niña years, giving way to air masses from the overheated western Pacific, which generate tropical cyclones (*typhoons*) between the Philippines and Japan, including most of the Pacific rimlands of China, during late summer and fall.

As in the case of China, observations of environmental conditions were conducted in Japan much earlier than in the West. The flowering dates of cherry trees were meticulously recorded, as well as the years of summer dryness that reduced rice yields and led to regional famines. Observations of the length and intensity of the winters—so pertinent for determining El Niño occurrences in the Pacific—were carried out especially by religious castes, who considered such natural events to be messages from their deities. Just as Zhu Kezhen collected ancient records in China, H. Arakawa compiled historical data concerning the flowering dates of cherry trees in Kyoto since A.D. 800, the days with snow cover in Tokyo since the 1600s, and the freezing dates of Lake Suwa since 1443. Using daily weather observations kept in the archives of local Han governments since the Edo era (1770–1880), Japanese climatologists have been able to establish the onset, duration, and intensity of the *Bai'u* rains as indicators of upset climatic conditions over the Far East (Yoshino and Murata 1988).

Several of these reconstructed environmental series were interpreted by B. M. Gray (1974) in an attempt to associate extreme temperature and rainfall events with climatic anomalies elsewhere. The surface of Lake Suwa, located west of Tokyo at an elevation of 500 meters, usually freezes at the beginning of January; an early date heralds a severe winter ahead, a late date—as well as short duration of the superficial ice—announces a benign winter. Thus the records of Lake Suwa can be used to infer the weather situations that generated the temperature conditions of the years considered. Winters that are warmer than normal coincide with the mature phase of ENSO in the tropical Pacific and the passage to cooler waters in the eastern tropical Pacific, and vice versa in the western Pacific. The latter occurred during the winters of 1578–79, 1614–15, 1624–25, 1652–53, 1701–2, 1804–5, and 1828–29, which were El Niño years. Short-lived periods of snow cover in Tokyo occur early during years with cold waters along the equatorial Pacific and late in January during warm ENSO years in the tropical Pacific. This was particularly patent in 1720–21, 1728–29, and 1791–92, which were conspicuous El Niño years according to Hamilton and García (1986).

The analysis of the *Bai'u* rains conducted by Yoshino offers insights into the variability of rainfall in Japan, the lower part of the Yangtze River in China, and southern Korea. It is interesting to note that during the first half of the 1700s early summer rains were more abundant than during the second. Toward the end of the eighteenth century, the warming that anticipated the end of LIA spawned more frequent warm ENSOs and resulted in a surge of precipitation in the Pacific Asia rimlands (Figure 7.10). The drop in precipitation caused by the ENSO tranquility period of 1820–40 and the dip that occurred after the active 1870s are also recognizable in these series.

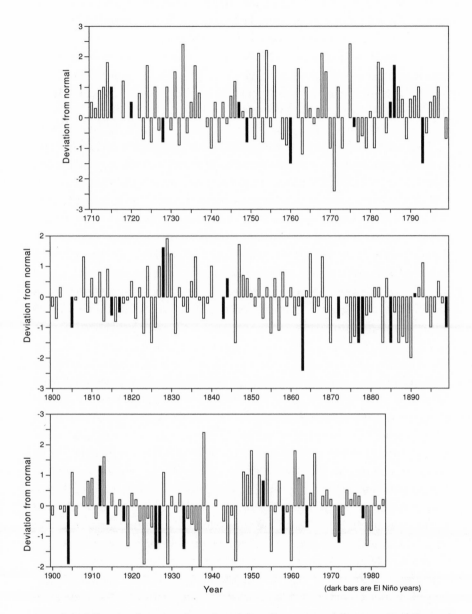

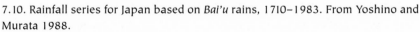

7.10. Rainfall series for Japan based on *Bai'u* rains, 1710–1983. From Yoshino and Murata 1988.

It is further possible to detect long-term trends from this proxy information. During warm periods in the last 1,500 years (when ENSO events were more frequent), central Japan showed warming tendencies, such as those of the first quarter of the 1500s, the early 1700s, the 1870s and 1880s, and the 1920s and 1940s (Lamb 1977). Cold periods with fewer ENSO occurrences, on the other hand, affected central Japan in the early 1600s (the height of LIA), in the late 1600s, and from the 1820s to the 1840s, thereby enhancing the tendencies toward drought and agricultural crises.

The interesting issue of relating cold and dry periods with harvest failures and ensuing famines has been tackled by Junsei Kondo (1988), using data from the Tohoku District in central Japan. He found that from A.D. 1300 to 1600, poor harvests were caused mainly by droughts and less often by untimely floods. During the seventeenth century, they were almost equally the result of floods and cold summers, droughts having been reduced by the construction of waterworks after the institution of the Tokugawa shogunate in A.D. 1600. The lean years and famines of the past 300 years seem to have been the consequence of cooler summers that affected the growing season of rice, and not so much of droughts or floods. Summer temperature drops on the order of 1.5°C reduced yields by up to 30 percent; in especially "lean" years, harvests were 80 percent below normal.

Kondo linked the cooler summers mainly to atmospheric dust from volcanic eruptions in the tropics and in Japan; the fine particles trap part of the incoming solar radiation and prevent the warming of the atmospheric layers below. He also noticed that the ocean off the District of Tohoku can be 1.5°C colder during these events than in normal years, which contributes to the cooling effect. Atmospheric temperature reductions are related to blocking conditions created by a persistent high pressure cell that will not allow the polar front's summertime northward shift—constituting another of the antecedents that reduced harvests and caused subsequent famines. The famines of 1783–86 in the wake of the eruption of Mount Asama in central Japan are famous; they were probably aggravated by the eruption of Mount Lakagiar on Iceland, where they also caused harvest shortages. It is interesting to note that a powerful El Niño was brewing in the Pacific during those two years. (As we will see in the last chapter, volcanic eruptions tend to precipitate the outbreak of ENSO events.) Another memorable famine, from 1835 to 1838, which was characterized by summer temperature reductions up to 2.5 °C, is linked by Kondo to the 1835 eruption of Mount Coseguina in Nicaragua; but in this case there was no ENSO development in the Pacific. The famous Krakatoa eruption in Indonesia, in 1883—which prompted a global cooling crisis but no immediate El Niño event—lowered summer temperatures and caused poor rice yields also in Japan. In 1902, by contrast, a reduced rice harvest coincided with volcanic eruptions in the Antilles (La Soufrière, St. Vincent) and in Guatemala (Mount Santa Maria), both of which have been associated with the onset of a moderate ENSO episode in that year. Kondo relates the poor harvests of 1912 to the eruption of the Novarupta-Katmai volcano in Alaska, the impact of which was probably compounded by the development of the 1911–12 El Niño in the tropical Pacific. A series of poor harvests in the early 1930s can be linked to the global climatic crisis that surrounded El Niño 1932, the dust bowl years in the North American Midwest being one of its manifestations. Kondo's data also reveals low rice yields during the early 1940s, when no volcanos erupted but one of the century's major El Niño events occurred, in 1940–42. In the recent past, reduced harvests coincided with the eruption of Mount St. Helens in 1980—when conditions in the Pacific basin were not altered—and the eruption of Mount El Chichón in Mexico in 1982 on the eve of El Niño 1982–83, the most powerful of the twentieth century.

In many particular details, the Chinese and Japanese studies reveal close ties between their countries' historical climatic variations and major anomalies in the tropical Pacific basin. This valuable evidence supports the assertion that El Niño effects have been felt not only in the present but also in the past, as attested by the severe food shortages and environmental crises that such phenomena imprinted in the history of these populous and ancient countries.

8

~

Traces in the Misty Past

El Niño—the name attesting to its Hispanic roots—is eminently a phenomenon of South American climatology. The effects of the perturbations of the tropical Pacific on nature and humans were observed first and foremost on the west coast of South America. Throughout this book it has been demonstrated that the effects of oceanic and meteorological El Niños can also be detected in distant regions by scrutinizing the historical sources of those regions for climatic crises. While going farther back in time than instrumental climatological series, the historical series are less reliable and seldom go beyond the last millennium—which is where, until recently, the search for traces of past El Niños ended. However, since the extremely strong El Niño occurrences in recent decades have provided a clearer picture of their environmental impact and allowed us to place their sequels in a coherent system, geochronological techniques have become a reliable and justifiable means of identifying traces of El Niño in the misty past.

The first attempts to unveil prehistoric El Niño events were undertaken by archeologists and sedimentologists associated with the Chicago Field Museum. From depositions left by swollen rivers during contemporary El Niño events in northern Peru, they inferred the existence of similar occurrences in fossil sediments (Nials et al. 1979). This initiative opened the door both for investigations of coastal lagoon depositions, marine faunal changes in littoral environments, and changes in river morphology that threw light on climatic changes along coastal Peru, and for ice core analyses that establish not only the sequences of mighty El Niño occurrences but also their approximate dates. In this way, Quinn's historical El Niño chronology could be complemented with a time series from ages for which no human testimonies exist. It was revealed that powerful El Niño–like phenomena had occurred before the arrival of the Spaniards and that these episodes had been particularly strong during certain periods in the first millennium A.D. and early in the second millennium. Some were not only intense but also of prolonged duration, so archeologists and geologists started to use the term *mega-Niño*. Their research unearthed such prehistoric mega-occurrences in A.D. 1000–1100, ± 600, and 511–14, which is close to a climatic period between 800 to 1300 called the Medieval Warm Period. During that period, as mild temperatures and warm summers became more frequent, settlements and plowland in northern Europe were pushed farther north. With the northern seas free of drifting ice, Norse navigators undertook voyages of discovery and colonization into Iceland and Greenland, and from there even ventured into Labrador and the St. Lawrence River in North America. New agricultural frontiers were opened in forested regions and high-altitude areas of central Europe in a process known as *Rodungsperiode*, deforestation period, which added more sustainable space for the growing populations. The rather benign period neared its end in northern Europe with spasmodic cold outbreaks in A.D. 1210 and 1320, announcing the coming of the Little Ice Age that established itself between the end of the 1400s and the mid-1500s.

What were the consequences of the Medieval Warm Period for the tropical belt in general and the tropical oceans in particular? The inferred global temperature increase between 0.8° and 1.4°C must also have raised temperatures in the tropical oceans, which activated water circulation in meridional (north-south) and zonal (east-west, west-east) directions. The ocean-mass exchanges, the energy and humidity exports, and the storminess that characterize contemporary El Niño episodes must have been maximized during the outbursts of mega-Niños in tropical latitudes. Likewise, the compensatory humidity deficits experienced in some tropical regions during El Niño episodes must have been exacerbated. In the Americas, prehistoric El Niños no doubt led to prolonged droughts in interior regions and increased rainfall in many Pacific rimlands.

Based on these considerations, this chapter presents three cases of cultural changes induced by mighty El Niños for which we have only archeological evidence. The examples chosen from coastal South America, the central Andes, and Amazonia have all been associated with anomalies that originated over the Pacific Ocean, but considering the present state of knowledge concerning the impact of prehistoric ENSOs, one can only speculate whether civilization collapses in Central America and Africa during those times were distant echoes of El Niño.

In Search of Mega-Niños

The search for powerful El Niños of the past begins with the assumption that imprints similar to those left on the landscapes and ecologies by major contemporary episodes are preserved in geological and paleoecological records and that, in areas considered as *prime regions* for contemporary El Niños, these imprints or scars are easier to recognize than in distant regions that receive only weak echoes of these disturbances. Therefore, the search for traces of mega-Niños has concentrated mainly on the waters and islands of the equatorial Pacific, on the coastal fringes of western South America—especially northern and southern Peru, as well as northern Chile—the Andean mountains and plateaus, and the lowlands of Amazonia. Given the tremendous impact of the El Niño events of 1997, 1982, 1972, and 1925 on the landforms, fauna, and flora of these regions and the voluminous scientific documentation produced, those years serve as models for the effects that past mega-Niños may have had.

Michael Moseley was one of the first archeologists interested in tracing pre-Hispanic El Niños. Observing the thick alluvia deposited by northern Peruvian rivers during rainy years of contemporary times, he realized that uncovering these types of depositions and establishing firm dating bases would enable him to recognize the impact of past El Niños on the ecology of northern Peru. Moseley and his coworkers identified thick river depositions from heavy rains—El Niño events—that seem to have occurred around A.D. 511–12, 546, 576, 600, 612, 650, 681, and 1100. Encouraged by these findings, scores of geologists flocked to coastal Peru in search of alluvions that might be traces of prehistoric El Niños. Their endeavors resulted in identifying El Niño–like episodes around A.D. 1450, 1300, 1100, 600, and 500 (Thompson, Mosley-Thompson, Thompson 1992). Moving the time sequence back even farther, geologists studying the sedimentation in a mountain lake in southern Ecuador (Rodbell et al. 1999) claim that El Niños occurred as long ago as 10,500 years B.P., while sedimentological studies from ponds on the Galapagos Islands—near the center of the prime El Niño region—detected traces of La Niña–like episodes from 6170 and 5070 B.P. (Steinitz-Kannan et al. 1998). For traces to be still recognizable today, they must have been left by extremely powerful and long-lived ENSO events, which raises the question whether prehistoric El Niños occurred with the same frequency as contemporary ones, that is, at intervals of three and a half to six years.

Geologists believe that the interval of recurrences before 5000 B.C. was fifteen years and that for this reason the traces of prehistoric El Niños are more discernable. How far back have these specialists been able to detect such anomalies? On this point, there is significant disagreement: while some claim that El Niños are traceable only after 5000 B.C.—that is, when our geological period, the Holocene, was well advanced (Sandweiss et al. 1996)—others move the temporal scale back as far as 8000 and even 40,000 years B.P., based on river deposits found interbedded with sediments that correspond roughly to those created by torrential rains in today's arid climate of coastal Peru (Wells and Noller 1997).

Adding to the controversy, two paleoecologists, L. E. Heusser and F. Sirocko, contend that climatological variations of the character and intensity of major contemporary El Niños can be traced back to 17,000 B.P., based on evidence gathered from pollen of conifers (pine and junipers) and oak species in marine sediments from the basin of Santa Barbara, California. These authors go so far as to relate these traces of major El Niños to similar deposits in the Indian Ocean and on the east coast of Asia, thus lending more credibility to the assertion that past El Niño events affected not only the whole Pacific basin and its rimlands but also the Indian Ocean, just as the major El Niño occurrences of the present do.

El Niño–like phenomena—both climatic and oceanic—have probably existed since the separation of the eastern Pacific Ocean from the western Atlantic Ocean. During the geological periods when the two oceans were connected (Figure 8.1), there must have been a steady circulation of warm

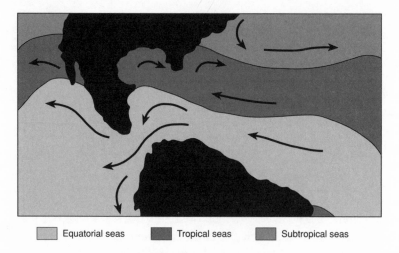

Equatorial seas   Tropical seas   Subtropical seas

8.1. Circulation between the Atlantic and the Pacific Oceans before the formation of the Central American land bridge

water from east to west and vice versa, so that no differentiation between them existed. With the formation of the land bridge between North and South America in the course of the mountain-building processes of the Andes and the chains of Central America, exchanges between tropical Atlantic and tropical Pacific came to an end. An oceanic circulation dictated by the new geography of the Pacific basin was established with two circuits on each side of the equator, rotating clockwise in the northern hemisphere and counterclockwise in the southern hemisphere. These impelled cool upwelling waters from high into low latitudes along the west coasts of North and South America and then westward north and south along the equatorial line (Figure 8.2). Complementary to the ocean circulation over the eastern Pacific, two powerful high pressure cells were established that became the sources of the trade winds over the tropics of the Pacific Ocean and propellers of the surface ocean circulations. This assumption is based on elaborations by the German paleoecologist Peter P. Smolka, who used fossil foraminiferal records to reconstruct sea temperatures for the geological period between 21 and 1 million years B.P. (Smolka 1991). In the period between 7 and 6 million years ago, he noted a suggestive difference in temperatures on the Atlantic and Pacific sides of what today is the Isthmus of Panama, and a conspicuously cooler Pacific Ocean. Is this an indication that by that time the Central American continental bridge was completed and the two oceans initiated their independent existence? If so, independent oceanic and meteorological developments for both oceans should have begun in the Neogene. Since El Niño is a condition inherent in the circulation patterns of the whole Pacific Ocean, it might be assumed that El Niño–like phenomena showed for the first time during that epoch. There remains the question of geochronological proof. Geological experts have been able to document the crucial transition from the warmer Tertiary to the cooler Quaternary with the help of sediment interpretation.

As to the impact of such major climatic changes on the lowlands east of the Andes, there are repetitive dry periods from the Caribbean shores of South America to the Rio de la Plata plains that point to the manifestations characteristic of El Niño in western South America. Pollen evidence from the tropical lowlands suggests that the dominant tropical forests were briefly replaced by savanna grasses in some locations, which must have prompted adaptations not only by plants and animals of the regions involved but also by the human populations. Studies by archeologists and environmentalists in the tropical lands of South America are yielding valuable clues about the ways in which paleo-Niños impacted that part of the continent.

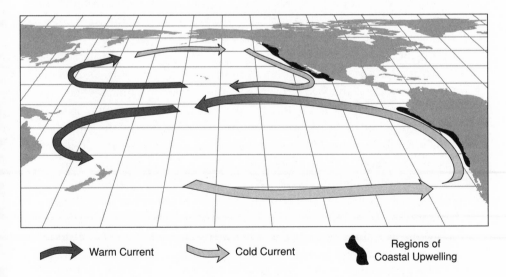

Warm Current   Cold Current   Regions of Coastal Upwelling

8.2. Anticyclonic circuits of the Pacific Ocean after its separation from the Atlantic Ocean

Floods and Devastation in the Chimor Land of Peru

The prehistoric significance of these phenomena for cultural transformations in northern Peru, especially the segment that is today the primary focus of El Niño, should not be downplayed. As presented in chapter 3, this is the region where Francisco Pizarro and his men initiated their thrust into the Inca empire and where we have the first coherent references to the climatic consequences of El Niño. Geological and cultural evidence strongly attests to the impact of these phenomena on nature and humans long before the arrival of the Spaniards.

Northernmost Peru depends on the sea and the rivers for its survival. The sea provides year-round fish and transportation, while the rivers born from the ice caps of the Andes supply water and sediments to the fertile oases. It is not surprising, therefore, that the earliest and most advanced coastal cultures of prehistoric Peru established themselves in these lands. The implications of being the "prime land" of El Niño became very clear to me during a survey of the region after the powerful 1972–73 and 1982–83 El Niño occurrences (Caviedes 1975, 1984). The sight of the devastations in the river oases caused by contemporary torrential downpours and floods raised questions about the damages of prehistoric El Niños and their impacts on cultural development and population expansion. So archeologists—starting with Fred Nials, Izumi Shimada, and Michael Moseley—focused their research on the implications of those events for cultural development.

Before the beginning of our era, communities of cultivators and fishermen were well established along the Lambayeque, Chicama, Moche, and Virú Rivers (Figure 8.3). Their subsequent cultural advancement is most notably reflected in the pyramids, goldwork, and pottery of the Moche, or Mochica, who migrated from the Moche River across the north coast during the first seven centuries after Christ. Agricultural land was expanded by extensive irrigation works to feed an increasing population. The Moche also erected pyramids of adobe bricks that served for religious ceremonies and as burial places for their rulers. Between the Piura River in the north and the Nepeña River in the south, ruins of such mud-brick constructions called *huacas* are found in practically every valley (Plate 8).

The continuance of the numerous Moche centers was repeatedly disrupted by floods, droughts, and earthquakes. El Niño episodes in A.D. 511–12, 546, and 576 severely damaged irrigation works and raised-field

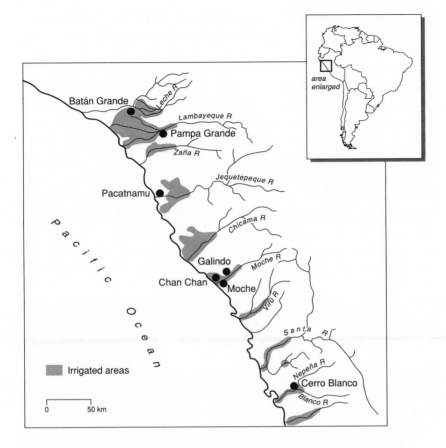

8.3. Irrigated river oases and cultural centers of northern Peru

structures, and an extended period of dryness from 562 to 594 devastated the oases and left the landscape deeply scarred (Moseley 1992). After severe flooding in A.D. 600, the capital at Cerro Blanco was abandoned, and a new center was established at Pampa Grande on the Lambayeque River, inland from modern Chiclayo. Further El Niño episodes in A.D. 612, 650, and 681 wrought havoc on the agricultural communities of the area and forced the political powers to move to Sipan, also on the Lambayeque River but closer to the coast. Around A.D. 700, the center at Pampa Grande was abandoned, the cultivated land destroyed or silted, and the raised fields ruined by the recurrent floods. Many of the carefully constructed canals were razed, and once fertile fields reverted to barren land.

Around A.D. 800, the Moche were assimilated by the Chimú, whose capital was Chan Chan, located near the mouth of the Moche River not far from the present city of Trujillo. The captial of the Chimú kingdom, which counted some 30,000 inhabitants at one time, had its share of natural catastrophes. Around A.D. 1100, a powerful El Niño was visited upon most of the tropical Pacific and tropical South America, changing the destiny of the people living there. The northern Chimú center at Batán Grande on the upper La Leche River was heavily flooded and became uninhabitable due to sediment accumulations. The town of Chotuna in the Lambayeque Valley was also devastated by the torrential rains and high floods, but, unlike Batán Grande, it was subsequently rebuilt. The same massive flooding caused the thriving center of Pacatnamu in the Jequetepeque Valley to break away from both the old Moche and the new Chimú cultural influences (Donnan 1987). During that major El Niño episode, the irrigation systems all along the Moche River and in the city of Chan Chan were severely damaged.

The magnitude of the A.D. 1100 mega-Niño in the circum-Pacific rimlands is reflected in a major cultural change on Easter Island around that time, probably associated with the arrival of a new wave of Polynesian settlers. On the shores of Lake Titicaca, the Tiwanaku culture underwent a rapid decline between A.D. 1100 and 1200, and a severe drought that caused profound cultural discontinuities in the Amazon lowlands has been reported by Betty Meggers (1994b).

Similar events around A.D. 1300 point to another major El Niño occurrence that has been archeologically documented in several places of coastal Peru. Those natural disasters ended the Chimú dominance at Pacatnamu (Donnan 1987), caused significant cultural disruptions in Chincha, several hundred miles south (Moore 1991), and left deep imprints on the landscapes and farming communities in the Casma Valley (Wells 1990). Entire portions of the Peruvian coast were elevated by tectonic activity; canals and waterworks were wrecked, and the abandonment of formerly productive land was accelerated (Moseley 1983).

In 1470, the Chimú state succumbed to the Inca from Cuzco, who exiled many of the Chan Chan artisans into that southern city. True to their inland origin, the Inca chose Catamarca in the northern Sierra and away from the sea as the site of their second capital. In Catamarca the fateful meeting between Francisco Pizarro and the Inca Atahualpa took place in 1533.

The reported sequence of catastrophic incidents shows the highest frequency of droughts and floods over the time span during which the power center moved from Cerro Blanco to Pampa Grande; that is, from A.D. 500 to 700. This period coincides with the inception of the Medieval Warm Period in Europe, during which—as explained in the previous chapter—the activated tropical circulation raised temperatures world-wide and effected changes in the wind and water circulations of the major oceans. The warm climate and favorable winds allowed the colonization of frontier lands in the North Atlantic (Iceland and Greenland) and made possible the landfall of Viking seafarers in North America. It is interesting to note that the scientific literature on climatic oscillations, cultural changes, and population displacements in pre-Hispanic South America mentions no El Niño events between 1100 and the early 1500s, except for the major El Niño of A.D. 1300—a reflection of the fact that the global cooling associated with the Little Ice Age was already setting in during that period, resulting in less energy transfers from overheated tropical oceans into the atmosphere and, therefore, a climatically less active tropical belt. El Niño signature phenomena returned again during the short warm interlude of the early 1500s, just in time to "welcome" the first Spanish conquerors to Peru.

The chronology of climatic crises and their cultural correlates applied in the north Peruvian oases is based chiefly on datings conducted by Lonnie G. Thompson and associates (Thompson and Mosley-Thompson 1992) of sediment carbon samples from the Quelccaya ice cap on the Eastern Cordillera of Peru, at latitude 14 °S. There, under the influence of the altiplano and the bend in the Andes chain, the imprints left by droughts and wet periods differ from those left between latitudes 4° and 7°S, where the air-flows are more zonal in character; that is, in the direction of the parallels. I believe that the ice cores of the Huascarán ice cap at latitude 9 °S are better suited for tracing the climatic crises that affected northern coastal Peru in pre-Hispanic times because they are not only closer to the Pacific Ocean but they reflect more accurately the effects of humid air flows coming from the interior of the Amazon basin. Also pertinent are the climate sequences inferred from the sediment accumulations at the bottom of Lake Pallcacocha in the southern Ecuadorean Andes at latitude 4 °S, where El Niño effects arrive straight from the equatorial Pacific. Sediment layers at the lake bottom depict a transition from cold depositions during the late glacial period in the Andes around 12,300 B.P. to storm-accumulated sediments more typical of the warmer times thereafter. Prolonged El Niño episodes of postglacial age are represented by coarser particles and more abundant sedimentation. The mega-Niños of pre-Hispanic times, mentioned above, emerge with greater precision, particularly those of A.D. 1100, 730, and 500, which means that Thompson's Huascarán-based chronology is more applicable to the major El Niño occurrences that affected the thriving communities of the northern coast (Thompson et al. 1995).

These detailed studies prove that the powerful El Niños between A.D. 1000 and 1100 were of great magnitude and prompted significant cultural revolutions and population movements among the peoples of South America and the South Pacific. The last two sections of this chapter will examine how the climatic oscillations during this time and a higher frequency of mega-Niños enticed Polynesian navigators to venture into the vastness of the eastern Pacific and eventually find Easter Island during one of those episodes.

Traces in the Ice and Lakes of the Andes

The search for prehistoric El Niños took us first to the prime region in northern Peru where ENSO disturbances triggered cultural evolutions or caused disruptions among the diverse communities living in that region. Archeological evidence, as well as absolute or relative dating techniques, enables us to establish with reasonable exactitude the times when extreme wetness and severe droughts occurred. In this manner, progress in archeological prospecting and geochronological sequencing has definitely increased the identification of these earlier El Niños. There are few places in South America and the Pacific rimlands where the results arrived at through these methodologies reflect climatic fluctuations and associated cultural changes without interference from other environmental factors; the high plateau of the altiplano is one of them.

The impact of climatic crises on the populations at this important South American crossroads has been studied by archeologists and geoscientists since it was realized that the Titicaca lakeshores were the cradle of one of the first organized societies of the Andes and the birthplace of the impressive Tiwanaku culture, the predecessor of the Inca. Abundant water from springs and temporary streams and large herds of guanacos (wild llamas) attracted early hunter-gatherer groups to the altiplano, where some 18,000 years ago, melting waters from Eastern Cordillera glaciers had created a lake system extending from the edge of the southern Peruvian Andes into northern Chile and northwestern Argentina (see Figure 5.4). As the climate at the "bend" of the continent became drier—probably because the cold Peru Current and the Pacific wind systems had been established—the lakes entered a process of punctuated desiccation. Connections between them were severed; the shallower ones became the salt flats of today, such as the Coipasa and Uyuni, and the larger ones—the muddy Lake Poopó and the clear-water Lake Titicaca—underwent a process of evaporation that has not yet ceased. Nineteenth-century naturalists, observing ancient shores perched above the contemporary lakeshore, suspected that the climate had been more humid and the lakes more extensive in the past. Pioneer archeologists of the altiplano, such as Max Uhle, realized that the humid conditions could have supported a much larger population and a flourishing culture in these now-parched lands.

References to lake levels as much as 100 feet higher at the time of the Tiwanaku culture's maximum splendor were exaggerations by early Spanish chroniclers, which nevertheless spawned the story that the Tiwanaku center, today some twenty kilometers from the lakeshore, was once situated by the lake and that the Tiwanaku people had spread their culture from this vantage point into southern Peru (Plate 9). There is no doubt that decisive fluctuations in the altiplano water balance played a crucial role in the cultural revolutions that took place, particularly in the Titicaca Lake basin.

Recent research by Mark Abbott and coworkers (1997) tackled the question of the connections between changes in the level of Lake Titicaca during the last 3.5 millennia and major climatic oscillations registered in the central Andes. A long column of lake sediments that spans these 3500 years revealed extended periods of desiccation starting 3500–3350 years B.P., followed by other lengthy episodes around 900–800, 400–200 B.C., A.D. 1–300, and 1100–1500. Since El Niño developments in the tropical Pacific correlate today with dryness in the altiplano, as explained in chapter 5, it is appropriate to assume that those dry periods mirrored powerful mega-Niños in the Pacific.

In the 1980s, when it became clear that the Pacific Ocean causes climatic variability across the tropical belt of South America and that dryness dominates east of the Andes during El Niño, glaciologists started to look for indications of past El Niños in the Quelccaya ice cap on the Eastern Cordillera of southern Peru, which receives its moisture from the sub-humid savanna lowlands of Bolivia and Brazil. It is not surprising that Lonnie Thompson and his collaborators detected thin ice sheet sequences containing larger amounts of microparticles and peculiar oxygen isotopes than on the Huascarán ice cores that indicate periods of drier-than-usual atmospheric conditions. By analogy with contemporary air flow conditions, they related these dry periods to El Niño episodes in the tropical Pacific, and the thicker ice sheets with fewer dust particles and plenty of oxygen to non–El Niño years, when the humidity is carried by strong winds from the east. Based on these distinctions, the researchers were able to trace in the Quelccaya ice cap and more recently in the Sajama ice cap, Bolivia, wet and dry climate periods as far back as 1500 B.P. It can be inferred that severe reductions in the water volume of Lake Titicaca should have occurred during dry periods around A.D. 524–40, 563–94, 636–45, and 1100–1450, whereas higher precipitation would have raised lake levels around A.D. 636–45 and from A.D. 1500 to 1700—the latter corresponding to the generalized wetter and cooler climate of the Little Ice Age.

The results of these investigations also underscore the role played by climatic variations as elicitors of cultural change in the central Andes. Since these fluctuations depend on ENSO occurrences in the tropical Pacific, the changed destinies of cultures in the altiplano and southern Sierras can be regarded as closely interwoven with those global phenomena. Analyzing depositions from the shores of Lake Titicaca, Michael W. Binford and his collaborators refined the coarse chronology established with the help of the Quelccaya ice cores, which enabled them to make cultural inferences from the changes found in the lake sediments. Before 1500 B.C., the environmental aridity of the altiplano—reflected in lower lake levels—prevented the development of agriculture, but several rebounds in lake levels thereafter and up to the beginning of our era indicate corresponding periods of generalized humidity (Figure 8.4). During those times, farming communities of the Chiripá culture established themselves around the lake, supplanting the herder and hunting bands of the preceding dry epoch. After a relapse to drier conditions at the beginning of our era that severely tested the survival capacity of the emerging Tiwanaku culture, the humidity increased again and attained particularly high levels between A.D. 350 and 500, when raised fields for farming purposes came into use on the lakeshores. These earthen platforms

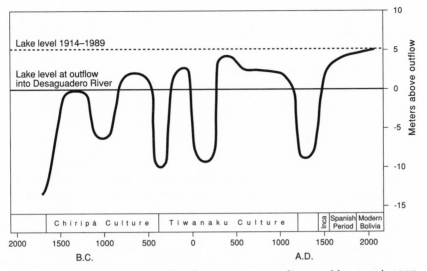

8.4. Lake Titicaca levels and cultural sequences according to Abbott et al. 1997

about one meter above the oscillating subsoil water level provide good drainage and aeration, while, at the same time, the humidity in the soil prevents drastic drops in temperature. It is estimated that the period of maximum raised-field construction lasted from about A.D. 600 to 1100, concurrent with the further development of the Tiwanaku culture and its expansion beyond the boundaries of the altiplano. Interestingly enough, the demise of that culture began toward the end of the 1100s due to a period of severe dryness that was experienced equally in the Amazon basin and the circum-Caribbean lowlands, while in the eastern Pacific, Polynesian scouts were landing on Easter Island.

Although rebounds in humidity over the altiplano caused lake levels to rise between A.D. 1230 and 1300—when the first symptoms of the Little Ice Age appeared in the northern hemisphere—the pervasive dryness from A.D. 1100 to 1450 is deemed responsible for the decay of the Tiwanaku culture and the relocation of the political power to the highlands of Cuzco, the heartland of the Inca empire. At the time of the Spanish arrival, the once flourishing agricultural communities of the altiplano still looked depressed, but the raised humidity corresponding to the beginning of the Little Ice Age was probably the reason for the proliferation of ephemeral lakes in these outlying confines of the Inca empire. With good reasons, Spanish colonial administrators called this region the Province of Charcas—*charca* being the Spanish word for "shallow pond."

We now leave the central Andean upland region and move on to the tropical lowlands east of the Andes, to examine the drying effects of pre-Hispanic El Niños on precipitation in this area and the cultural disruptions they caused among its populations.

Population Contractions in Prehistoric Amazonia

Not until the occurrence of El Niño 1972–73 was much attention paid to the rainfall anomalies caused by this phenomenon in other regions of South America. After that event, while I was reviewing the monthly precipitation data for the tropical lowlands east of the Andes, the values from the station of Uaupés caught my eye, because during El Niño years the summer rainfall there was lower than during other summers. The records of Uaupés (now Cachoeira de São Gabriel)—on the first rapids of the Uaupés River, which originates in the eastern Andes of Colombia—reflected quite accurately the rainfall decreases during El Niño years and the increases during known La Niña years (Figure 8.5). Subsequent El Niño occurrences in 1982–83 and 1992–94, and data from several other Amazonian stations with records prior to the 1970s, confirmed this tendency, indicating that most of the central Amazon region responds negatively—that is, with decreased humidity—to warm ENSO episodes in the tropical Pacific.

Archeologists investigating prehistoric sites and cultural sequences in the Amazon basin subsequently detected the cultural impact of severe dry episodes and dated them using carbon-14 techniques. The environmental effects caused by contemporary climatic anomalies permit a visualization of what could have happened during past major El Niño events (mega-Niños). The investigations of anthropologist Betty Meggers of the Smithsonian Institution into the link between El Niño events and droughts in the Amazon basin and other tropical regions east of the Andes provide a fascinating example of archeological findings being interpreted in the light of, and serving to corroborate, El Niños that occurred in the mist of time.

Meggers (1994b) postulates that periodic displacements of native populations as well as cultural innovations during the last two millennia occurred in response to subsistence stress caused by catastrophic droughts that need not have been of prolonged duration to exert lasting effects. These crises, which are also registered in pollen profiles from tropical sites indicating temporary vegetation alterations, must have been triggered by climatic oscillations similar to those of the present, since no large-scale climate changes have taken place in the Amazon basin during the past 6,000 years (Colinvaux and Oliveira 2000). The same ecological defacements that have been observed in the rain forest and peripheral sub-humid savannas during recent El Niño events must have affected the sedentary communities that sustained their livelihood through agriculture, hunting, and fishing. Agricultural productivity shrinks, game diminishes during dry episodes, fish populations dwindle, and natural forests as well as planted fields are constantly threatened by wildfire.

Reasonably accurate pollen chronologies coupled with reliable absolute dating techniques have identified episodic overlappings of forests and savannas in peripheral regions of the Amazon basin around 1500, 1200, 700, and 400 B.P. (Absy 1985; Bush 1991) Betty Meggers suggests that these episodes identify droughts inflicted by mega-Niños, which are also reflected in abrupt discontinuities in the archeological sequences of the Amazon basin and peripheral landscapes. The term *discontinuity* is applied in varied ways. It may mean: terminations or interruptions in the occupational sequence of a locality due to temporary abandonment; changes in styles of material culture elements, particularly ceramics, that attest to intrusions by other natives or to stimulation through contacts with outside groups; or linguistic diversification as a consequence of migrations precipitated by climatic stress. Since language is an appropriate criterion for identifying relationships among the various peoples who inhabited the Amazon basin and contiguous tropical grasslands, we will include this topic in our discussion.

Languages in Amazonia display an amazing heterogeneity for such a vast but homogeneous landscape. This diversity evolved due to frequent displacements, deculturation (by contact with alien groups, including the Spaniards and Portuguese), as well as genetic intermixing and cultural interbreeding. Two major linguistic branches are recognized in the tropical lowlands of South America: (1) the Gé-Pano-Carib speakers, who dwell mainly in the open woodlands and tropical savannas of eastern Brazil (home of the Gé), western Amazonia (area of the Pano), and the northeastern tropical lowlands and Caribbean Islands (domain of the Caribs); (2) the Arawakan and Tupian speakers, who intruded from the west and established themselves along the Amazon River and its tributaries, forcing the original inhabitants into peripheral locations (Figure 8.5).

Studies of language differentiation in time—glottochronology—place the beginning of diversification into sublanguages within the first branch some 5000 years ago, with the most recent diversifications taking place around 1500, 1000, and 700–500 B.P., which also correspond to climatic crises that affected the interfaces of forests and tropical grasslands mentioned above. In addition, the diversity and spatial distribution of the language groups in the South American tropical lowlands are accompanied by genetic differentiations that followed the dispersal and subsequent isolation of segments of formerly unified populations. Thus the crises provoked by past mega-Niños had profound implications even for the nonmaterial cultures of the people of Amazonia.

As to elements of material culture, multiple discontinuities occurred in ceramic styles, consisting of abrupt changes from earlier traditions to derivative new ones; this suggests fragmentation of original communities followed by cultural drift or replacement of the original community or its assimilation by newcomers (Meggers 1994a). The carbon-14 dates indicate the changes took place within short periods of time about 1500, 1000, 700, and 400 B.P., which coincide with the dry periods and some of the linguistic discontinuities mentioned above. Meggers identifies sudden replacements of ceramic styles or traditions in peripheral areas, such as the Llanos de Mojos in eastern Bolivia and on the island of Marajó on the lower Amazon, as well as along major tributaries of the Amazon River, showing the wide extent of these disruptions. Even more compelling is her evidence of climate-induced discontinuities in ceramic traditions from the Caribbean region that point not only to changes in material culture but also to episodes of dispersion in the search for alternative food sources when the communities were threatened by drought, and reoccupation once the climatic stress was over. These material culture findings also serve as confirmation of rain deficiencies north of the Amazon basin caused by contemporary El Niño events. In regions close to the Orinoco River, the largest stream north of the Amazon, indications of cultural discontinuities and site abandonments seem to be concurrent with mega-Niños in 1500, 1000, and 700 B.P. Discontinuities are dated around 1500 and 1000 B.P. at El Cuartel on Venezuela's Caribbean coast, and the site was abandoned around 700 B.P. Clearly indicative of the ecological bottlenecks caused by the droughts of mega-Niños in these coastal locations is the fact that populations turned from using mainly terrestrial food resources (game, fowl, berries) to exploiting marine resources, an alterna-

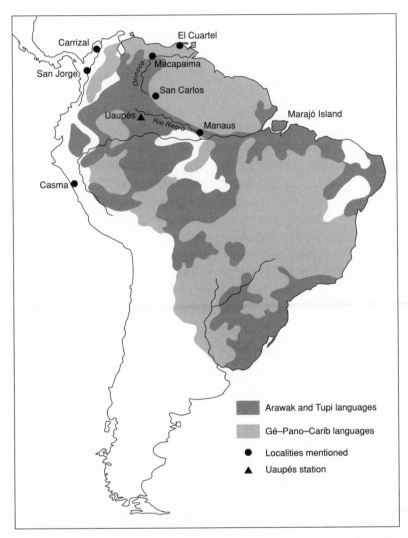

8.5. Major language families of Amazonia and places mentioned in this chapter. Adapted from Meggers 1994a.

tive not available to the native communities in the interior. Findings from the even drier environments of northern Colombia attest to the severe effects of mega-Niños around 1000, 700, and 500 years B.P. that caused devastating droughts, site abandonments, and reoccupations by groups with new ceramic traditions as on the San Jorge River and at Carrizal in the swampy lowlands south of the Caribbean coast.

As further evidence for these distant effects of past El Niños, Meggers mentions pollen profiles that document climatic changes as far back as 4000 years B.P., indicating brief but change-inducing periods of dryness in 1500, 1200, 700, and 400 B.P. Residues of catastrophic conflagrations are also interpreted as evidence of strong El Niño episodes. Recent examples of the ecological effects of forest burnings are the fires that broke out in the Rio Negro area in 1912—at the end of the ENSO episode of 1911—claiming the lives of hundreds of rubber collectors; the forest fire of 1926, which burned out of control for a full month during the decaying phase of the 1925 El Niño; and the wildfires of the early 1940s in concurrence with the extended ENSO of 1940–42. In the course of the 1972 El Niño event, the cultivation plots of Yanomama Indians were destroyed by fires, and the natives were forced to leave their villages and revert to gathering-and-hunting activities for their survival. Charcoal residues in the soil at San Carlos in southern Venezuela—the site of a widespread conflagration at the height of the major 1982–83 El Niño—are also related by Meggers to droughts caused by prehistoric El Niños which in the Casma Valley, northern Peru are reflected by mighty river sediments from catastrophic floods. Close temporal proximity between catastrophic events of different natures in these two distant places appear again around A.D. 500, 1330, 1460, 1628, and 1750, with the first two events fitting well the archeological discontinuities already mentioned and lending more support to the argument that the occurrence of severe droughts in the eastern lowlands of South America can be inferred from linguistic fragmentations, cultural differentiation, pollen profiles, and catastrophic fires.

West Winds Sweep Polynesians toward New Lands

Ben Finney loves his profession and is very resolute in his research. An anthropologist at the University of Hawaii, he wanted to find out how prehistoric navigators from the ancestral home of the Polynesian culture conducted long-distance travel in the open ocean and even crossed the dreaded equatorial calms to finally arrive in the Hawaiian archipelago.

Not satisfied with academic theory, Finney set out to discover for himself how this feat was accomplished. In 1976, he assembled a group of Hawaiians of Polynesian ancestry with the purpose of sailing from Hawaii to Tahiti in a traditionally built double-hull canoe, the *Hōkūle'a*, and using traditional Polynesian navigating techniques. On the thirty-two-day (5,370 kilometer) voyage, the navigators took advantage of the north hemispheric northeast trades to sail into the region of the equatorial calms—where they idled for nearly a week—and then moved faster toward Tahiti, sailing diagonally to the south hemispheric southeast trades. The return leg was accomplished in only twenty-two days due to a more expeditious passage through the equatorial calms and to the steadiness of the northeast trades (Finney 1977). The experience of sailing first southward diagonally to the northern trades, then idling in the equatorial calms, and finally slanting across the southern trades proved the feasibility of prehistoric Polynesian vessels to sail against the wind and prepared Finney's crew to undertake another venture in the *Hōkūle'a* at the end of 1985, this time within the confines of the South Pacific.

The purpose of the new voyage was to test the factual background of an oral tradition among the Maori of New Zealand's North Island, which tells of ancestors coming from Hawaiki (Tahiti) via Rarotonga, and to confirm the Rarotongan dialect's similarity to the Maori language. During a sixteen-day voyage in late November and early December 1985, the navigators of the *Hōkūle'a* had to deal head-on with the changing seasonal winds and storms that arise over the warm ocean during the southern summer (Figure 8.6); still, on December 8, they sailed into the Bay of Islands on New Zealand's North Island (Bayaban et al. 1987).

Before proceeding any farther, we should have some knowledge of the process by which the islands throughout the vast expanses of the Pacific were populated. The first inhabitants arrived on the western Pacific islands in the third millennium B.C. probably from the Malayan peninsula. Around 1500 B.C. these Proto-Polynesians—the ancestors of today's South Seas inhabitants—were established on the string of islands east of New Guinea called Melanesia, and around 1300 B.C. they seem to have reached Fiji. In successive "hops" they proceeded to the Tonga archipelago and colonized the islands of Samoa probably at the beginning of the first millennium B.C. Larger in size and richer in resources, Samoa

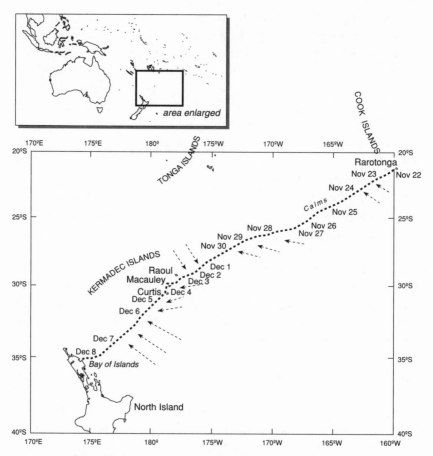

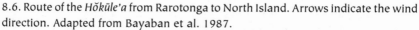

8.6. Route of the *Hōkūle'a* from Rarotonga to North Island. Arrows indicate the wind direction. Adapted from Bayaban et al. 1987.

became the cradle of this now genuine "Polynesian" civilization. From Vava'u (Samoa), audacious seafarers undertook further voyages of discovery and colonization to the north, where they eventually happened upon the Hawaiian Islands; to the southeast to Rarotonga and Aotearoa (the North Island of New Zealand); and westward to Tahiti and the Marquesas Islands.

At the beginning of our era, population pressures seem to have sent Polynesian navigators roaming the Central Pacific in search of new lands. Their vessels were now bigger: double canoes more than sixty feet long, equipped at times with double decks, fit with large sails, and amazingly maneuverable. Early European explorers of the South Pacific, like François La Pérouse and James Cook, report seeing fleets of these vessels transporting large groups of people. François La Pérouse describes in detail the circuslike performances that the "religious" entertainers of the Arioi fraternity performed on most inhabited places of the Society Islands.

In view of the Polynesians' societal and navigational advancements, it is obvious that the search for and colonization of new islands were deliberate acts and not the result of some unlucky fishermen's being swept away from their home islands. The incentives are also easily understandable: rapidly expanding populations on islands with limited resources sparked internecine struggles for survival, the losers being forced to leave. For these one-way scouting and colonization voyages, young people of both sexes were chosen, their canoes (double as well as single) well provisioned with taro, yams, coconuts, breadfruit, gourds (used as canteens), chickens, and South Asian pigs.

Early European as well as contemporary travelers extol the Polynesians' expertise in reading the stars, in inferring from waves and swells the locations of reefs and islands, and in foreseeing weather and climate changes based on their observations of seabird-, fish-, turtle-, and sea mammal-behavior, and on the general aspect of the ocean. While sailing downwind expedited navigation toward a known destination, the Polynesian seafarers were also expert at tacking against the wind, but—as Ben Finney experienced—it took twice as much time and effort as in a modern yacht. In view of such accomplished mastery of the sea, it can be posited that the Polynesians were limited in their search for new lands only by the number of islands and not by the vastness of the ocean.

During his 1,650-mile voyage from Rarotonga to New Zealand's North Island in the early summer of 1985, Finney experienced firsthand the strength of the steady easterlies in that part of the South Pacific and wondered how prehistoric navigators could have sailed against the winds when they left Samoa or Tahiti in search of new lands to the east. Faced with the reality that most of the inhabited Polynesian islands east of Samoa and the Society Islands are located in regions of the eastern Pacific where the dominating trade winds or easterly winds are stronger and steadier than between Rarotonga and New Zealand, Finney decided to tackle this problem also. In two articles published in 1985 and 1989, he argued that during certain years the southern trades and the equatorial easterlies are interrupted by anomalous flows from *west* to *east* that could have facilitated the discovery and colonization of the easternmost islands of Polynesia, the Marquesas Islands, and the Tuamotu archipelago. These special years, he wrote, were those in which a phenomenon called El Niño affected the coast of distant South America.

To prove his contention, Finney took the *Hōkūle'a* on yet another trip, this time from Samoa to Tahiti, during the southern winter of 1986 when a moderate El Niño was in progress. Even though the southern winter is not the season when this condition manifests itself strongly, navigators can rely on some breaks in the normally steady southeast trades caused by transient depressions, to facilitate sailing eastward with the help of temporary westerly flows.

The first 650 nautical miles, between Samoa and Aitutaki in the Cook Islands, were covered in only nine days due to occasional westerly winds associated with the passing of winter depressions (Figure 8.7). The second leg, from Aitutaki to Rarotonga, was undertaken in early August when the temporary resumption of the southeast trades allowed the *Hōkūle'a* to sail southward to Rarotonga. The final 720 miles, from Rarotonga to Tahiti, were to be completed around mid-August. The strategy was again to wait for disruptions in the easterlies and southeast trades to take advantage of the strong westerly winds that would push the watercraft eastward. It could not be helped, though, that the stars would be hidden behind clouds and prevent the navigators from ascertaining their progress. The expected disruptions occurred during the final days of the southern winter: several low pressure cells and troughs developed in the South Pacific, spawning westerly flows so powerful that after eight days, Finney's crew found themselves near the island of Mehetia, 80 miles southeast of their destination, and had to take a northwesterly course—now helped by the southeast trades—to reach Tahiti. Still, sailing 720 miles in unknown open seas in merely eight and a half days had been a record performance.

During the voyage, the modern Polynesian seafarers encountered situations that their ancestors had probably exploited. Several times when there was no land in sight, they noticed seaweed floating past, which indicated the proximity of an island or reef. Or they sighted boobies and white terns, which, like other marine birds of the Pacific, make long daily excursions from coastal nesting places, their morning and evening routes also providing clues about the location of land to those who could "read"

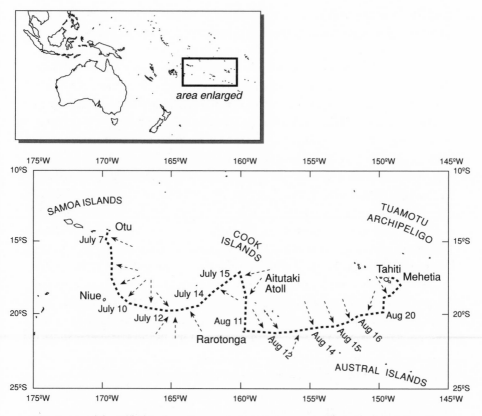

8.7. Route of the *Hōkūle'a* from Samoa to Tahiti. Arrows indicate the wind direction. From Finney et al. 1989

these signs. In addition, contemporary fishermen and seafarers of Micronesia have preserved the skill of inferring from wave and swell deflections in the open seas the location of atolls or reefs that cannot be seen from the low decks of their watercraft or of islands beyond the horizon.

Yet another contributing factor helped ancient Polynesian seafarers in their discovery quests. According to their geological origin, the minor islands of the Pacific are classified as volcanic islands and coral islands, or atolls. The latter consist of coral reefs ringing beautiful lagoons and rise just a few feet above sea level. Only coconut palms and undemanding tubers grow on the nutrient-poor sandy soils. Farmland is not extensive because the island center is occupied by the lagoon. Volcanic islands, on the other hand, are the tips of extinct volcanoes or lava flows, and their bizarre peaks form landscapes of unique beauty, as on Bora-Bora, Tahiti, and the Marquesas. Of larger size than the coral islands, they heat up considerably during daylight hours, thereby drawing in humid winds from the sea. The rising warm air forms distinctive cloud pennants above, which can be seen from the ocean long before the land itself comes into view (Plate 10). Another boon to the volcanic islands is that the steady inflow and rising of maritime air produces abundant rainfall, which feeds numerous creeks and the lush vegetation on the nutrient-rich volcanic soils. The combination of fertile soils and the growth of tall native trees constitutes the basis for inferring that the early colonizers departed from volcanic, not from coral, islands because, once the supporting capacity of the islands was exhausted and outmigration became neceessary, the tall trees (which still grow on many of these islands) provided the lumber to build the big canoes needed for the long voyages ahead. The coconut palms that abound on the coral islands, on the other hand, have never been suitable for the construction of watercraft, not even for rafts.

The next section tells the story of the Polynesian colonization of Easter Island, where climatic and ecological constraints did not allow the growth of major arboreal vegetation. Unable to leave, these people were condemned to extreme isolation, which ultimately led to the collapse of a culture deprived of external stimuli and smothered by a population that surpassed the limited biotic resources of that small speck of land.

The Extraordinary Discovery of Rapa Nui

Easter Island is the most isolated inhabited island of the world, 1,000 miles from unpopulated Ducie, the nearest Polynesian island in the Tuamotu archipelago to the west, and 1,800 miles from the coast of South America to the east. Triangular in shape, the island is slightly more than 8 miles at its base and 4 miles at its tip. Obtuse volcanic cones sit on each of the three corners, the Maunga Terevaka at 1350 feet above sea level being the highest (Figure 8.8). The discovery of this tiny island in the immensity of the South Pacific Ocean is a major feat of humankind. Not only the island's small size conspires against its easy finding, but its location in a part of the South Pacific where the prevailing winds and ocean currents flow from east to west must have discouraged navigators approaching from the opposite direction and sailing *against* the winds and currents.

In December 1978, aboard a Chilean jetliner en route from Easter Island to Tahiti, I was pondering these difficulties when the first atolls of the

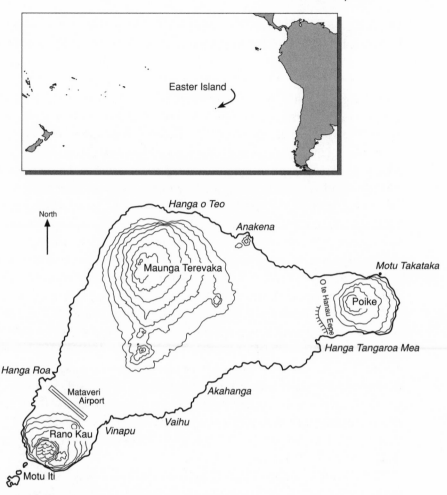

8.8. Topography of Easter Island. The volcanoes, main anchorages, and Mataveri airport are also shown.

Tuamotus came into view below. More a geographer than an anthropologist and without the sailing experience of Ben Finney, I could think of only one way for navigators of the past to have come close to Easter Island: with the help of winds blowing from the west; that is, during El Niño occurrences, when the usual trades and easterlies flowing from the strong South Pacific high are temporarily reversed.

To substantiate this hypothesis, I knew that I had to find solid proof of the interruption of the normal air circulation by a west-east flow of winds and ocean currents in that part of the Pacific. In the 1960s, the Americans had established a satellite-tracking station on the island, and in the early 1970s, the Mataveri airstrip was built for use by jetliners flying between Santiago de Chile and Melbourne, Australia. The air observations required for the safety of these operations would allow me to check the validity of my thesis, but it was not until 1986 that I finally secured the data—a series of wind observations conducted at six-hour intervals—that permitted an evaluation of the winds faced by the early discoverers at the *point of arrival*. Computer-animated wind roses generated with the wind direction and speed data processed by our colleague Peter Waylen confirmed that the wind over Easter Island comes predominately from the southeast during normal years and that this pattern intensifies during La Niña years. However, in 1982–83, when one of the most powerful El Niño events of the century struck, the wind patterns changed completely for several weeks. Altered conditions began during April (midfall in the southern hemisphere), when the first break in the dominating southeast and east winds was registered. After a recovery of the easterlies during the core of the southern winter, abnormal winds began to blow from the west and northwest. In the early spring of 1982, as El Niño was gaining strength in the tropical eastern Pacific, these winds reached unusual intensity and subsided only at the end of January 1983. Daily wind graphs showed that the dominating westerlies occurred in clusters of days, some of them lasting uninterruptedly up to five weeks. Only after October 1982 did the clusters break up into intermittent periods of westerly winds (Caviedes and Waylen 1993).

This detailed picture of the wind changes during a major El Niño event in the eastern South Pacific could now be used to check the Easter Islanders' legends pertaining to their origin. It may be due to the extreme isolation that the traditions about their provenance and the events surrounding their arrival have been so cherished and passed on to subsequent generations with other ledgendary accounts.

The first European to set foot on Easter Island was the Dutch voyager Jacob Roggenween, who arrived in 1622. The island was visited by several navigators during the eighteenth century, among them François La Pérouse and James Cook. They marveled at the huge stone statues standing and lying all over the island and were intrigued that the people they encountered appeared to be too primitive to have carved these magnificent figures (Plate 11). Sadly, postdiscovery contacts with Europeans proved to be catastrophic for the islanders: sailors infected the women with Western diseases, and the men acquired the reputation of being devious thieves. The original islanders were further decimated by raids from Peruvian guano entrepreneurs eager to procure labor for their ventures in coastal Peru. It was only toward the end of the nineteenth century that the world became concerned about this decaying outpost of Polynesian civilization. Literary personalities, anthropologists, and missionaries rushed in to collect the oral traditions from the few remaining islanders in an effort to preserve at least the memories of this fascinating culture and find answers to its origin and the causes of its decay. The most valuable compilation of the oral legends concerning the discovery, populating, internal warfare, and decline of Rapa Nui—as the natives called the island—was undertaken by the Capuchin missionary Sebastian Englert. Due to their methodological robustness, the interpretations of the first-arrival legends by anthropologist Thomas Barthel are equally valuable. Matching the circumstances described in the oral traditions with the time of year suggested by the wind analyses mentioned above allows a plausible conjecture as to when and how the early settlers arrived on Easter Island.

The incentive for undertaking such a voyage came from a dream of a certain Hau Maka, who lived in Hiva—Hiva Oa or Fatu Hiva being places on the Marquesas Islands. In the dream, his soul flies in the direction of the rising sun until it finds new land. Upon awakening, Hau Maka relates his dream to the local chief, Hotu Matu'a, who commands a party of seven young men to leave immediately in search of that land. "Traveling east" in search of mystical lands is a constant in Polynesian folklore, according to Barthel; the title of his book *The Eighth Land* refers precisely to such an island which, in Polynesian cosmology, lies in the eastern confines of the Pacific. So the scouting party sails eastward and eventually finds the island of Hau Maka's dream. On their voyage, the scouts are followed by a mythical sea turtle, which turns out to be an evil spirit that causes the death of one of the young men.

The element of inevitability that pervades this legend of discovery was probably inserted into the account once the people were already established on the island; the dream is at the same time an omen and a command given by fate, the latter being reinforced by the presence of the sea turtle, which indicates the very special circumstances under which the voyage was made. The fear of undertaking a voyage against the prevailing winds and currents around Hiva—normally considered senseless and suicidal—is definitely overridden by the supernatural imperative of the dream. The sea turtle swimming eastward is an indication that the voyage took place at a time when the waters of the eastern Pacific were warming up, since these creatures are uncommon in the cooler waters of the eastern Pacific. The order to sail in the direction of the rising sun expresses the fateful certainty that no other than the island of Rapa Nui is awaiting discovery.

From the vantage point of the Marquesas Islands (at 10°S/140°W), Easter Island (at 27°S/110°W) lies due southeast at sunrise during the summer months. Hence it can be surmised that these events occurred at the onset of an unusual summer when the winds (the means by which Hau Maka's soul traveled) and the ocean currents (the sea turtle's medium) were flowing in an eastward direction. Chief Hotu Matu'a's peremptory order to depart immediately is consistent with our plotting of the winds on Easter Island during El Niño 1982, which showed the first signs of altered flows in the fall of that year. Hundreds of generations of experience had probably taught the Polynesians that such early deviations from the norm heralded major air and ocean alterations ahead. Thus, when they noticed the first symptoms of the abnormalities we today know as El Niño, they had time to send out scouting parties and prepare for major colonization expeditions in the upcoming spring and summer when the changes in the direction of the winds and currents would be firmly established.

According to the legends, Chief Hotu Matu'a did *not* wait for the seven scouts to return but arrived on the island in two canoes with an organized party of colonists just when the young men were about to embark on their return voyage. The fact that cultivated plants, such as taro, yams, sweet potatoes, bananas, and sugarcane, as well as chickens were supposedly in the canoes indicates that the expedition had been thoughtfully planned. Another indication that the voyage was undertaken with the intent of founding new settlements is the legendary detail that two women aboard gave birth shortly before the party landed. Had this been just an exploratory voyage, pregnant women would not have been taken along.

In his analysis of the legends about the arrival on Easter Island, Thomas Barthel found several clues concerning the time of year when this happened. The mention of Vaitu Nui (April)—the first month of agrofishing activities in the Polynesian calendar—as the month when the scouting party departed coincides with the time when the early symptoms of a major El Niño event are manifested. Their arrival at the beach of Anakena on Rapa Nui (Plate 12) is reported to have occurred in early Maro (June), which means the journey took roughly five weeks, a period so short that even Barthel suggested that this could not have been achieved without the help of favorable winds from the west. As to April being the month of departure, this is in keeping with Easter Island's contemporary wind patterns: our studies revealed that during the onset of El Niño 1982, the first reversals in wind direction occurred in April. The legends do not mention the weather conditions when the main colonizing group landed, but it can be assumed that they arrived during one of the prolonged periods of strong winds from the northwest, which tend to occur in August and September of El Niño years, as the 1982 wind data show. Incidentally, the beach of Anakena is open to the northwest.

Many details in the Easter Island legends compiled by Father Englert and Thomas Barthel denote a preoccupation with the past that is not frequently found in the folklore of the rest of Polynesia. The details serve to embellish or sublimate actual events in order to keep alive the islanders' thoughts about the homeland and strengthen their sense of identity. They also constitute proof that the discoverers and colonizers of Easter Island were Polynesians and not Indians from South America, as Thor Heyerdahl insisted. Recently, his thesis has been definitely refuted by DNA studies proving the Easter Islanders' genetic affiliation with Polynesian peoples. As to the language spoken by the Easter Islanders, it has greater affinity to Marquesan than to the Matarevan spoken in the Tuamotu archipelago, although the Marquesas Islands lie 2,000 miles *northwest* of Easter Island.

We have discussed the Polynesian origin of the Easter Islanders and prosed that their journey of discovery seems to have occurred during an El Niño event in the distant past; what remains to be clarified is the approximate date of their arrival. Based on carbon-14 datings of organic remains, Thor Heyerdahl placed that event around A.D. 380, and contemporary archeologists propose that the early settlement occurred around A.D. 400, findings which direct the search for clues about altered global climatic conditions toward the end of the fourth century. According to Hubert Lamb (1995), those were turbulent times in climatic history. In Europe, summers were becoming increasingly warmer and drier, and as polar ice melted, sea levels rose flooding vast coastal areas in both the North

Atlantic and the Mediterranean. Italy, Greece, and Asia Minor suffered pronounced drought, and the water level of the Caspian Sea dropped considerably. In northeast Africa, the Nile experienced low levels, and a Christian kingdom in Nubia (Sudan) seems to have foundered due to food scarcity. As repeatedly stated in this book, these unusual weather conditions coincide with upset conditions in the tropical Pacific, meaning that warm ENSO events occurred frequently and individual El Niño events occurred with similar or even greater intensity than at present. The repeated reversals in the direction of the winds and ocean currents probably encouraged exploratory voyages from the eastern outposts of Polynesia to an unprecedented degree—and one of these voyages resulted in the discovery of Easter Island.

There is, however, a controversial point in this story of the settlement of Easter Island. The legends collected by Sebastian Englert (1970) suggest that there was more than one wave of arrivals. At some unspecified time after the arrival of Hotu Matua's group, whose descendants called themselves Hanau Momoko (lizard men), a second group allegedly arrived—the Hanau Eepe (the heavyset men)—whose long earlobes have been perpetuated in all *moai*, Easter Island's famous stone figures. Size and prolongation of the earlobes point to their origin in the Marquesas where large earlobe rings were worn. Relations between the two groups were never good, and in the confrontation at the ditch of O te Hanau Eepe, the Hanau Eepe were totally annihilated, while the remaining victors descended to the low cultural levels that discoverers and early navigators found hard to reconcile with the monumental statuary of the island.

Of interest to us is the arrival date of this second wave of colonists. If changes in stone carving styles are an indication of new influences, the Hanau Eepe probably arrived between A.D. 1000 and 1100, the transition period from the "settlement phase" (A.D. 400 to 1100) to the "Ahu Moai phase" (A.D. 1000 to 1500), according to JoAnne Van Tilburg (1987). The period from A.D. 1000 to 1100 has been mentioned repeatedly as a time of global warming and abrupt climatic changes that peaked around A.D. 1200. As discussed in earlier sections of this chapter, it was also the time of decisive cultural turnarounds in coastal Peru, in the Bolivian altiplano, and in the Amazon basin, probably the consequence of mega-Niño events. Thus Easter Island can be included with other regions whose cultural histories were notably influenced by major changes in the climatic and oceanic circulations of the eastern Pacific. If there was a global warming trend around A.D. 1000–1100, it can be posited that reversals in the sea and airflow circulations of the South Pacific occurred just as they do today in El Niño years, and also with similar frequency, which is what probably encouraged the Polynesians to undertake more scouting missions.

The last point raises another intriguing question. If the eastern Polynesian islands were discovered during those special years, why were there no further exploratory endeavors during subsequent El Niño occurrences? Nobody can prove that there weren't. Peter Waylen conducted an enlightening experiment using the wind data of Mataveri airstrip. Sequencing the six-hour wind observations, he produced simulations of the tracks that would be taken by balloons propelled by those winds (Figure 8.9). During years of normal circulation in the southeastern Pacific (such as 1980 and 1984), the balloons drifted, as expected, from the Marquesas Islands—the Easter Islanders' assumed ancestral home—to the west and northwest into central Polynesia. However, under the wind conditions dominating in 1982, a balloon starting from the Marquesas in May would have taken a southeasterly course and would have passed slightly west of

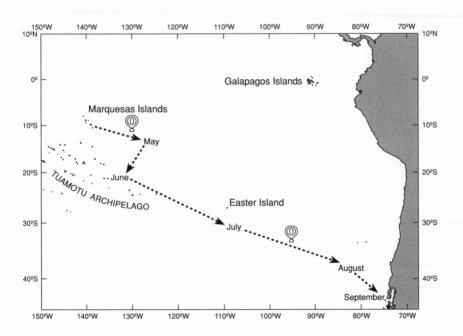

8.9. Route followed by a simulation balloon from the Marquesas Islands to Easter Island. Adapted from Caviedes and Waylen 1993

Easter Island by the end of the month. Returning now to the actual scenario of the Polynesians' exploratory voyages: when they reached a location equivalent to that hypothetical point where the balloon had drifted, these experienced seafarers might have been alerted to the proximity of land by sightings of seabirds or of the cloud pennants that usually hover over the volcanic islands of the South Pacific.

The experiment also proved the feasibility of an assumption advanced by some specialists in transoceanic contacts: namely, that Polynesians could even have reached the South American continent at some time in the past. After passing southwest of Easter Island, the balloon in the simulation continued drifting *eastward* for several weeks and would have reached the west coast of South America by early September, provided the winds persisted. This means that if the Polynesians—once established on Easter Island—ever continued sailing to the east in search of the legendary "Eighth Land," the westerly winds prevailing during El Niño years could have taken them to the coast of southern Chile.

Then why are there no traces of Polynesians to be found in South America? Certainly the favorable winds were not lacking, for as we know, westerlies erupt frequently in the South Pacific. The reason lies elsewhere. Easter Island is a tiny speck of land located precisely at the center of the South Pacific anticyclone, which is characterized by sinking dry air. The island has never been significantly more humid than it is today, and arboreal vegetation was neither dense nor tall, as evidenced by pollen analysis (Flenley et al. 1991). This means that Easter Island did not possess large trees from which canoes similar to those built by the original colonists back on Hiva could be fashioned. When their original vessels deteriorated in the course of time, they had no way of replacing them and were faced with the certainty of never being able to leave again. Nostalgia for their homeland "to the sunset" is the tenor of their legends, as indicated by Father Englert. When the environmental dryness increased with the advent of cooler centuries, and because of the pressure on wood resources by the growing population, the few existing tall trees disappeared. Subsequent El Niños came and went, but without suitable vessels and slowly losing the seamanship of their forefathers, the people lost all hope of ever escaping the confining isolation of the island. If there were successful landfalls in South America during the early centuries of occupancy, the traces of their presence were probably erased by assimilation into the local populations. As in the case of other South Pacific islanders, those who were forced to leave because of dwindling resources, warfare, and increasing population pressures did so without a return ticket.

A team of European environmentalists recently published a study suggesting the possibility of South American Indians coming to Easter Island between A.D. 1300 and 1450 (Dumont et al. 1998). Might this event—which, interestingly enough, coincided with the end of the *moai*-carving period—have been responsible for the sudden appearance on the island of *totora* reed (*Schoenoplectus californicus*), which is widespread on the western margin of South America, and for changes in the microzoa populations of the island's few lakes? This possibility would support Thor Heyerdahl's theory that the original islanders came from that continent, but the researchers themselves concede that the islanders' DNA shows no signs of the intermixing that should have occurred with these Indians, so other explanations for these sudden changes must be explored.

These conjectures all add to the many mysteries surrounding the origin of humans on Easter Island, the emergence of its magnificent statuary, and the precipitous decay of its culture. What seems to be incontestable, however, is that the navigating feats of eastern Pacific islanders and the destiny of the people on Rapa Nui are intricately linked to the changes in ocean and wind conditions brought about by El Niño phenomena during the last two millennia.

9
~

Where Else to Look?

As we have seen throughout this book, climatic variations provide additional interpretive keys for explaining actions taken by the protagonists of history. Of course, human fate is not solely determined by external circumstances, but since the dawn of civilization, environmental fluctuations have had stronger influences than normally assumed. As for the future, it can be expected that in spite of our attempted mastery over our surroundings, climatic variations will continue to interfere with human designs.

The examples presented in this book have brought to the surface the manifold effects of past El Niños for which there were no explicit references in conventional historical accounts. There are many more cases of climate crises with serious implications for societies, and we can find clues about their occurrence in a variety of surrogate historical sources. The question is where and what to look for in such sources. References to harvest failures, famines, inclement winters, devastating floods, and pest outbreaks are indications of weather gone awry due to worldwide alterations in the balance of the atmosphere. In many cases, it seems that these disasters are not related to concomitant climate variations, but this can be only the result of the fact that connections to global crises have not been sufficiently established. Although in recent times many such references have been uncovered, more clues about such crises still await discovery in archives, travelers' accounts, natural hazards reports, and personal diaries. The British writer Mike Baillie tied seemingly unrelated critical events from around the world to global cooling of the atmosphere precipitated either by volcanic eruptions or by impacts of celestial bodies with the earth's atmosphere (Baillie 1999). In the same vein, his colleague David Keys purports that in A.D. 540 the collision of a dying comet with our planet had deleterious consequences for incipient cultures in western Europe (Keys 2000). This book has not focused on a single catastrophic event that may have caused historical turnabouts, but it has produced proofs that climatic oscillations, such as El Niño, are persistent and recurrent. Based on the varied manifestations of El Niño or La Niña during contemporary times, we are now well equipped to sift through historical and unconventional sources for traces of similar oscillations in the distant past.

The present understanding of ENSO phenomena has also contributed to demonstrate the universal applicability of their effects. Studies of El Niño foster the public recognition of the globality of climate, which, in practical terms, is a truer expression of universalism than globalism in politics, economics, or fashion. While the concept has been trivialized by the media and some academicians, the celebrations that marked the beginning of the third millennium proved the validity of globalism as the entire world celebrated its advent as an integrated community. Something similar has happened with El Niño. It took long years before the countries of the world, immersed as they were in their own affairs, recognized and accepted the broader implications of these anomalies. Advances in teleconnections since the 1970s, when El Niño emerged as the major modulator of tropical climates, helped to reveal its vast influences on human affairs beyond political, economic, or ideological boundaries. El Niño has also enhanced the realization that major disasters prompted by climatic oscillations do not occur in isolation, as pointed out by sequels, such as catastrophic flooding, fish and coral mortality, droughts, storms, and shipwrecks—which, in turn, affect all humankind. It is difficult for us, thinking that we have grown more independent of nature's constraints, to recognize at what point the decision-making power of earlier societies was restrained by climatic fluctuations.

For many individuals interested in global environments and deeply committed to their preservation, the vast array of interconnections in the natural world that become patent whenever El Niño or La Niña strikes is the clearest expression of the *wholeness of nature*. A schematization of the multiple linkages between climate, the biosphere, human settlements and activities, as well as political and historical developments was presented in chapter 2. Such an integrated view of the workings of contemporary El Niño is a useful departure point for understanding how past events may have interlaced with natural changes and human affairs. For example, I was amazed when I realized that all the scourges that characterized El Niño–related droughts in northeastern Brazil—famines, pests, plagues, rural depopulation, locust outbursts—also appeared in Ethiopia each time it experienced a drought when the monsoons failed. In both cases, under the blue skies of these tropical countries similar tragedies were in the making, thousands of miles apart. Another indication of the convergence of effects produced by El Niño pertains to the discovery that in temperate semiarid environments of the Americas—such as the U.S. Southwest and Chile's arid Norte Chico—the copious winter rains triggered by El Niño unleash an unusual greening of shrub vegetation and a parallel explosion of rodents, including the carriers of the lethal Hanta virus. Had it not been for the common denominator of El Niño, this coincidence might never have been realized. Along the same lines, we might speculate that the outbreaks of Black Plague in medieval Europe, transmitted by similar carriers, also coincided with times of climatic stress.

Another insight revealed by the most recent El Niño occurrences pertains to the role of tropical oceans as pacesetters of climate in middle and high latitudes. Warm or cold water developments in the Pacific, Atlantic, and Indian oceans are now regarded as crucial for determining global trends. The amount of humidity transferred to the atmosphere and the final outcome of the constant struggle between cold air from the polar regions and warm air from the tropics depend on the seasonal or interannual changes in the location of their interfaces. Understanding how ocean temperature variations stimulate the global climate requires some knowledge of the process by which the atmosphere receives energy from the oceans and the sun: while energy input into land and water masses is proportional to surface area, the effect is not uniform. Natural systems are said to have "short" or "long" memories. Systems with "short memories" respond almost immediately to caloric inputs, such as when continents reach the highest temperatures right after the summer peak and cool down quickly with the arrival of fall and winter. In systems with "long memories" it takes more than a season—and at times several years—before the effects are manifested. The latter happens with some prolonged periods of ocean warming and cooling, or with the Quasi Biennial Oscillation (QBO), which—as the name suggests—takes nearly two years to change signs. Because of these properties of natural systems, the wet episodes and the droughts detailed in this book could be linked to El Niño/Southern Oscillation variabilities even if they occurred within one year before or after.

Using a historical perspective to investigate El Niño has shed light on the pertinence of changing geographies to human affairs, meaning that certain landscapes experience a change of appearance over time, so that what we see today in a place is not what past peoples contended with. Geography is the backdrop against which history plays out, and in this drama the scenarios may change frequently. Historical analysts tend to underplay certain environmental imperatives on the actions of leaders and the designs of conquering societies, since this detracts from human initiative. We have documented the stimuli posed by the changing geography of the Amazon basin, or the lands contiguous to Lake Titicaca, and the impact that catastrophic flooding and dryness have played on human settlements and cultural differentiation in coastal Peru. On a much vaster scale, and during the geological time when humans had not made yet their appearance in the Americas, the emergence of the Isthmus of Panama meant a drastic change of geography: it interrupted the continuity of the tropical Atlantic into the tropical Pacific and favored the establishment of an independent system of air and ocean circulation in the latter. It is very likely that primeval El Niños began to occur in the Pacific basin far earlier than assumed by some geologists and archeologists. Only the utilization of the concept of past geographies allows the interpretation of human crises that appear inexplicable in the face of contemporary environmental conditions.

In view of the evidence that former El Niños were elicitors of environmental crises and human disasters, the reader may be wondering how El Niño–induced changes will affect the climates of the future and which indicators can be used to forecast these changes. Concerning climatic oscillations in general, specialists distinguish three basic causes: (1) entry into the atmosphere of carbon dioxide and other gases from volcanic eruptions and human pollutants; (2) periodic and irregular fluctuations of solar radiation; and (3) energy exchanges between the ocean and the atmosphere. Geophysicists focus on these conditioners to predict ENSO developments and future scenarios assuming that the gas input keeps up, the global warming continues, and the frequency of El Niño or La Niña events increases.

A commonly held view is that El Niño phenomena have become more frequent in recent decades, following the rising carbon dioxide content in the atmosphere. Lending support to this argument are instrumental measurements that indicate a sharp increase in carbon dioxide levels since the early 1900s. However, the global warming and cooling periods from 1860 onward (presented in Figure 9.1) illustrate that this tendency might not be related exclusively to augmented carbon dioxide content, for there are noticeable dips in temperature throughout the second half of the nineteenth century and a punctuated surge only after the 1930s. Even the rising tendency of global temperatures since the 1940s has been interrupted by cold recurrences, which demonstrates that this has not been a linear development. It is only since around the 1970s and following El Niño 1982–83 that global warming has become sustained and El Niño events have occurred with greater frequency and intensity (Figure 9.2).

Using a sophisticated computer model, Gerald Meehl and Warren Washington (1996) investigated the possible effects of increased carbon dioxide levels on the recurrence of warming episodes in the tropical Pacific and reached the conclusion that "we cannot definitely attribute the recent warming in the Pacific (associated global warming of the 1980s and early 1990s) to increased levels of CO_2 in the atmosphere." In fact, they noticed that the said warming was more related to cloud absorption and reflection of incoming solar energy than to the increase of heat-absorbing gases in the atmosphere. Given this inconclusive proof of the importance of carbon dioxide for global warming and, from there, for a higher frequency of warm ENSO events, researchers must look for other causes. Some clues may be coded in the periodicity with which these phenomena occur, because periodicity in systems that depend on the energy of the sun is determined by semiregular fluctuations in the latter's intensity.

Studies in general climatic history based on reliable dating techniques are establishing that past warm occurrences—particularly prehistoric El

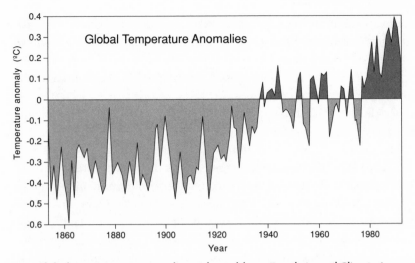

9.1. Global temperature anomalies. Adapted from *Fourth Annual Climate Assessment 1992*, NOAA, 1993.

Niño events—have been irregular in frequency and return intervals. From 15,000 to 7,000 B.P., ENSO episodes were weaker and spaced farther apart, which suggests that the thermal differences between the now-colder eastern and the warmer western Pacific were less accentuated than at present, as were the wind systems in the tropical Pacific, so that they

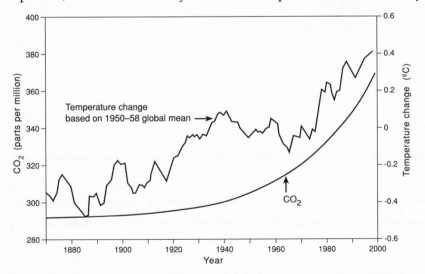

9.2. Carbon dioxide in the atmosphere and global temperatures since 1860. From Mann et al. 1999.

did not cause the dramatic reversals typical of El Niño–La Niña transitions today. It appears that oceanic and atmospheric conditions similar to the present ones became established in the Pacific Basin some 5,000 years ago, which is when the ENSO episodes ingrained in those circulations started to take on clearer contours.

David Enfield and Luis Cid (1991) found that El Niño phenomena seem to have occurred independently of major climatic changes and that the ENSO return intervals have not varied since the height of the Little Ice Age (1525–1747). These authors suggest that the return intervals of El Niño are ruled by changes in the intensity of solar radiation. In periods of high solar activity, major El Niños occur at 11.8-year intervals—minor episodes every 3.5 years—while in periods of low solar activity, the intervals are reduced to 7.8 and 3.1 years, respectively. The "11.8-year" periodicity brings to mind the 11-year cycle of sunspots that modulates the solar energy arriving at our planet's atmosphere and is suspected to be the elicitor of climate variations. However, solar energy influences the earth's heat budget indirectly through the very sensitive stratosphere. It is there that the peculiar Quasi Biennial Oscillation originates, which is responsible for the reversal of high elevation flows that regulate hurricane development in the Atlantic and the cooling and warming phases in the tropical Pacific. It seems that when solar activity is reduced and the QBO relaxes, the Pacific-born ENSO fluctuations are more likely to keep their rhythm because there is less interference from the stratosphere. Conversely, the periods of recurrence in the ocean and atmospheric interactions ingrained in ENSO are lengthened when both solar activity and the QBO are strengthened. Blaming the sunspots for climate variations is nothing new. They were cited in the past as catalysts for droughts in northeastern Brazil by Adalberto Serra, and for variations in the water level of Lake Titicaca by Felix Monheim.

Thus El Niño emerges as the final outcome of the convergence of several rhythms: the annual summer-winter cycle, the almost 2-year cycle of the QBO, the 3.1-and 7.8-year periodicities of El Niño, and the 11-year sunspot recurrences. At such peak moments, the mega-El Niños of the past might have also occurred, if one considers that major El Niños of the present have burst out at such intervals.

Volcanic eruptions are also involved in the origin of an El Niño, provided they occur in the tropical belt, as experiences from the last 200 years suggest. These eruptions inject fine ash, gases, and water vapor into the upper atmosphere, where they absorb incoming solar radiation and thus affect the heat budget of the tropical atmosphere, which in turn triggers the onset of El Niños. Citing volcanic activity and its involvement with the tropical energy budget as the causes of the beginning of a warm ENSO event is not always applicable, however, for many El Niños, such as those of 1957, 1940, and 1925, were not preceded by volcanic eruptions, although those of Pinatubo (1991), El Chichón (1982), Agung (1963), Santa María in Guatemala (1912), and Krakatau (1883) were. In the same vein, the outpouring of submarine lava through vents in the Pacific Ocean floor has been suggested as an elicitor of El Niño. Glowing lava would spread along the ocean floor, heating the surrounding water masses and triggering sea warming (Walker 1988). But long-term observations of the mechanisms that explain the origin and propagation of warm surface waters in the tropical Pacific do not support the possibility of water heated by contact with submarine lava causing an oceanic El Niño development. A further disclaimer is the fact that the occurrences of geophysical hazards, such as volcanic eruptions and outpourings of submarine lava, do not exhibit the cyclical periodicities exhibited by the atmospheric components of ENSO events.

Among all these possible causes, one begins to realize that no single one is sufficient to cause an El Niño outburst; only the convergence of several atmospheric, oceanic, and geophysical circumstances makes this happen. Since most inhabitants of the subtropics and high latitudes adjust their activities to the seasonal cycles, it may be difficult for them to acknowledge the existence and accept the consequences of other cycles. Thus, when faced with oddities, such as El Niño, the general tendency is to regard them as *anomalies*, that is, events outside what is considered normal or expected. In nature, however, there is no such thing as "outside the normal." (This point was explained in chapter 6 with the help of catastrophe and chaos theories.) There is a place in nature for what usually is called "disorder." The credit goes to Poincaré, Thomm, Lorenz, and other mathematicians for providing models that explain "catastrophe" and "chaos" as proper, albeit peculiar, forms of change in the physical world, where events do not necessarily progress in a linear fashion. In some natural processes, a certain increase in input may not result in a commensurate effect. In climatology, the regularity of natural cycles has often been disrupted by sudden energy inputs leading to El Niño or La Niña, but their failure to occur despite the appearance of certain "predictors" reveals its unpredictable nature. Thus, trying to predict the various phases of ENSO or the imminence of an El Niño has been difficult, notwithstanding the availability of the most advanced computer facilities and sophisticated modeling techniques for generating Global Climate Models (GCMs). In these complex constructs, every measurable parameter associated with weather development is entered in multiple equations and iterations to establish interactions and simulate probable scenarios of climatic change. Among the most difficult problems for global climate modeling are the quantities and magnitudes to be assigned to the numerous parameters in order for them to trigger an El Niño event. So far, no model has been satisfactory, and it is still difficult to predict the onset of an ENSO more than twelve months ahead of time. This uncertainty is definitely related to the influence of random factors on their genesis, such as volcanic eruptions, and secondary cycles, such as those of sunspots and QBO.

Analysts of global climate change speak of a *climate systems complex* when referring to the stimuli and feedback between land and ocean masses, air and sea temperatures, pressures, winds, humidity, solar radiation, and other weather elements. The behavior of these components is ruled by physical laws that commonly ensure stability but also leave room for randomness, which may result in apparently "chaotic" responses. The balance between these two opposing tendencies (persistence and sudden change) presides over the interesting concept of *oscillatory states in nature*, which explain the quasi stability of atmospheric states from one season to the other, or from one year to the next (Rind 1999). A system with these properties has been in operation since life developed on earth, so it is appropriate to postulate that climatic variations of El Niño style have been occurring for a long time and that they will not overturn the established order of nature in the foreseeable future. This is not to say that the consequences will not become more serious than they are today. Population growth has forced people into occupying unsafe coastal locations, unstable mountain sites, and the fringes of arid lands where inter-annual climatic oscillations have the detrimental consequences that we have seen in Africa, India, China, and South America.

The cases presented in the preceding chapters reveal that some climatic anomalies, such as floods, cold outbreaks, heat waves, and droughts, are not tied to ENSO but depend on local or regional climatic controls. There is no doubt, though, that the large-scale deforestations in Amazonia or tropical Southeast Asia and the pulsations of the ozone hole over the Antarctic affect atmospheric stability, the full implications of which are still far from being understood. Nevertheless, one should also not blame every climatic mishap on El Niño. Since being "discovered" by the industrialized societies in 1982–83, El Niño has been held responsible for far too many unpleasant climate developments and, fueled by a sensationalist media, has been demonized for many nonclimatological phenomena and ecological mishaps.

Climatic variations—secular and inherent characteristics of this planet—have been operating on earth since long before humankind appeared. Our ancestors were obviously much more vulnerable to the whims of nature than we are today. Even examples from contemporary Sahelian Africa, or from nineteenth-century India, Ethiopia, and China, demonstrate the power of climatic imperatives on recent history. Reading Arnold Toynbee's *A Study of History* in my student years, I was fascinated by Toynbee's thesis of environmental challenge and human response as propelling forces in history. He contends that climate crises of the past altered natural environments to an extent that elicited mass migrations—Toynbee uses precisely the German word *Völkerwanderungen* when referring to peoples' displacements. Movements on such a grand scale modified the course of history, as exemplified by the invasion of the Roman Empire by Goths, Slavs, Teutons, and Vandals, the attacks of the Huns and Turks that precipitated the fall of Byzantium, and the onslaught of Mongol hordes that prompted the erection of the Great Wall but could not prevent repeated deposals of Chinese dynasties by warlords from the Asian steppes.

Supporting Toynbee, this book has also explored how climatic crises of ENSO signature sparked migrations that produced language differentiation and changes in ceramic styles in the Amazon basin and helped Polynesian seafarers reach new islands in the eastern Pacific. In a similar manner, recent droughts associated with El Niño have caused social and political unrest in sub-Saharan countries, social tension and outmigration in northeastern Brazil, and declines in food production in India, China, and Japan. Thus not only do El Niño effects have global dimensions, but they function as a major natural catalyst of recent and subrecent history.

If this book were to have a didactic purpose, it would be to raise awareness about the human implications of climatic fluctuations and to instill in readers the desire to scour the pages of history books and even fiction in search for hidden references to El Niño conditions. For example, *Little*

House on the Prairie, which I read with my young son while living in western Canada, gave me a better understanding of how the severe climate of the North American prairies (with its inclement winters, scorching summers, droughts, tornadoes) molded the personalities of those who made a home there. Fiction can be a very valuable means for conveying a personalized sense of weather and the harshness of climate. To mention a few other examples, there is Leo Tolstoy's classic *War and Peace,* which depicts the cruelty of the Russian winter in the years of Napoleon's campaign, and several twentieth-century Russian novels expose the human brutality and climatic inclemency of the siege of Stalingrad with stark realism. The traumatic German experience has been fictionalized in Hans Dibold's *Doctor at Stalingrad* and in a similar novel by Heinz G. Konsalik. Recently, while reading Stephen Ambrose's account of the continental crossing in *Lewis & Clark Voyage of Discovery* I noticed repeated references to the severity of the winter of 1805 in North America; that year, according to numerous sources, an El Niño occurred in the Pacific waters, and I might have overlooked its pertinence to global climatic history in a casual reading of Lewis and Clark's journey. More such hints pointing to the local and regional effects of past El Niño occurrences may be hidden in other literary pieces just waiting to be discovered.

In the tapestry of history there are telltale threads that attest to the recurrence of El Niño phenomena. Individuals who are fond of environmental history could comb written sources for passing references to climatic variabilities, similar to those of contemporary El Niño or La Niña events, that served as a backdrop for notable historical circumstances.

Bibliography

Abbott, M. B., M. W. Binford, M. Brenner, and K. R. Kelts. "A 3500 14C Yr. High-resolution Record of Water Level Changes in Lake Titicaca, Bolivia/Peru." *Quaternary Research* 47 (1997): 169–80.

Absy, M. L. "Palynology of Amazonia: The History of the Forests as Revealed by the Palynological Record." In *Amazonia*, ed. G. T. Prance and T. E. Lovejoy, pp. 72–82. Oxford: Pergamon Press, 1985.

Acosta, Joseph de. *Historia Natural y Moral de las Indias*. Mexico: Fondo de Cultura Económica, 1940.

Addis, J., and M. Latif. "Amazonian Arthropods Respond to El Niño." *Biotropica* 28 (1996): 403–8.

Alves de Andrade, F. *Agronomia e Humanismo*. Fortaleza: Impensa Universitária do Ceará, 1967.

Andrade, Lopes de. *Introduçao a sociologia das sêcas*. Rio de Janeiro: Editora A Noite, 1948.

Arntz, W. E., and E. Fahrbach. *El Niño: Klimaexperiment der Natur*. Basel: Birkhäuser Verlag, 1991.

Avila, L .A., and G. B. Clark. "Atlantic Tropical Systems of 1988." *Monthly Weather Review* 117 (1989): 2260–65.

Baillie, Mike. *Exodus to Arthur. Catastrophic Encounters with Comets*. London: B. T. Batsford, 1999.

Barthel, Thomas. *The Eighth Land: The Polynesian Discovery and Settlement of Easter Island*. Honolulu: University Press of Hawaii, 1978.

Bayaban, C., B. Finney, B. Kilonski, and N. Thompson. "Voyage to Aotearoa." *Journal of the Polynesian Society* 96 (1987): 161–200.

Beevor, Antony. *Stalingrad.* New York: Viking, 1998.

Bennett, E. B. "Influence of the Azores High on Sea Level Pressure and Wind, and on Precipitation, in the Eastern Tropical Pacific Ocean." *Inter-American Tropical Tuna Commission. Bulletin* 12 (1966): 1–23.

Berlage, H. P. "Fluctuations of the General Atmospheric Circulation of More Than One Year, Their Nature and Prognostic Value." *Koningl. Neder. Meteor. Institute. Meded. en Verhand* 69 (1957): 152 pp.

———. "The Southern Oscillation and World Weather." *Koningl. Neder. Meteor. Institute. Meded. en Verhand* 88 (1966): 151 pp.

Bhalme, H. N., D. A. Mooley, and S. K. Jadhav. "Fluctuations in the Drought/ Flood India and Its Relationships with the Southern Oscillation." *Monthly Weather Review* 111 (1983): 86–94.

Binford, M. W. "Climate Variation and the Rise and Fall of an Andean Civilization." *Quaternary Research* 47 (1997): 235–48.

Birch, J. R., and J. R. Marko. "The Severity of the Iceberg Season on the Grand Banks of Newfoundland: An El Niño Connection?" *Tropical Ocean-Atmosphere Newsletter* 36 (1986): 18–22.

Bjerknes, Jacob. "El Niño Study Based on Analysis of Ocean Surface Temperatures 1935–57." *Inter-American Tropical Tuna Commission. Bulletin* 5 (1961): 219–307.

———. "Survey of the El Niño 1957–58 in Its Relation to Tropical Pacific Meteorology." *Inter-American Tropical Tuna Commission. Bulletin* 12 (1966): 1–62.

———. "Atmospheric Teleconnections from the Equatorial Pacific." *Monthly Weather Review* 97 (1969): 163–72.

———. *Preliminary Study of the Atmospheric Circulation during the Period Preceding the 1972–73 El Niño.* Department of Meteorology, University of California, Los Angeles, 1974.

Black, D. A., et al. "Eight Centuries of North Atlantic Ocean Atmosphere Variability." *Science* 286 (1999): 1709–13.

Brooks, Reuben H. "Drought and Public Policy in Northeastern Brazil." *Professional Geographer* 25 (1973): 338–46.

———. "Drought and Adjustment Dynamics in Northeastern Brazil." *GeoJournal* 6 (1982): 121–28.

Brown, Leslie H. "Biology of Pastoral Man as a Factor in Conservation." *Biological Conservation* 3 (1971): 93–100.

Bryson, Reid, and T. J. Murray. *Climates of Hunger: Mankind and the World's Changing Weather.* Madison: University of Wisconsin Press, 1977.

Burman, José. *Great Shipwrecks off the Coast of Southern Africa.* Capetown: Struik, 1967.

Bush, M. B. "Modern Pollen Rain Data from South America and Central America: A Test of the Feasibility of Fine-resolution Lowland Tropical Palynology." *The Holocene* 1 (1991): 162–67.

Carranza, L. "Contracorriente marítima observada en Paita y Pacasmayo." *Boletín de la Sociedad Geográfica de Lima* 1 (1891): 344–45.

Carrillo, Camilo N. "Disertación sobre las corrientes oceánicas y estudios de la corriente peruana o de Humboldt." *Boletín de la Sociedad Geográfica de Lima* 2 (1892): 72–110.

Cavazos, Tereza, and S. Hastenrath. "Convection and Rainfall over Mexico and Their Modulation by the Southern Oscillation." *International Journal of Climatology* 10 (1990): 377–86.

Caviedes, César N. "Secas and El Niño: Two Simultaneous Climatological Hazards in South America." *Proceedings Association of American Geographers* 5 (1973): 44–49.

———. "El Niño 1972: Its Climatic, Ecological, Human and Economic Implications." *The Geographical Review* 65 (1975): 439–509.

———. "Five Centuries of Winter Storms in the Southeastern Pacific." In *Abstracts of the Annual Meeting of the Southeastern Division of the Association of American Geographers (SEDAAG)*, p. 13. Blacksburg, Va., 1980.

———. "On the Genetic Links of Precipitation in South America." *Forschritte landschaftsÖkologischer und klimatologischer Forschungen in den Tropen. Freiburger Geographische Hefte* (ed. D. Havlik and R. Mäckel) 18 (1982a): 55–77.

———. "Natural Hazards in South America: In Search of a Method and a Theory." *GeoJournal* 6, no. 2 (1982b): 101–11.

———. "El Niño 1982–83." *Geographical Review* 74 (1984): 267–90.

———. "South American and World Climatic History." In *Environmental History: Critical Issues in Comparative Perspective*, ed. Kendall E. Bailes, pp. 135–52. Washington: University Press of America, 1985.

———. "Five Hundred Years of Hurricanes in the Caribbean: Their Relationship with Global Climatic Variabilities." *GeoJournal* 23 (1991): 301–10.

Caviedes, César N., and P. R. Waylen. "Chapters for a Climatic History of South America." Festschrift zur Ehre von Professor Wolfgang Weischet's 70. Geburtstag (1991). *Freiburger Geographische Hefte* 32: 149–80.

———. "Anomalous Westerly Winds during El Niño/Southern Oscillation Events: The Discovery and Colonization of Easter Island." *Applied Geography* 13 (1993): 123–34.

Chenoweth, Michael. "Ship's Logbooks and 'the Year without a Summer' (1816)." *Bulletin American Meteorological Society* 77 (1996): 2077–94.

Chung, J. C. "Correlations between the Tropical Atlantic Trade Winds and Precipitation in Northeastern Brazil." *Journal of Climatology* 2 (1982): 35–46.

Claxton, Robert H. "Climate and History: From Speculation to Systematic Study." *Historian* 55 (1982): 220–36.

Clemens, S. C., D. W. Murray, and W. L. Prell. "Nonstationary Phase of the Plio-Pleistocene Asian Monsoon." *Science* 274 (1996): 943–47.

Cole, J. E., G. T. Shen, R. G. Fairbanks, and M. Moore. "Coral Monitors of El Niño/Southern Oscillation Dynamics across the Equatorial Pacific." In *El Niño. Historical and Paleoclimatic Aspects of the Southern Oscillation*, ed. H. F. Diaz and V. Markgraf, 349–75. New York: Cambridge University Press, 1992.

Colinvaux, P. A., and P. E. de Oliveira. "Paleoecology and climate of the Amazon basin during the last glacial cycle." *Journal of Quaternary Science* 15 (2000): 347–56.

Colls, Keith. "Assessing the Impact of Weather and Climate in Australia." *Climatic Change* 25 (1993): 225–44.

Craig, A. K., and I. Shimada. "El Niño Flood Deposits at Batán Grande, Northern Peru." *Geoarcheology* 1 (1986): 29–38.

Craig, William. *Enemy at the Gates. The Battle for Stalingrad.* New York: E. P. Dutton and Co., 1973.

Diaz, Henry F., and Vera Markgraf, eds. *El Niño. Historical and Paleoclimatic Aspects of the Southern Oscillation.* New York: Cambridge University Press, 1992.

Doberitz, R. "Cross-spectrum Analysis of Rainfall and Sea Temperatures at the Equatorial Pacific Ocean. A Contribution to the El Niño Phenomenon." *Bonner Meteorologische Abhandlungen* 8 (1968): 61 pp.

Doberitz, R., H. Flohn, and K. Schütte. "Statistical Investigations of the Climatic Anomalies of the Equatorial Pacific." *Bonner Meteorologische Abhandlungen* 7 (1967): 76 pp.

Donnan, Christopher B. *The Pacatnamu Papers.* Los Angeles: Museum of Cultural History/University of California, 1987.

Dumont, H. J., C. Cocquyt, M. Fontugne, M. Arnold, J.-L. Reyss, J. Blomendal, F. Oldfield, C. L. M. Steenbergen, H. J. Korthals, and B. A. Zeeb. "The End of Moai Quarrying and Its Effect on Lake Rano Raraku, Easter Island." *Journal of Paleolimnology* 20 (1998): 409–22.

Dupon, Jean-François. "Where the Exception Confirms the Rule: The Cyclones of 1982–1983 in French Polynesia." *Disasters* 8 (1984): 34–47.

Eguiguren, Victor. "Las lluvias de Piura." *Boletín de la Sociedad Geográfica de Lima* 4 (1894): 241–58.

Elliot, W. P., and J. K. Angell. "Evidence for Changes in Southern Oscillation Relationships during the last 100 Years." *Journal of Climate* 1 (1988): 729–37.

Encina, Francisco. *Historia de Chile.* Santiago: Editorial Nascimento, 1952.

Enfield, David B. "Progress in Understanding El Niño." *Endeavour* 11, no. 4 (1987): 197–204.

Enfield, David B., and L. Cid. "Statistical Analysis of El Niño/Southern Oscillation over the Last 500 Years." *TOGA Notes* 1 (1990): 1–4.

———. "Low Frequency Changes in El Niño-Southern Oscillation." *Journal of Climatology* 4 (1991): 1137–46.

Englert, Sebastian. *Island at the Center of the World.* New York: Charles Scribner's Sons, 1970.

———. *Leyendas de Isla de Pascua.* Santiago: Ediciones de la Universidad de Chile, 1980.

Evans, M. N., R. J. Fairbanks, and J. L. Rubenstone. "A Proxy Index of ENSO Teleconnections." *Nature* 394 (1998): 732–34.

Finney, Ben R. "Voyaging Canoes and the Settlement of Polynesia." *Science* 196 (1977): 1277–85.

———. "Anomalous Westerlies, El Niño, and the Colonization of Polynesia." *American Anthropologist* 87 (1985): 9–26.

Finney, B. R., P. Frost, R. Rhodes, and N. Thompson. "Wait for the West Wind." *Journal of the Polynesian Society* 98 (1989): 261–303.

Fitz-Roy, Robert. *Narrative of the Surveying Voyages of His Majesty's Ships Adventure and Beagle, between 1826 and 1836, Describing Their Examination of the Southern Shores of South America and the Beagle's Circumnavigation of the Globe.* London: Henry Colburn, 1839; reprint, New York: AMS Press, 1966.

Flenley, J. R., A. S. M. King, J. Jackson, C. Chew, J. T. Teller, and M. E. Prentice. "The Late Quaternary Vegetational and Climatic History of Easter Island." *Journal of Quaternary Science* 6, no. 2 (1991): 85–115.

Flohn, Hermann. "Lessons from Climatic History." *Contributions to Atmospheric Physics* 53 (1980): 204–12.

———. "Singular Events and Catastrophes: Now and in Climatic History." *Naturwissenschaften* 73 (1986): 136–49.

Flohn, Hermann, M. Hantel, and E. Ruprecht. "Investigations on the Indian Monsoon Climate." *Bonner Meteorologische Abhandlungen* 14 (1970): 99 pp.

Florescano, Enrique. *Precios del maíz y crisis agrícolas en México (1708–1810).* Mexico: El Colegio de México, 1969.

———. "Una historia olvidada: la sequía en México." *Nexos* 32 (1980): 9–18.

Francou, Bernard, and Luis Pizarro. "El Niño y la sequía en los altos Andes centrales (Perú y Bolivia)." *Bulletin de l'Institute Français d'Études Andines* 15, no. 1/2 (1985): 1–18.

Fraedrich, Klaus. "An ENSO impact on Europe?" *Tellus* 46–A (1994): 541–52.

Fraedrich, Klaus and K. Müller. "Climate anomalies in Europe associated with ENSO extremes." *International Journal of Climatology* 12 (1992): 25–31.

Gao, Shiying, and Jinsun Wang. "Tropical Cyclones in the Northwest Pacific and El Niño." *Tropical Ocean and Atmosphere Newsletter* 35 (1986): 6–7.

Gimeno, L., R. Garcia, and E. Hernandez. "Precipitations in the Canary Islands in the Seventeenth Century and the Relationship with El Niño Events." *Bulletin of the American Meteorological Society* 79 (1998): 89–91.

Glantz, Michael H. *Value of Reliable Long Range Climate Forecast for the Sahel: A Preliminary Assessment.* Boulder: IFIAS and NCAR, 1976.

———. *Currents of Change.* New York: Cambridge University Press, 1996.

———, ed. *Desertification: Environmental Degradation in and around Arid Lands.* Boulder: Westview Press, 1977.

Glantz, Michael H., R. Katz, and N. Nicholls, eds. *Teleconnections Linking Worldwide Climatic Anomalies.* New York and Cambridge: Cambridge University Press, 1991.

Glyn, Peter W., and Mitchell W. Colgan. "Sporadic Disturbances in Fluctuating

Coral Reef Environments: El Niño and Coral Reef Development in the Eastern Pacific." *American Zoologist* 32 (1992): 707–19.

Gootenberg, Paul. *Between Silver and Guano.* Princeton: Princeton University Press, 1989.

Gordon, Neil D. "The Southern Oscillation and New Zealand weather." *Monthly Weather Review* 114 (1986): 371–87.

Gray, B. M. "Early Japanese Winter Temperatures." *Weather* 29 (1974): 103–7.

Gray, W. M. "Atlantic Seasonal Hurricane Frequency. Part 1. El Niño and the 30 mb Quasi Biennal Oscillation (QBO)." *Monthly Weather Review* 112 (1984a): 1649–68.

———. "Atlantic Seasonal Hurricane Frequency. Part 2. Forecasting Its Variability." *Monthly Weather Review* 112 (1984b): 1668–83.

Gregory, Stanley, ed. *Recent Climatic Change: A Regional Approach.* London and New York: Belhaven Press, 1988.

Grove, Richard E. "Global Impact of the 1789–93 El Niño." *Nature* 393 (1998): 318–20.

Gu, Daifang, and S. G. H. Philander. "Secular Changes and Interannual Variability in the Tropics during the Past Century." *Journal of Climate* 8 (1995): 864–75.

Hagelberg, E., S. Quevedo, D. Turbon, and J. B. Clegg. "DNA from Ancient Easter Islanders." *Nature* 369 (1994): 25–27.

Hameed, S., W. M. Yeh, M. T. Li, R. Cess, and W. C. Wang. "An Analysis of Periodicities in the 1470–1974 Beijing Precipitation Record." *Geophysical Research Letter* 6 (1983): 436–39.

Hamilton, Kevin. "Evidence for Tropical–Mid Latitude Teleconnections in the Eighteenth and Ninenteenth Century." *Tropical Ocean-Atmosphere Newsletter* 30 (1985): 1–2.

Hamilton, Kevin, and Rolando R. Garcia. "El Niño/Southern Oscillation Events and Their Associated Midlatitude Teleconnections." *Bulletin of the American Meteorological Society* 67 (1986): 1354–61.

Hancock, Graham. *Ethiopia. The Challenge of Hunger.* London: Victor Gollancz, 1985.

Hastenrath, Stefan. "Decadal-scale Changes of the Circulation in the Tropical Atlantic Sector Associated with Sahel Drought." *International Journal of Climatology* 10 (1990a): p. 459–72.

———. "Tropical Climate Prediction: A Progress Report, 1985–90." *Bulletin of the American Meteorological Society* 71 (1990b): 819–25.

———. "Recent Advances in Tropical Climate Prediction." *Journal of Climate* 8 (1995): 1519–32.

Heathcote, R. L. "Drought in Australia: A Problem of Perception." *Geographical Review* 59 (1969): 175–94.

Heusser, L. E., and F. Sirocko. "Millenial Pulsing of Environmental Change in Southern California from the Past 24 k.y.: A Record of Indo-Pacific ENSO Events?" *Geology* 25 (1997): 243–46.

Hisard, P. "Centenaire de l'obervation du courant côtier El Niño, Carranza, 1892. Contributions de Krusenstern et de Humboldt a l'obervation du phénomène

ENSO." In *Paleo-ENSO International Symposium*, ed. L. Ortlieb and J. Macharé, 133–41. Lima: ORSTOM-CONCYTEC, 1992.

Hobbs, J. E. "Recent Climatic Change in Australasia." In *Recent Climatic Change: A Regional Approach*, ed. Stanley Gregory, 285–97. London and New York: Belhaven Press, 1988.

Hocquenghem, Anne-Marie. "Los españoles en los caminos del extremo norte del Perú en 1532." *Bulletin de l'Institut Français d'Études Andines* 23, no. 1 (1994): 1–68.

Hocquenghem, A.-M., and L. Ortlieb. "Pizarre n'est pas arrivé au Pérou durant une année El Niño." *Bulletin de l'Institut Français d'Études Andines* 19, no. 2 (1990): 327–34.

Ingram, Charles W. N. *New Zealand Shipwrecks, 1795–1970*. Wellington, New Zealand: A. H. Reed and A. W. Reed, 1972.

Jáuregui, Ernesto. "Algunos aspectos de las fluctuaciones pluviométricas en México en los últimos cien años." *Boletín del Instituto Geográfico de la Universidad Nacional de México* 9 (1979): 39–64.

Jones, P. D., T. M. Wigley, and P. B. Wright. "Global Temperature Variations between 1861 and 1984." *Nature* 322 (1986): 430–34.

Kates, Robert W. *Drought Impact in the Sahelian-Sudanic Zone of West Africa: A Comparative Analysis of 1910–1915 and 1968–1974*. Department of Geography, Clark University, Worcester, Mass., 1981.

Kessler, Albrecht. "Das El Niño-Phänomen under Titicacaseepiegel." *Festschrift für Wendelin Klaer zum 65. Geburtstag. Mainzer Geographische Studien* 34 (1990): 91–100.

Keys, David. *Catastrophe. The Quest for the Origin of the Modern World*. London: Ballantine Books, 2000.

Kondo, Junsei. "Volcanic Eruptions, Cool Summers, and Famines in the Northeastern Part of Japan." *Journal of Climate* 1 (1988): 775–88.

Lamb, Hubert H. *Climate. Present, Past and Future*. London: Methuen, 1977.

———. *Weather, Climate and Human Affairs*. London: Routledge, 1988.

———. *Historic Storms of the North Sea, British Isles and Northwest Europe*. Cambridge: Cambridge University Press, 1991.

———. *Climate, History and the Modern World*. 2nd ed. London: Methuen, 1995.

Lara, A., and R. Villalba. "A 3620-Year Temperature Record from *Fitzroya cupressoides* Tree Rings in Southern South America." *Science* 260 (1993): 1104–6.

Lawrence, M. B., and J. M. Gross. "Atlantic Hurricane Season of 1988." *Monthly Weather Review* 116 (1989): 2248–59.

Lobell, M. G. "Some Observations of the Peruvian Coastal Current." *Transactions of the American Geophysical Union* 2 (1942): 332–36.

Loney, Jack K. *Victorian Shipwrecks*. Melbourne: Hawthorn Press, 1971.

Lough, J. M. "Tropical Atlantic Sea Surface Temperatures and Rainfall Variations in sub-Saharan Africa." *Monthly Weather Review* 114 (1986): 561–70.

Lumbreras, Luis G. *Arqueología de la América Andina*. Lima: Milla Batres, 1981.

Mann, M. E., R. S. Bradley, and M. K. Hughes. "Northern Hemisphere Temperatures during the Past Millenium: Inferences, Uncertainties and Limitations." *Geophysical Research Letters* 26 (1999): 759–62.

Marret, Robert. *Peru*. London: Ernest Benn, 1969.

Marshall, Don B. *California Shipwrecks: Footsteps in the Sea*. Seattle, Wash.: Borrego, 1978.

Martins Pinheiro, Luiz C. *Notas sobre as sêcas*. Rio de Janeiro: Direçao de Obras Contra as Sêcas DNOCS, 1960.

Mears, Eliot G. "The Ocean Current Called 'The Child.'" In *Annual Report, Smithsonian Institution for 1943*, 245–51. Smithsonian Institution, Washington, D.C., 1944.

Meehl, G. A., and W. M. Washington. "El Niño–like Climate Change in a Model with Increased CO_2 Concentrations." *Nature* 382 (1996): 56–60.

Meggers, Betty J. "Archeological Evidence for the Impact of Mega-Niño Events on Amazonia during the Past Two Millennia." *Climatic Change* 28 (1994a): 321–28.

———. "Biogeographical Approaches to Reconstructing the Prehistory of Amazonia." *Biogeographica* 70, no. 3 (1994b): 97–110.

———. "Possible Impact of the Mega-Niño Events on Precolumbian Populations in the Caribbean." In *Ponencias del Primer Seminario de Arqueología del Caribe*, ed. Marcio Veloz Maggiolo and Angel Caba Fuentes, 156–76. Altos de Chavon: Museo Arqueológico Regional and Organización de Estados Americanos, 1996.

Melero, Marcos T. *Los huracanes de la Isla de Cuba*. Havana: n.p., 1870.

Merriman, Daniel. "El Niño Brings Rain to Peru." *American Scientist* 43, no. 1 (1955): 63–76.

Metcalfe, Sarah. "Historical Data and Climatic Change in Mexico—a Review." *Geographical Journal* 153 (1987): 211–22.

Millás, J. C. *Hurricanes of the Caribbean and Adjacent Regions, 1492–1800*. Miami: Academy of the Arts and Sciences of the Americas, 1968.

Minard, Charles Joseph. 1861. "Carte figurative de pertes successives en hommes de l'Armée française dans la campagne de Russie 1812–1813." In Edward R. Tufte, *The Visual Display of Quantitative Information*. Cheshire, Conn.: Graphic Press, 1983.

Monheim, Felix. "Beiträge zur Klimatologie und Hydrologie des Titicacabeckens." *Heidelberger Geographische Arbeiten* 1 (1956): 152 pp.

Moore, J. D. "Cultural Responses to Environmental Catastrophes: Post El Niño Subsistence on the Prehistoric North Coast of Peru." *Latin American Antiquities* 2 (1991): 27–47.

Moseley, Michael, E. *The Maritime Foundations of Andean Civilization*. Menlo Park, Calif.: Cummings, 1975.

———. "The Good Old Days Were Better: Agrarian Collapse and Tectonics." *American Anthropologist* 85 (1983): 773–99.

———. *The Inca and Their Ancestors*. London: Thames and Hudson, 1992.

———. "Climate, Culture, and Punctuated Change: New Data, New Challenges." *Review of Archaeology* 17 (1997): 19–27.

Moura, Antonio D., and Jagadish Shukla. "On the Dynamics of Droughts in North-eastern Brazil: Observations, Theory and Numerical Experiments with a General Circulation Model." *Journal of the Atmospheric Sciences* 38 (1981): 2653–75.

Murphy, Robert C. "Oceanic and Climatic Phenomena along the West Coast of South America during 1925." *Geographical Review* 16, no. 1 (1926): 26–54.

Nafziger, George F. *Napoleon's Invasion of Russia.* Novato, Calif.: Presidio Press, 1998.

Namias, Jerome. "Influence of Northern Hemisphere General Circulation on Drought in Northeast Brazil." *Tellus* 24 (1972): 336–43.

National Oceanic and Atmospheric Administration. *Fourth Annual Climate Assessment 1992.* Camp Springs, Md.: NOAA/Climate Analysis Center, 1993.

Neumann, C. H., B. R. Jarvinen, and A. C. Pike. *Tropical Cyclones of the North Atlantic Ocean, 1871–1986.* Historic Climatology Series 6–2. Asheville, N.C.: National Center for Atmospheric Research, 1988.

Newell, John P. "Sea-ice and Atmospheric Circulation Anomalies in the Labrador Sea Region Associated with the Extremes of the Southern Oscillation." *International Journal of Climatology* 16 (1996): 63–71.

Nials, F. L., E. E. Deeds, M. E. Moseley, S. G. Pozorski, T. G. Pozorski, and R. A. Feldman. "El Niño: The Catastrophic Flooding of Coastal Peru." *Field Museum of Natural History, Bulletin* 50, no. 7 (1979): 4–14 and 50, no. 8 (1979): 4–10.

Nicholls, Neville. "Impact of the Southern Oscillation on Australian Crops." *Journal of Climatology* 5 (1985): 4553–60.

———. "A Method for Predicting Murray Valley Encephalitis in Southeast Australia Using the Southern Oscillation." *Australian Journal of Experimental Biological and Medical Science* 64 (1986): 587–694.

———. "Historical El Niño/Southern Oscillation Variability in the Australasian Region." In *El Niño. Historical and Paleoclimatic Aspects of the Southern Oscillation,* ed. Henry F. Diaz and Vera Markgraf, 151–92. New York: Cambridge University Press, 1992.

Nicholson, Sharon E. "An Analysis of the ENSO Signal in the Tropical Atlantic and Western Indian Ocean." *International Journal of Climate* 14 (1997): 345–75.

Pankhurst, Richard. *The History of Famines and Epidemics in Ethiopia prior to the Twentieth Century.* Addis Ababa: Relief and Rehabilitation Commission, 1990.

Parthasarathy, B., N. A. Sontakke, A. A. Monot, and D. R. Kothawale. "Droughts/ Floods in the Summer Monsoon Season over Different Meteorological Subdivisions of India for the Period of 1871–1984." *Journal of Climatology* 7 (1987): 57–70.

Peña, O., and H. Romero. "Rutas ciclonales en el Pacífico Sur: Situaciones de primavera y verano." *Revista del Pacífico Sur* 5 (1976): 113–27.

Philander, S. G. "El Niño and La Niña." *American Scientist* 77 (1989): 451–60.

Poey, André. "Chronological Table of Cyclonic Hurricanes." *Journal of the Royal Geographical Society* 25 (1856): 291–328.

Quinn, William H. "A Study of the Southern Oscillation-Related Climatic Activity for A.D. 622–1900 Incorporating Nile River Flood Data." In *El Niño. Historical and Paleoclimatic Aspects of the Southern Oscillation*, ed. Henry F. Diaz and Vera Markgraf, 119–49. New York: Cambridge University Press, 1992.

Quinn, William H., V. T. Neal, and Santiago Antúnez de Mayolo. "El Niño Occurrences over the Past Four and a Half Centuries." *Journal of Geophysical Research* 92, no. C13 (1987): 14449–63.

Quinn, William H., D. A. Zoff, K. S. Short, and R. Kuo Yang. "Historical Trend and Statistics of the Southern Oscillation, El Niño, and Indonesian Droughts." *Fishery Bulletin* 76 (1978): 663–78.

Ramage, Colin. "El Niño Variability and Tropical Cyclones." *Tropical Ocean-Atmosphere Newsletter* 30 (1985): 3–5.

Rasmusson, Eugene M., and John M. Wallace. "Meteorological Aspects of the El Niño/Southern Oscillation." *Science* 222 (1983): 1195–1202.

Rawe, J., and A. Crabtree. *Shipwrecks of the Southern Cape*. Capetown: Atlantic Underwater Club, 1978.

Reading, Alison J. "Caribbean Tropical Storm Activity over the Past Four Centuries." *International Journal of Climatology* 10 (1990): 365–76.

Reason, C. J. C., R. J. Allan, and J. A. Lindesay. "Dynamic Response of the Oceanic Circulation and Temperature to Interdecadal Variability in the Surface Winds over the Indian Ocean." *Journal of Climate* 9 (1996): 97–114.

Richardson, Howard C., and D. J. Nemeth. "Hurricane-Borne African Locusts (*Schistocerca gregaria*) on the Windward Islands." *GeoJournal* 23 (1991): 349–57.

Rind, D. "Complexity and Climate." *Science* 284 (1999): 105–7.

Romero, H. "The 1988 Drought in Chile." *Tropical Ocean-Atmosphere Newsletter* 52 (1989): 5–6.

Ryan, Christopher J. "Costs and Benefits of Tropical Cyclones, Severe Thunderstorms and Bushfires in Australia." *Climate Change* 25 (1993): 355–67.

Salivia, Luis A. *Historia de los Temporales de Puerto Rico y las Antillas (1492 a 1970)*. San Juan, P.R.: Editorial Edil, 1972.

Sallnow, Michael J. *Pilgrims in the Andes. Regional Cults in Cusco*. Washington, D.C.: Smithsonian Institution Press, 1987.

Sandweiss, D. H., J. B. Richardson, E. J. Reitz, H. B. Rollins, and K. A. Maasch. "Geoarcheological Evidence from Peru for a 5000 Years B.P. Onset of El Niño." *Science* 273 (1996): 1531–33.

Schneider, Hans J. "Drought, Demography, and Destitution: Crisis in the Norte Chico." *GeoJournal* 6 (1982): 111–19.

Schütte, Karin. "Untersuchungen zur Meterologie und Klimatologie des El Niño-Phänomens in Ecuador und Nordperu." *Bonner Meteorologische Abhandlungen* 9 (1968): 140 pp.

Schweigger, Erwin. *Die Westküste Südamerikas im Bereich des Peru-Stroms*. Heidelberg: Keysersche Verlag, 1959.

———. "Bosquejo histórico de la teoría sobre la Corriente Peruana." *Publicaciones del Instituto de Geografía de la Universidad Nacional Mayor de San Marcos*. Serie I. Monografías y Ensayos Geográficos No. 2 (1960), 40 pp.

Sears, A. E. "The Coast Desert of Peru." *Bulletin of the American Geographical Society* 27 (1895): 256–71.

Serra, Adalberto. *Aspectos estatisticos das sêcas nordestinas.* Rio de Janeiro: Conselho Nacional de Pesquizas/Departamento Nacional de Meteorologia, 1973.

Shimada, I., C. B. Schaaf, L. G. Thompson, and E. Mosley-Thompson. "Cultural Impacts of Severe Droughts in the Prehistoric Andes: Application of a 1,500-Year Ice Core Precipitation Record." *World Archeology* 22 (1991): 247–70.

Sirocko, Frank. "Past and Present Subtropical Summer Monsoon." *Science* 274 (1996): 937–38.

Smolka, P. P. "Neogene Ozeane." *Die Geowissenschaften* 9:11 (1991): 347–51.

Stahle, D. W., M. K. Cleaveland, D. B. Blanton, M. D. Therrell, and D. A. Gay. "The Lost Colony and the Jamestown Droughts." *Science* 280 (1998): 564–67.

Steinitz-Kannan, M., M. A. Riedinger, W. Last, M. Brenner, and M. C. Miller. "Un registro de 6000 años de manifestaciones intensas del fenómeno de El Niño en sedimentos de lagunas de las islas Galápagos." *Bulletin de l'Institut Français d'Études Andines.* 27:3 (1998): 581–92.

Suplee, Curt. "El Niño and La Niña: Nature's Vicious Cycle." *National Geographic* 195, no. 3 (1999): 73–95.

Swan, S. L. "Mexico in the Little Ice Age." *Journal of Interdisciplinary History* 11 (1981): 633–48.

Taulis, Emilio. "De la distribution de pluies au Chile." *Materiaux pour l'étude des calamités* (Societé de Géographie de Genève) 1, part 1 (1934): 3–20.

Thompson, L. G., and E. Mosley-Thompson. "Reconstructing Interannual Climate Variability from Tropical and Subtropical Ice-core Records." In *El Niño. Historical and Paleoclimatic Aspects of the Southern Oscillation,* ed. Henry F. Diaz and Vera Markgraf, 295–322. New York: Cambridge University Press, 1992.

Thompson, L. G., E. Mosley-Thompson, M. E. Davis, P.-N. Lin, K. A. Henderson, J. Cole-Dai, J. F. Bolzan, and K.-b. Liu. "Late Glacial Stage and Holocene Ice Core Records from Huascarán, Peru." *Science* 269 (1995): 46–50.

Thompson, L. G., M. E. Davis, E. Mosley-Thompson, T. A. Sowers, K. A. Henderson, V. S. Zagorodnov, P.-N. Lin, V. N. Mikhalenko, R. K. Campen, J. F. Bolzan, J. Cole-Dai, and B. Francou. "A 25,000-Year Tropical Climate History from Bolivian Ice Cores." *Science* 282 (1998): 1858–61.

Thompson, L. G., E. Mosley-Thompson, and K. A. Henderson. "Ice-core Paleoclimate Records in Tropical South America since the Last Glacial Maximum." *Journal of Quaternary Science* 15 (2000): 377–94.

Tourré, Y., and E. Rasmusson. "Tropical Atlantic Region during the 1982–83 Equatorial Pacific Warming Event." *Tropical Ocean-Atmosphere Newsletter* 25 (1984): 1–2.

Trenberth, Kevin E. "Atmospheric Circulation Climate Changes." *Climatic Change* 31 (1995): 427–53.

Tyson, Peter D. "Synoptic Circulation Types and Climatic Variation over Southern Africa." In *Recent Climatic Change: A Regional Approach,* ed. Stanley Gregory, 202–14. London and New York: Belhaven Press, 1988.

Vallis, Geoffrey K. "El Niño: A Chaotic Dynamical System?" *Science* 232 (1986): 243–45.

Van Tilburg, JoAnne. "Symbolic Archaeology on Easter Island." *American Anthropologist* 40 (1987): 26–33.

Vidal-Gormaz, Francisco. *Algunos naufragios ocurridos en las costas de Chile desde su descubrimiento hasta nuestros dias.* Santiago: Imprenta Elseviriana, 1901.

Vogel, Coleen H. "A Documentary-Derived Climatic Chronology for South Africa, 1820–1900." *Climatic Change* 14 (1989): 291–307.

Walker, Daniel E. "Seismicity of the East Pacific Rise: Correlations with the Southern Oscillation?" *EOS Transactions of the American Geophysical Union* 9 (1988): 857–65.

Walsh, John. "Return of the Locust: A Cloud over Africa." *Science* 234 (1986): 17–19.

Wang, C., and S. Wang. "The Fluctuation of Precipitation Amount in China for the Last 5000 Years." *Science Sinica* B1 (1987): 104–12.

Wang, Shao-Wu. "El Niño and Summer Temperatures in Northeast China, 1860–1980." *Tropical Ocean-Atmosphere Newsletter* 25 (1984): 4.

Wang, S. W. and Z. C. Zhao. "Droughts and Floods in China, 1470–1979." In *Climate and History*, ed. T. M. Wigley, M. Ingrasham, and G. Farmer, 271–88. Cambridge: Cambridge University Press, 1981.

Wells, L. E. "Holocene History of El Niño Phenomena as Recorded in Flood Sediments of Northern Coastal Peru." *Geology* 18 (1990): 1134–37.

Wells, L. E., and J. S. Noller. "Determining the Early History of El Niño." *Science* 276 (1997): 966.

Whetton, P. H., A. M. Fowler, M. R. Haylock, and A. B. Pittock. "Implications of Climate Change due to the Enhanced Greenhouse Effect on Floods and Droughts in Australia." *Climatic Change* 25 (1993): 289–317.

Whetton, Peter H., and Ian Rutherfurd. "Historical ENSO Teleconnections in the Eastern Hemisphere." *Climatic Change* 28 (1994): 221–53.

Wolde-Mariam, Mesfin. *Rural Vulnerability to Famine in Ethiopia. 1958–1977.* London: Intermediate Technology Publications, 1986.

Wooster, Warren S. "El Niño." *California Cooperative Oceanic Fisheries Investigations, Reports*, vol. 7, new series 1175 (1957): 557–59.

Wyrtki, Klaus. "Surface Currents of the Eastern Tropical Pacific Ocean." *Inter-American Tropical Tuna Commission. Bulletin* 9 (1965): 270–304.

———. "Teleconnections in the Equatorial Pacific Ocean." *Science* 180 (1973): 66–68.

———. "Equatorial Currents in the Pacific 1950 to 1970 and Their Relations to the Trade Winds." *Journal of Physical Oceanography* 4 (1974): 372–80.

Yoshino, Masatoshi M. "Rainfall, Frontal Zones and Jet Streams in Early Summer over East Asia." *Bonner Meteorologische Abhandlungen* 3 (1963): 126 pp.

Yoshino, Masatoshi M., and A. Murata. "Reconstruction of Rainfall Variation in the Bai'u Rainy Season in Japan." In *Recent Climatic Change: A Regional Approach*, ed. Stanley Gregory, 272–83. London and New York: Belhaven Press, 1988.

Yoshino, Masatoshi M., and T. Yasunari. "Climatic Anomalies of El Niño and Anti-El Niño Years and Their Socio-economic Impacts in Japan." *Science Reports of the Institute of Geoscience, University of Tsukuba. Section A: Geographical Sciences* 7 (1986): 41–53.

Zhang, J., and T. J. Crowley. "Historical Climate Records in China and Reconstruction of Past Climates." *Journal of Climate* 2 (1989): 833–49.

Index

César N. Caviedes is professor of geography at the University of Florida. He is author of several books on Latin America, including *South America* (1994), *The Persisting Ecological Constraints of Tropical Agriculture* (1993), and *Elections in Chile* (1991) and of numerous chapters and articles on El Niño.